BY MEMBERS OF THE POTOMAC CORRAL OF THE WESTERNERS

GREAT WESTERN
INDIAN FIGHTS

THE DEFINING BATTLES

MJF BOOKS
NEW YORK

Published by MJF Books
Fine Communications
322 Eighth Avenue
New York, NY 10001

Great Western Indian Fights
LC Control Number 96-78822
ISBN-13: 978-1-56731-171-6
ISBN-10: 1-56731-171-7

Printed in the United States of America.

MJF Books and the MJF colophon are trademarks of Fine Creative
Media, Inc.

QM   10   9   8   7   6   5   4   3   2

Contents

THE WRITERS   7

LIST OF ILLUSTRATIONS   15

LIST OF MAPS   16

    Chapter 1—The Indian Wars of the West   19
        by John C. Ewers

PART I—FUR TRADING DAYS, 1832   27

    Chapter 2—The Pierre's Hole Fight   30
        by Bradley H. Patterson, Jr.

PART II—UNDER THE LONE STAR, 1841   39

    Chapter 3—Battle of Bandera Pass   41
        by O. Clark Fisher

PART III—FIGHTING IN THE FAR WEST, 1858–60   47

    Chapter 4—The Indians Have an Inning   50
        by Jack Dodd

    Chapter 5—The Soldiers Have Theirs   61
        by Jack Dodd

    Chapter 6—The Battle of Pyramid Lake   73
        by Arthur W. Emerson

PART IV—THE CIVIL WAR PLUS, 1861–65   83

    Chapter 7—The Battle of Wood Lake   86
        by Noel M. Loomis

    Chapter 8—Canyon de Chelly   94
        by Clinton P. Anderson

    Chapter 9—The First Battle of Adobe Walls   102
        by Lawrence V. Compton

PART V—ACTION ON THE BOZEMAN TRAIL, 1866–67   109

    Chapter 10—The Fetterman Fight   117
        by Roy E. Appleman

    Chapter 11—The Hayfield Fight   132
        by Roy E. Appleman

    Chapter 12—The Wagon Box Fight   148
        by Roy E. Appleman

PART VI—POST CIVIL WAR: SOUTHERN PLAINS, 1868   163
    Chapter 13—The Fight at Beecher Island   165
       by James S. Hutchins
    Chapter 14—Battle of the Washita   175
       by Lawrence Frost
PART VII—PAWNEE VS. SIOUX, 1873   183
    Chapter 15—The Battle of Massacre Canyon   185
       by Ray H. Mattison
PART VIII—THE MODOC WAR, 1872–73   189
    Chapter 16—Blood on the Lava   192
       by F. G. Renner
PART IX—THE SOUTHERN PLAINS, 1874   201
    Chapter 17—The Second Battle of Adobe Walls   203
       by J. C. Dykes
    Chapter 18—The Battle of Palo Duro Canyon   214
       by J. C. Dykes
PART X—THE NORTHERN PLAINS, 1876   221
    Chapter 19—The Battle of the Rosebud   225
       by J. A. Leermakers
    Chapter 20—The Battle of the Little Bighorn   235
       by Robert M. Utley
PART XI—APACHES VS. APACHES, 1871–86   255
    Chapter 21—The Apache Scouts Who Won a War   257
       by D. Harper Simms
PART XII—TROUBLE IN THE MOUNTAINS, 1877–79   267
    Chapter 22—The Bannack Indian War of 1878   270
       by Frederick A. Mark
    Chapter 23—Besieged on Milk Creek   281
       by Jack P. Riddle
PART XIII—THE CHEYENNES GO HOME, 1878   293
    Chapter 24—Massacre of the Dull Knife Band   295
       by B. W. Allred
PART XIV—THE GHOST DANCE, 1891   303
    Chapter 25—Tragedy at Wounded Knee   307
       by George Metcalf
BIBLIOGRAPHY   318
APPENDIX   327
INDEX   329

The Writers

B. W. (BILL) ALLRED, resident member, is a native of Utah. He has B.S. and M.S. degrees from Utah Agricultural College and took additional graduate work at the University of Nebraska. He was a cowboy in Utah, a sheepherder in Wyoming, and a county agent in Colorado before joining the Soil Conservation Service in 1935. He is now the Ranch Planning Specialist in the Washington office of the Soil Conservation Service. He collects Western Americana, specializing in books on range life. He is the author of *Range Conservation Practices for the Great Plains* (Washington, D.C., 1940); *Practical Grassland Management* (San Angelo, Texas, 1950); (with J. C. Dykes) *Flat Top Ranch* (Norman, Oklahoma, 1957); and over four hundred articles and book reviews.

CLINTON P. ANDERSON, resident member, United States Senator from New Mexico, has lived in the West since 1917 and is known as an authority on Western history. He is one of the best-known collectors of Western Americana in the country. He first entered public life in 1933 when he was appointed state treasurer of New Mexico. He served three terms in the House of Representatives beginning in 1940, and was Secretary of Agriculture, 1945–1948. He has served in the Senate since 1948, and is currently chairman of the Joint Congressional Committee on Atomic Energy. He is a member of the Senate Committees on Finance, Interior and

Insular Affairs, Aeronautical and Space Sciences, and of the Select Committee on Water Resources. He is also a member of the Joint Committee on Navajo-Hopi Administration, the Outdoor Recreation Resources Review Commission, and the Board of Regents of the Smithsonian Institution.

ROY E. APPLEMAN, resident member and sheriff (president) in 1959, is a professional historian. He has degrees from the University of Ohio and Columbia University and has done additional graduate work at Yale. He was District Historian of the National Park Service in New York in 1935–36; Regional National Park Service Historian at Richmond, Virginia, in 1936–42; and since 1946 has been Staff Historian at the Washington, D.C., office. He has been responsible for the research, administration, and travel connected with many of the National Park Service historical projects. He served with distinction in the Pacific during the war, rising from private to Major. He was Combat Historian for the Philippines, Okinawa, and Japan. He was called back for the Korean conflict and graduated to the rank of colonel. He is a close student of the Indian Wars.

LAWRENCE V. COMPTON, resident member, is a graduate of the University of Kansas and has a master's degree from the University of California. He spent many years in the Southwest as a wildlife conservationist. For the past nine years he has been the Principal Biologist of the Soil Conservation Service with headquarters in Washington, D.C. He is the author of numerous articles and bulletins on wildlife and its conservation.

JOHN B. (JACK) DODD, a resident member until the fall of 1959 and now a corresponding member, was born in Spokane, Washington. His grandparents on both sides homesteaded in the Big

Bend country of Washington when it was still a territory. He is a graduate of the University of Idaho and was a forester for the National Park Service for many years. He is now Assistant Superintendent of the Everglades National Park, Homestead, Florida. His hobbies are antique guns, collecting Indian artifacts and handicraft, and Western history, particularly that dealing with Washington Territory. He served in World War II and is now a lieutenant colonel in the U.S. Army Reserve.

J. C. (JEFF) DYKES, resident member, is a native of Texas. He is a graduate of the Texas Agricultural and Mechanical College and a former faculty member of his alma mater. He is now Assistant Administrator of the Soil Conservation Service. He is an ardent collector of Western books and an outstanding authority on Western Americana. He is the author of *Billy the Kid: The Bibliography of a Legend* (Albuquerque, New Mexico, 1952); the introduction to Pat Garrett's *The Authentic Life of Billy the Kid* (Norman, Oklahoma, 1954); (with B. W. Allred) *Flat Top Ranch* (Norman, Oklahoma, 1957); and numerous articles and papers on Western books and conservation. Since 1950 he has been an associate editor of *The Brand Book*, the official monthly publication of the Chicago Corral, The Westerners.

ARTHUR W. EMERSON, corresponding member, is a professional writer. He was born in the sand hills of Nebraska of pioneer stock. His grandfather Emerson operated the first store in Deadwood, South Dakota. He is a graduate of the South Dakota School of Technology and spent several years in sales and promotion work in Chicago, Cleveland, and Minneapolis. He mined gold in Montana and was a free-lance writer on many subjects. For three years he was in charge of educational relations with seventeen Indian reservations on the Northern Great Plains. He is now Information Specialist for the Soil Conservation Service in the West, with headquarters at Berkeley, California.

10 THE WRITERS

JOHN C. (JACK) EWERS, resident member and sheriff in 1958, is a native of Ohio. He has A.B. and M.A. degrees from Dartmouth College, New Hampshire. He was the first curator of the Museum of the Plains Indians on the Blackfoot Reservation in Montana and won the confidence of the elders of that tribe. He is the author of numerous publications on the Blackfeet and other Indians including *The Horse in Blackfoot Culture* (Washington, D.C., 1955) and *The Blackfeet* (Norman, Oklahoma, 1958). He is one of the top Indian historians in the country and a member of the Smithsonian staff. His present job is that of Assistant Director, Museum of History and Technology, Smithsonian Institution, Washington, D.C.

O. CLARK FISHER, resident member, is the Congressman for the Twenty-first Texas District. He was born on a ranch in Kimble County, Texas. His father was a trail driver and the first cousin of King Fisher, the highly publicized Texas gunman and Deputy Sheriff. Clark attended Baylor University and the University of Texas and holds the LL.B. degree. He was County Attorney, District Attorney, and State Representative prior to being elected to the Seventy-eighth Congress. He is now serving his eighteenth year in Congress and, like his father, is a Kimble County rancher. He has been interested in pioneer and frontier history since his youth. He is the author of *It Occurred in Kimble* (Houston, Texas, 1937), one of the best Texas county histories.

LAWRENCE FROST, corresponding member, is a nationally known foot surgeon who lives in Monroe, Michigan. Monroe was the birthplace of Mrs. George A. (Elizabeth B.) Custer and the adopted home of the Custers. Dr. Frost is an avid collector of Custeriana and serves as curator of the Custer Room of the Monroe County Historical Museum. He is a corresponding member of the New York Posse of The Westerners.

JAMES S. HUTCHINS, corresponding member, is in the automobile sales and service business in Columbus, Ohio. He is a graduate of U. S. Military Academy, West Point, New York. He is an ardent student of the evolution of the equipment, clothing, and weapons used by the U. S. Army throughout its service in the trans-Mississippi West. He collects all manner of objects worn and used by the soldiers on the Western frontier, particularly saddles and other horse gear. He also collects books, pamphlets, and other written material having to do with these subjects. His articles on the Indian-fighting soldiers and their equipment have appeared in such publications as *Military Collector and Historian, Montana, the Magazine of Western History* and *The Brand Book* of the Chicago Corral, The Westerners.

J. A. LEERMAKERS, corresponding member, is assistant director of the Research Laboratories of the Eastman Kodak Company, Rochester, New York. He is a native of Nebraska but attended college in Iowa and California. He earned his Ph.D. in Chemistry at the California Institute of Technology. His interest in Western history has extended over a period of twenty years. He has made a particular study of the transcontinental trails and has spent parts of several summers exploring them. He collects firearms associated with American history and is the proud owner of a Hawken rifle, found near Deadwood, South Dakota. He writes about his hobbies and makes wonderful color photographs to illustrate his articles.

NOEL LOOMIS, corresponding member, was born in Indian Territory (Oklahoma) but now lives at Descanso, California. He is a member of the English faculty at San Diego State College and one of the best known Western novelists. He is a past president of the Western Writers of America and is now serving as the secretary-treasurer of that organization. He has written four hundred short stories and fifty novels, including *Short Cut to Red River* (New York, 1958) which won the Spur Award of the W.W.A. for the best Western novel of 1958. He is also the author of a distinguished book of history, *The Texan-Santa Fe Pioneers* (Norman, Oklahoma, 1958). Noel is at work on a 1200-page novel of the days of the Republic of Texas.

FREDERICK A. MARK, corresponding member, is the Assistant State Conservationist, Soil Conservation Service, Spokane, Washington. He was born in Montana but lived on a ranch near the Fort Hall Indian Reservation in Idaho as a boy. He holds the B.S. and M.S. degrees from the University of Idaho. He was an appraiser for the Federal Land Bank before beginning his quarter-of-a-century career in the Soil Conservation Service in the Northwest. He is a collector of Western Americana with emphasis on Idaho and the Northwest. He is a resident member of the Spokane Corral, The Westerners. He is the author of numerous articles and papers on Western history and conservation.

RAY HAROLD MATTISON, corresponding member, is a professional historian with the National Park Service, Omaha, Nebraska. He has a B.A. degree from the State Teachers College at Wayne, Nebraska, and a M.A. in History from the University of Nebraska. He is a member of the Nebraska State Historical Society, the State Historical Society of North Dakota, the Mississippi Valley Historical Association, and the Nebraska Writers' Guild. He is a corresponding member of the Chicago Corral, The Westerners. In addition to the official publications he has written, Ray has contributed about twenty-five articles to historical quarterlies in the Northern Plains States. Several of these articles have been reprinted as separates, including *Ranching in the Dakota Badlands* (Bismarck, North Dakota, 1952); *Roosevelt and the Stockmen's Association* (Bismarck, 1950); and *Roosevelt's Dakota Ranches* (Bismarck, 1956).

GEORGE METCALF, resident member, is on the staff of the Smithsonian Institution, Washington, D.C. He is a native of Nebraska. He was a member of the party that excavated and studied the sites of the ancient Indian villages on the Missouri River in South Dakota. He is an ardent student of the history of the American Indians. His present position at the Smithsonian is that of museum aide in archeology. He is the author of numerous technical reports.

BRADLEY H. PATTERSON, JR., resident member, is a native of Massachusetts, but anything of historical importance that evolved from the "winning of the West" is his meat. He is a mountain climber and camper in the far reaches of the West during summer vacations. His special interest is retracing and visiting the transcontinental routes of travel our pioneers followed as they migrated west. It was on such a summer exploration that Brad visited Pierre's Hole and became interested in its history. He is a member of the White House staff, serving as assistant to the Secretary of the Cabinet.

F. G. (FRED) RENNER, resident member and sheriff in 1957, is a native of Montana, where his father was a rancher on the Missouri River above Great Falls. He holds degrees from the University of Washington and the University of California. His entire professional career has been devoted to range conservation with the Forest Service and, for the last twenty-five years, the Soil Conservation Service. He is the outstanding authority in the country on the art of Charles Marion Russell, the great Montana cowboy artist. He is the technical advisor to the C. M. Russell Memorial Museum at Helena and the Trigg-C. M. Russell Galleries at Great Falls. He owns a number of Russell originals and is the nation's premier collector of the published works of Russell. Fred is the author of *Rangeland Rembrandt* (Helena, Montana, 1958); *A Selected Bibliography on Management of Western*

Ranges, Livestock, and Wildlife (Washington, D.C., 1938); and numerous articles and papers on range conservation.

JACK P. RIDDLE, corresponding member, was on duty with the U. S. Army as a captain in Washington, D.C., for several months and a frequent visitor at the Potomac Corral meetings. He is a native of Colorado and was educated in the Denver schools. After fifteen years' service in the Army, he is back in Denver, where he is a photographer for the Denver *Post*. He is a close student of Western history and has completed the research for a series of three books on Colorado.

D. HARPER SIMMS, resident member, was born on the Mescalero Apache Indian Reservation in New Mexico. His father and grandfather were Indian Missionaries. He has two degrees, one in Journalism, from the University of Missouri. He is a student of Indian history, with a special interest in the Apaches. He was in information work in Albuquerque for many years and for the last nine years has been Chief of the Information Division, Soil Conservation Service, Washington, D.C. He is the editor of *Corral Dust*, the official publication of the Potomac Corral.

ROBERT M. UTLEY, corresponding member, was formerly a resident member. He is a professional historian and is now Historian in the Region Three Office, National Park Service, at Santa Fe, New Mexico. He was born in Arkansas but reared in Pennsylvania and Indiana. He graduated from Purdue University and then earned his M.A. in history at the University of Indiana. During his college days he spent his summers at the Custer Battlefield National Monument in Montana, where he served as ranger-historian. He was a historian in the Historical Section, Joint Chiefs of Staff, 1954-1957. He is the vice-president of the Historical Society of New Mexico.

LIST OF ILLUSTRATIONS

Following page 120

Trappers en route to Rendevous—*Paul Rockwood*
Gunpowder and Arrows—*Charles M. Russell*
Lieutenant Grummond's Even Chance—*Charles Schreyvogel*
Indian Charge—*Charles Schreyvogel*
Diorama of the Wagon Box Fight—*Photograph*
The Death of Roman Nose—*Charles M. Russell*
Forsyth's Fight on the Arickaree—*Frederic Remington*
Cavalry Charge—*Frederic Remington*
The Battle of the Lava Beds—*Charles M. Russell*
Mackenzie's Scout Finds the Winter Camp—*William Loechel*

Following page 216

Probably the Last Photograph of Lieutenant Colonel George A. Custer
The Indian Leaders—Red Cloud, Gall, Sitting Bull, Crow King—*Photographs*
Apache Scouts Stripped for Battle—*Photograph*
The Renegade Apaches Kill a White Rancher—*Frederic Remington*
Miles Followed Orders and Tried to Win with the Regulars—*Frederic Remington*
Kayetah and Martine, the Scouts Who Negotiated the Surrender—*Photograph*
The Army's Umatilla Allies—*Photograph*
Bannacks Captured by General Miles—*Photograph*
The Milk Creek Battle Monument—*Photograph*
Dull Knife's Defiance—*Maynard Dixon*
Burying the Dead at Wounded Knee—*Photograph*

MAPS

Page

Great Western Indian Fights (location map)
Military Campaigns against the Spokane, Palouse, and
   Couer d'Alene Indians—1858   52
Bozeman Trail, 1866-1868   110
Fort Phil Kearny and Vicinity   118
Fort C. F. Smith and Vicinity   136
Beecher's Island   168
Battle of the Rosebud   229
The Battle of the Little Bighorn   247
The Chiricahua Apache Campaign   261
Bannack Indian War   274
Wounded Knee Battlefield   312

Note: The maps, with one exception, were prepared by William Loechel. The map of the Battle of the Little Bighorn was drawn by Walter Vitous.

GREAT WESTERN INDIAN FIGHTS

1. THE INDIAN WARS
OF THE WEST

JOHN C. EWERS

"Before the west could be settled it had to be won." So wrote vigorous Theodore Roosevelt seventy years ago. Throughout the greater part of the nineteenth century hostile Indians, the descendants of the aboriginal occupants of the region, provided the major obstacle to the winning of the American West beyond the Mississippi River. There many desperate Indian tribes made their heroic last stands to preserve their traditional hunting grounds from the intrusions of American trappers, overland emigrants, miners, cattlemen, and farmers. There many valiant whites, both soldiers and civilians, laid down their lives in the struggle to transform an undeveloped Indian country into a safe abode for civilized men and women and for their children. History has recorded no more dramatic conflicts than the battles which were fought between red men and white on the plains, in the deserts, and in the mountains of the American West during the nineteenth century.

The theater of warfare was a vast one. It extended from Minnesota westward to the Pacific Coast, from the Canadian boundary southward to Mexico. Throughout this region the overrunning of Indian lands by white men proved a fundamental cause of irritation and alarm to the Indians. It did not always lead to open warfare. But so basic and so constant was this cause of friction that a minor incident could and sometimes did trigger a bitter, prolonged, and costly Indian war.

Long before the western Indian country was invaded by American trappers and settlers this area had been a battleground of warring Indian tribes. In these intertribal wars the larger and stronger tribes expelled the smaller, weaker ones from choice hunting territories. Mobile, nomadic tribes preyed upon the farming Indians, who lived in more sedentary villages and grew crops in the river valleys nearby. Bitter animosities engendered by generations of intertribal feuds prevented the many Indian tribes of the West from uniting in defending their homeland against white intruders. These long-standing conflicts between neighboring tribes aided the whites during the period of Indian Wars. For example, in the Sioux Wars members of the Pawnee, Crow, and Shoshone tribes, which had long suffered from the aggression of the mighty Sioux, joined the whites in their efforts to pacify a common enemy. Later, in the Southwest, friendly Apache scouts helped the Army to seek out elusive, hostile Apache bands.

Indian warfare had been a major deterrent to the expansion of white settlements in America since colonial times. It has been said that it took a hundred years of forest-felling and Indian fighting for white settlement to move the first hundred miles inland from the Atlantic coast. In the Middle West, under the leadership of such great chiefs as Pontiac, Tecumseh, and Black Hawk, the Indians delayed but could not stop the relentless westward movement of settlers. In the woodlands of the South the Creeks and Seminoles had resisted with equal courage and stubbornness. But they could not stem the rising tide of white home-seekers.

A small skirmish involving a few members of the Lewis and Clark expedition far beyond the frontier of settlement produced the first casualty in the Indian Wars of the West. In the summer of 1806, Meriwether Lewis led a detachment of three enlisted men northward from the Missouri River to search for the sources of the Marias River. He had no desire to encounter any of the dread Blackfeet. But on Badger Creek, on the present Blackfoot Reservation, he met a party of eight Piegan (Blackfoot) warriors, and he couldn't avoid spending the night with them. Early the next morning the Indians tried to steal the soldiers' arms and horses. In the ensuing melee He-who-looks-at-the-Calf, one of the Piegans, was stabbed in the heart.

Shortly thereafter American beaver trappers fanned the flames of Blackfoot animosity by trespassing upon their lands and taking beaver from their streams. Throughout the period of the Rocky Mountain fur trade the Blackfeet and their Gros Ventre allies fought many a small-scale battle with the hardy trappers. The most famous of these engagements, the Battle of Pierre's Hole, is described in this book.

Not until the decline of the fur trade in the early 1840s did American settlers become a major source of irritation to western Indians. On the expanding frontier of Texas the wild Comanches met the six-shooter-toting Texas Rangers. Farther north emigrant wagon trains bound westward for Oregon, California, and Utah killed and frightened game in the plains country through which they passed and roused the hostility of the powerful Sioux. When the government established forts at strategic points along the overland trails through the Indian country, the Army inherited the enmity of these Indians.

During the 1840s and '50s the frontier of white settlement expanded rapidly in Minnesota and in the region beyond the Rockies. The invasion of Indian lands by white farmers and miners precipitated numerous local Indian Wars in widely scattered areas of the West—in California, Washington Territory, Utah, Nevada, the Southwest, and Minnesota. In some of these areas of conflict the settlers organized volunteer forces to fight the Indians. But the Army continued to bear the major responsibility for pacifying hostile tribes on the far-flung frontier.

The decade of the 1860s witnessed the negotiation of numerous treaties with western Indian tribes under the terms of which the Indians nominally agreed to cede portions of their lands and to limit their own activities to the reservations left to them. But many tribes, both large and small, had difficulty making a living through traditional pursuits upon their reservations and refused to be confined to them. Many of the hardest-fought battles of the West were waged by desperate, restless "Reservation Indians" during the decade of the '70s. The Army fought the Sioux, Cheyennes, Arapahoes, Kiowas, and Comanches on the Great Plains, the Apaches in the Southwest, and the Modocs, Nez Perces, and Bannacks in the Northwest. Not until the middle '80s did the last die-hard Apache "hostiles"—as unfriendly Indians were called—finally surrender and lay down their arms.

In the pacification of the Plains Indians the Army had a cruel and effective ally—starvation. From time immemorial the buffalo had been the staff of life of these Indians. But the rapid extermination of the buffalo in the decade of the '70s left the warriors of the Plains little choice between surrender and starvation. Nearly a decade after the buffalo were gone the mighty Sioux, led to believe that through participation in the ceremonies of a new religion called the Ghost Dance they could make the buffalo return and the white men disappear, caused white authorities to believe another Indian War might be imminent. The subsequent Battle of Wounded Knee proved to be the swan song of the long and bitter Indian Wars of the West.

Surely no opposing forces ever differed more radically than did the Army of the United States and the hostile Indians of the West in the years 1850–90. The leaders of the blue-coated soldiers were professional military men who had studied the great battles of history at West Point. Many of them had demonstrated their mastery of the arts of civilized warfare on the battlefields of the Mexican War, the Civil War, or both. Yet in the leaders of the warring Indian tribes they encountered stubborn, intelligent men who were not impressed by the white officers' military reputations, who refused to fight according to the white men's rules, and who possessed an ability to embarrass their professional opponents by eluding or defeating the soldiers sent against them. When impatient, cocky young officers, eager to earn reputations for themselves, underestimated the leadership and fighting qualities of illiterate Indians, they invited disaster and paid for their mistakes with their lives. Older heads soon learned, as did General William T. Sherman, that in fighting Indians the Army was engaged in "an inglorious war, not apt to add much to our fame or personal comfort; and for our soldiers, to whom we owe our first thoughts, it is all danger and extreme labor, without one single compensating advantage."

In the Indian warrior the soldier found a worthy foe. What the Indian lacked in formal schooling he made up in native cunning and courage, in combat experience, and in thorough knowledge of the country in which he fought. He hunted men much as he hunted other big game. He was an expert in luring unsuspecting animals or enemies into an ambush. He was skilled in concealing his own movements. As the wild old frontiersman Jim Bridger said, "Where there ain't no Injuns, you'll find 'em thickest." In his prolonged intertribal wars the Indian gained intimate knowledge of tactics in small-scale, hit-and-run raiding, by which he harassed his enemies and kept them off balance. As a horseman the Indian of the Plains and the Northwest had few equals. His fleet, tough little ponies gave him the mobility he needed to elude large, slow-moving bodies of troops. He could evade conflict save under conditions which appeared favorable to him. It is no wonder that the successful formula for defeating and pacifying the Plains Indians which was adopted by the Army included both the winter surprise attack on hostile villages (when the Indians' superior horsemanship was of no advantage to him) and the immobilization of the Indian through the capture or destruction of his horses.

Much has been written about the horrors of Indian warfare—the Indians' penchant for torturing prisoners and mutilating the dead. But these cruelties did not originate during their wars with the whites. Long before white settlers and soldiers overran the western Indian country, redskinned warriors disfigured male prisoners and scalped and hacked to pieces their fallen foes in hard-fought intertribal battles. Most commonly these actions followed a revenge raid against enemies who had killed a prominent chief or a goodly number of warriors of the vengeance-motivated tribe.

Nor was savagery in the Indian Wars limited to the practices of the Indians. No war could be more savage than race warfare. And at times the Indian Wars degenerated to that level. Color of skin alone became the distinguishing mark of the hated enemy. Peaceful bands of Indians were attacked and their women and children killed in the indiscriminate slaughter that ensued.

The primitive Indian warrior made a contribution to the art of warfare. His swift, silent, harassing, small-scale operations were the forerunners of the commando raids in World War II. At least one description of western Indian raiding tactics was used in the training of American troops for action in the Pacific. General Douglas MacArthur paid tribute to the Indian as an efficient fighting man. "As a warrior, his fame is world-wide. Many successful methods of modern warfare are based upon what he evolved centuries ago. Individually he exemplified what the line fighter could do by adaptation to the particular countryside in which he fought."

Many books and articles have been written about various aspects of the Indian Wars in the West. Some of these works, such as George Bird Grinnell's *The Fighting Cheyennes*, John C. Ewers' *The Blackfeet*, R. N. Richardson's *The Comanche Barrier to South Plains Settlement*, have traced the participation of particular tribes in these wars. Books have been devoted to the Modoc War and to the Nez Perce War. The literature on the Battle of the Little Bighorn alone is extensive and widely scattered. No single volume could adequately describe all the hundreds of engagements, large and small, fought between Indians and whites in the American West during the nineteenth century.

This book is the first to combine in one volume descriptions of the most outstanding battles in the Indian Wars of the West. Each battle is described by a thorough student of that engagement. The writers have studied the historic records bearing on the fight, including official reports of field officers (if the Army was involved) and the testimony of participants who survived the fighting. They have considered and evaluated the interpretations of the battle made by previous writers. In the great majority of cases they have carefully examined the ground on which the battles were fought.

In *Great Western Indian Fights* the reader may relive some of the most stirring episodes in American history.

PART I
Fur Trading Days
1832

Introduction

No western Indians were more hostile toward white traders and trappers during the early decades of the nineteenth century than were the Gros Ventres (Big Bellies). This small tribe of little more than three hundred lodges hunted buffalo on the northwestern plains from the valley of the Saskatchewan southward beyond the Missouri River. They were allies of the three powerful Blackfoot tribes who lived between them and the Rocky Mountains to the westward. Yet their language differed markedly from that of their Blackfoot neighbors. Their closest relatives were the Arapaho Indians south of the Platte.

British traders on the Saskatchewan early learned to distinguish between the strong but friendly Blackfeet and the weaker but more irritable Gros Ventres. The Blackfeet neither feared nor fought the traders on the Saskatchewan. The Gros Ventres vacillated between friendship and enmity. In 1793 they attacked South Branch House and killed all but one of the inhabitants of that post. The very next year they pillaged Manchester House on the Saskatchewan. And thirty-one years later they fell upon Chesterfield House on the Red Deer River in present Alberta.

Early American trappers in the Upper Missouri country knew the Blackfeet and Gros Ventres as desperate and implacable enemies. Knowing both only as hostiles, they had little reason to distinguish Gros Ventres from Blackfeet. So they were inclined to call them all "Blackfeet," even though many of the Indian depredations upon American trappers who dared to trap beaver around the headwaters of the Missouri between the years 1808 and 1840 were committed by the Gros Ventres.

27

John Colter, first of the mountain men, was also the first American trapper to face the dread "Blackfeet" (really Gros Ventres) in battle. That was in 1808, when he helped a large party of Crows to repulse a "Blackfoot" attack. Repeated Blackfoot and Gros Ventre attacks prevented Americans from gaining a foothold in or near their country for more than twenty years thereafter. Even after the American Fur Company made peace with the Blackfeet and established a trading post on the Missouri near the mouth of the Marias in 1831, these Indians continued their relentless forays against American trappers. They clearly distinguished between traders, who offered the Indians useful goods in exchange for their furs and peltries, and trappers who exploited the rich fur resources of the high country with no profit to the Indians. And their war parties ranged far south and west of their own hunting grounds in search of these trapper-intruders.

Following their attack upon Chesterfield House in 1826, a considerable portion (but probably not the entire tribe) of the Gros Ventres fled southward to escape the wrath of the Hudson's Bay men and to join their kinsmen, the Arapahoes, south of the Platte. During the next five years American trappers and Santa Fe traders encountered the Gros Ventres as far south as the Cimarron, more than eight hundred miles from their northern homeland. They were making life miserable for overland parties of Americans and Mexicans alike.

Nor could this contentious little tribe long remain at peace even with their Arapaho relatives. A hot-headed Gros Ventre chief killed a chief of the Arapahoes. This led to more bloodshed before peace could be restored between the two tribes. The tribes decided to separate, and the Gros Ventres started on the long trek northward to their homeland. They passed through North Park to Bridger's Pass, and thence northward along the west side of the Rockies. So it was that in mid-July these battle-hardened, trapper-hating, red-skinned warriors entered the valley of Pierre's Hole west of the Three Tetons.

But it takes two sides to make a good fight. Now let's look at the other one. The other backdrop for the battle in Pierre's Hole was the annual reunion and bacchanal of the Rocky Mountain trappers called the Rendezvous. Hostile Indians (the Arikaras and

Blackfeet in the early 1820s and before) and competing trappers (the American Fur Company in the late 1820s) had forced a whole fraternity of American mountain men to abandon the earlier water route along the Upper Missouri. The Rocky Mountain Fur Company (which had its beginnings with the Ashley men of 1823–26) was compelled to change its former system of using a series of fixed trading posts at strategic river forks, and to devise an alternative method of gathering the furs, exchanging them for supplies, and transporting the supplies westward and the furs to St. Louis. This alternative, which was started by General Ashley himself in 1825, was called the Rendezvous system. Every summer, from 1825 to 1840 (except 1831), Company trappers, unaffiliated ("free") trappers and friendly Indians would meet, usually in July, at some selected Hole or junction point.

This was a once-a-year time for unbending and carousing, for seeing old comrades again, for spinning whopping tales or grimmer obituaries, for taking part in sporting contests or grudge fights, for picking a squaw bride, perhaps, and for planning the next year's trapping campaigns. The prime reason for Rendezvous, however, was logistical. To each such boisterous convention would come a caravan of supplies, westward from St. Louis, along the Platte, and over South Pass—across what was later to become the Oregon Trail route. (Irony it was that the hostility of the Upper Missouri Indians forced these early supply lines to go overland. They quickly discovered the flat, easy South Pass; when the thousands of settlers of the next decades headed for Oregon, the route was waiting for them.)

With the caravan's arrival, Rendezvous would get started in earnest. Beaver furs ("plews"), bundled into packs, were the commodity offered by the trappers and Indians. In exchange the supply train sold blankets, guns, powder, lead, knives, "forfurraw" (decorative trinkets for the extra-friendly squaws), and whiskey—everything marked up from five hundred to two thousand per cent over St. Louis prices. The Indians also traded mocassins and buckskins, pemmican and horses. In a few quick days the typical trapper would dispose of all his year's catch of furs and be back in debt to the Company—a debt to be worked off by still another year's hunting in the lonely mountains, waist-deep in icy streams.

2. THE PIERRE'S HOLE FIGHT

BRADLEY H. PATTERSON, JR.

Near the northwest edge of Wyoming, three sharp peaks spiral into the expansive sky. Here is the triumvirate of the American Alps: to the caravans of westward-crawling explorers, "the pilot knobs"; to the lonely French trappers, *"les trois Tetons."*

Down from the steel-blue granite fastness of the Teton Range lie two valleys—crowded these days with July tourists, but shouting with history from the mere century and a quarter back when solitary bands of beaver-hunters were the only white men in the western half of the continent. Then, as now, the Tetons looked down—to the east into Jackson's Hole, a crossroads of the trappers' wilderness, to the west into Pierre's Hole, meeting place and battleground.

There was no reason to use the elegant word "valley" when the mountain man's one-syllable "hole" would mean much the same: a plain, ringed with sheltering mountains where there were convenient streams, grass, game, and firewood. The early West was dotted with "holes" (the bigger ones were "parks") and in these protected flats the mountain men camped, wintered, and held their yearly fur-for-supplies Rendezvous.

Whereas in Jackson's Hole (named for an early fur-trapper) the Teton escarpment plummets dramatically eastward with nary a foothill between summit and sagebrush, on the Pierre's Hole side the mountains come down to the plain in a tumble of basins, ridges, and draws. Across this Hole, forming its western and southern boundaries, are the Big Hole and the Palisade Ranges. The waters in Pierre's Hole (the south fork of the Teton River) flow northward, emptying into the Henry's Fork of the Snake River near present-day Rexburg, Idaho.

Pierre's Hole immortalizes the name of *"le vieux Pierre Tivani-tagon."* This worthy, also known as *"le grand Pierre,"* was one of the leaders of the considerable number of Iroquois Indians whom the British Northwest Company imported from near Montreal into the Pacific Rocky Mountain area. The British purpose here was to use these Indians, already superb canoeists, as trappers also, and it is stated that a full third of the Northwest Company employees were Iroquois. These Indians gave the British as much trouble as assistance; both McKenzie and Alexander Ross complain about them, and in 1825 Pierre and several of his colleagues were among the eleven Indians and twelve trappers who, with their seven hundred pelts, deserted Britisher Peter Skene Ogden and joined Etienne Provost's band of Ashley men. Pierre himself was killed by the Blackfeet in the winter of 1828 while serving with an Ashley brigade. We do know that Pierre and his Iroquois comrades had trapped extensively in this Upper Snake River region, at times with Alexander Ross, at times "on their own," during the years 1823–24.

In 1832, not satisfied with establishing its trading-post monopoly along the Upper Missouri, the American Fur Company was intensifying the competition. This summer (and the next) it too would be represented some ninety strong at the Rendezvous; it too would outfit a supply train and, sending it from the Company's steamboat wharves at Fort Pierre or Fort Union, would try to beat the Rocky Mountain Fur Company caravan to the Rendezvous. The reason was elementary: the first supply train to get to Rendezvous would get much of the business and most of the furs for that year.

Thus the setting in early July of 1832: the three Tetons looking westward over their lofty shoulders to see foregathering in the upper part of Pierre's Hole some 250 trappers, plus some 200 lodges of Nez Perce, Flathead, Snake, and Bannack Indians. In a cloud of dust, coming across Green River Valley, was the Rocky Mountain supply caravan—180 mules loaded with trade-goods and 110-odd men, captained by William Sublette, himself a trapper. In the Big Horn Valley farther to the north, and in an equal hurry, was the rival supply train of the American Fur Company, under Lucien Fontenelle. (From Rendezvous the Rocky Mountain Fur partisans successively sent two advance parties out to hurry Sublette's caravan along. The American Fur Company men likewise sent scouts for Fontenelle.)

But coming up from the south was a large band of Gros Ventre Indians. Here were 150–200 men, women, and children, heading homeward after one of their tribe's periodic visits with their former neighbors and kinsmen, the Arapahoes of Colorado. Wanting to avoid their mortal enemies, the Crows, and perhaps to get a few shots at their less feared enemies the Flatheads, this band of Gros Ventres was traveling west of the Divide—on a course which would lead them straight through Pierre's Hole.

On its trek westward, the Sublette and Campbell supply train found itself being augmented. At Independence, Sublette consented to have Nathaniel J. Wyeth (of Cambridge, Massachusetts) and his band of twenty-three other eastern greenhorn entrepreneurs travel with his train. (The western fur trade was getting crowded.) Six of the Wyeth party turned back before they were across South Pass. Near Laramie Fork, Tom (Broken Hand) Fitzpatrick came riding up to meet them, to urge them to hurry, since they were being raced to Rendezvous this year and the race was crucial.

Broken Hand then wheeled about and rode off west again to

tell the waiting trappers and Indians that Sublette was on his way. But a single man in the mountains was fair game for any lurking Indians, and the Gros Ventres were on the move in the vicinity. Some of them spied Fitzpatrick at Green River, chased him, wore out his horse, and would have had his scalp had he not hidden artfully under some rocks and brush for thirty-six hours until the coast was clear enough for him to continue on foot. His raft on the Snake upset, too, but when his searching companions found him, though he had only a knife with him, he was still heading straight for Pierre's Hole. He was badly emaciated and, although he still had his scalp, its reported metamorphosis was to give him a new name—White Hair.

Where the Sweetwater freshens the North Platte, a group of trappers came into camp—bedraggled and starving. They were from a small, independent, and nearly bankrupt St. Louis outfit (Gant and Blackwell) and had come out the year before. They sold their furs and joined the caravan. Near Green River came still another addition—Alexander Sinclair and thirteen free trappers. At Green River, the mathematics were different. Around midnight on July 2 the supply-train camp was attacked by Gros Ventres. Ten horses were subtracted.

Six days later, at noon of July 8, 1832, the Sublette caravan came boisterously jangling into Pierre's Hole from the south, amid a fusillade of celebrative rifle shots. They had won their race with Fontenelle. The Rocky Mountain Company reaped a wealth of plews that summer (actually, the last great harvest of the fur trade). Bill Sublette learned there was more money in the supply business than in the fur-hunting itself.

The trading and revelry went on for more than a week. Then—back to the year's business. For Bill Sublette, his packs heavy with furs, back to St. Louis. For the trappers, lightheaded and empty-handed, back to the Green River, the Snake River, and the Yellowstone, to the Owyhee and the Humboldt, back to the Salmon and the Bear, to the Wind and the Bighorn. The aspens would soon be gold again, the beavers' coats would be thickening. There would be autumn campfires with hump-rib and beavertails roasting and "boudins" spitting in the coals. The snow would soon whiten a thousand peaks, the wind blasting the leaves from the cottonwoods. With pack animals and spare horse, the scattered brigades would be threading their way along a hundred mountain trails—wagon routes of the next decade, roads of the next century. Some of the mountain men would take new squaws with them, for warmer, less lonely nights in winter quarters in South Park or on the Popo Agie. Some would see each other again at next summer's Rendezvous on Horse Creek; a few would rendezvous only with a Blackfoot arrow or a grizzly's fang. This was life in the American West in the 1830s—but it would go on only as long as hats were made of beaver.

On July 17 the Rendezvous began to break up. Bill Sublette's brother Milton led a band of thirteen trappers up to the end of the Hole on their way southwestward. With them were Sinclair and fifteen of his men, and Wyeth and ten of his. They camped eight miles south of Rendezvous. When breaking camp next morning, they espied a long file of approximately 150–200 Indians, some on horseback but mostly on foot, coming down a gap in the mountains ahead of them. Not Fontenelle and his caravan, but Gros Ventres.

The trappers did two things immediately—they threw up emergency breastworks (the packs from their mules) and sent two riders off down the Hole to the Rendezvous, to round up white and red reinforcements.

Most of the Gros Ventre women and children retreated to the mountains; the braves prepared for an attack in force on what they supposed was only a small brigade of trappers. To gain time, the Gros Ventres sent forward a war chief, unarmed, with red blanket and peace pipe. The veteran trappers recognized this ruse for what it was. One of Sublette's men was Antoine Godin, an Iroquois half-breed, whose father had been killed by the Blackfeet two years back. Godin rode forward and with him rode a Flathead brave whose tribe had been subject to years of Gros Ventre and Blackfoot marauding.

The Gros Ventre chief stretched out his right hand; Antoine took it. To his Flathead companion, he shouted "Fire!" and the chief was killed on the spot. They scalped him, took the richly decorated blanket as booty, and galloped back to the group of trappers. A new *modus operandi* for Cambridge; Wyeth's brother exclaims in writing, "This was Joab with a vengeance—art thou in health, my brother?" But one will remember what the Gros Ventres were like.

The furious Indians at once dove into a deep, swampy woods and began to pile up a fortification of logs and branches, their women digging trenches behind it. This seemed too redoubtable a stronghold to take by storm, and the trappers skirmished at long range. It wasn't long before Bill Sublette came riding up with eager reinforcements from the Rendezvous—one or two hundred trappers and four or five hundred Nez Perces and Flatheads.

Bill Sublette took charge, irritated that more decisive action had not already been taken. He ordered Wyeth's Boston greenhorns to stay back, then led Wyeth himself, Sinclair, Campbell, and some sixty other red and white volunteers into the willow grove. Sublette and Campbell made verbal wills as they advanced, making each the other's executor. Unnecessary for them, as it turned out, but one hopes that Sinclair had made one—he was hit as they went forward and died later after Campbell had carried him out of the woods.

Sublette saw a small hole between the logs, and an Indian's eye behind—a literal bullseye when Sublette shot at it. Then it was his turn to get shot—a wound in the arm took him out of the battle, though for a time he kept on shouting commands. The attacking trappers had now split into two enfilades, but in the 1830s there were no walkie-talkies. They got on opposite sides of the stockade, and there was some highly unfortunate cross fire.

When the lead began to get low (the mountain men had to come back the next day to dig bullets out of the trees), epithets were used as supplements. The trappers threaded nearer and nearer through the woods, brush, and vines. "The idea of a barbed arrow sticking in a man's body, as we had observed it in the deer and other animals, was appalling to us all, and it is no wonder that some of our men recoiled from it," John Wyeth later wrote. Occasionally a Flathead would rush forward, fire, and snatch a blanket from the defending breastworks as a trophy. One trapper, high-"spirited," climbed onto the top, peered down, then fell in with two bullets through his skull. The trappers then

decided on an old Blackfoot custom—to set fire to the woods.
Their red accomplices protested vehemently—not that it wasn't
sporting, not that they minded Blackfoot incineration, but fire
would endanger what was really important—the plunder and
booty they were thirstily anticipating. The mountain men overruled these objections and instructed the squaws to gather fag-
gots.

The Gros Ventres now tried a ruse. They shouted to the attackers that they might die in flames, but let the trappers beware—
there were four hundred more lodges of their Gros Ventre breth-
ren who were near and who would avenge them. The Gros
Ventres at this point got an unexpected assist from the translating
department. This final admonition was circuitously rendered into
English by Flathead and Nez Perce interpreters—and came out
that four hundred lodges of Gros Ventres were at that moment
attacking and plundering the rendezvous camp itself, back down
the Hole. Some trappers with poor judgment plus many more
who were just as happy to extricate themselves from this encounter immediately rushed off to save their main camp, leaving only
a small watch-party.

Those staying behind retreated to the edge of the grove. Night
fell. Some hours later the main body of trappers shamefacedly
returned; they had found the rendezvous camp unmolested. Now
it was too dark and forbidding to charge in again at the Gros
Ventres; the trappers mounted guard until morning.

With the morning sun they advanced again toward the Indian
breastworks. There was silence; no opposition. Closer they came
—still no response. Finally they rushed behind the stockade. They
found the Indians gone. The Gros Ventres had made good their
escape in the middle of the night, carrying off their wounded on
litters that left bloodstains on the trailside branches. In the stockade there were twenty or thirty dead horses and nine dead Indians. More corpses were found through the woods, including
bodies of several children, according to some reports. There were
some white dead—mutilated, Indian style. There was a wounded
white man who died shortly, and a wounded Gros Ventre squaw
whom the Flatheads dispatched without hesitation.

The trappers' red allies got their plunder, too; the escaping

Gros Ventres had left a trail of blankets, tepees, and other possessions as they fled. A little farther into the mountains the trappers found a herd of forty-five horses where the Gros Ventre squaws had hidden them. Bill Sublette recognized some of these horses as his, proving that it had been members of this same Gros Ventre band who had attacked his camp at Green River on July 2.

The mountain men buried the dead behind the breastworks and counted up the final score—five trappers and seven friendly Indians killed, six whites and seven red allies wounded. The Gros Ventres later admitted they had lost twenty-six of their band— which in savage reporting systems probably meant a good many more.

There continued to be violent repercussions in the aftermath of the fight. The trappers and their allies all went back to Rendezvous and waited a few days, taking care of Bill Sublette's wound. The leader of the Gant and Blackwell trappers (whom Sublette had met on the Platte) decided that Sublette had gypped him. His name was Stephens and he, plus four free trappers and three of the Wyeth party who had had enough, started eastward ahead of Sublette—over Teton Pass. Two of this party were Daniel Boone's grandsons. The Gros Ventres were waiting for them. One trapper and one Bostonian gave their scalps to the Gros Ventres and their bones to the forest, there overlooking Jackson's Hole on one of the most scenic mountainsides in America. Stephens himself was mortally wounded and, with the luckier survivors, came back across the pass to die in Pierre's Hole.

In the Hoback River country, latecomer Fontenelle, still en route with the American Fur Company's supply caravan, came head-on into the retreating Gros Ventres. Fontenelle, however, was suspicious and on guard, and the Gros Ventres were still licking their wounds. After a formal parley, Fontenelle sent fifteen of the Gros Ventres down the Green River a ways to where Captain Benjamin Eulalie de Bonneville of the Seventh Infantry U.S. Army, out fur-trapping on a two-year leave, was building a frontier trading post. Bonneville treated the murderous Gros Ventres civilly though watchfully, in spite of being egged on to slaughter them all by several Crows who were simultaneously paying the new fort a visit. The fifteen got neither scalps nor horses.

The Sublette and Campbell train, loaded with 168 packs of beaver pelts worth $85,000, made an intentional detour in order to avoid any second encounter with the Gros Ventres—and miscalculated. Sublette ran into the main Gros Ventre body, who had heard of their relatives' defeat; they were now wearing war paint, ready for trouble. The veteran Sublette, however, subtracted twenty-five pounds of tobacco from his wares and negotiated his way out of danger.

Yet after their great defeat and these lesser frustrations, the Gros Ventres' worst tribulations were still ahead of them. The survivors of the Pierre's Hole battle rejoined the main tribal body and, shunted off course by the fight, continued their migration northward—east of the Divide—in Crow country. Here, in the Absaroka Mountains, men, women, children, and possessions fell to the Crows—traditional enemies of all Blackfeet. What few surviving members of the migrating Gros Ventres finally got into the Upper Missouri home country told their story to their other Blackfoot neighbors, with lasting effect.

For the next two decades these two tribes strongly resisted any attempts at white settlement in their homeland. They sought out and killed the lone hunters and trappers and raided wagon trains. In fact, the echoes of the shots fired over the Pierre's Hole breastworks were heard in the Upper Missouri country for a long time.

PART II

Under the Lone Star
1841

Introduction

The problems of the infant Republic of Texas were many—and none were more troublesome than the raids of the Mexicans and Indians on the western and northern border settlements. The Republic was badly in debt and it seemed impossible to maintain an army to deal with the numerous frontier raids. The Congress of the Republic authorized the organization of a number of companies of rangers (Stephen F. Austin had used this same plan to defend the frontier before Texas won its independence from Mexico).

The rangers furnished their own horses, guns, and clothing and were enrolled for relatively short periods of service—six months and never more than twelve. They were not very well paid (sometimes just not paid) and there never were very many of them at any one time, but what a job they did! They patrolled, fought Mexicans and Indians, recovered stolen women, children, horses, and cattle, followed the Comanches far into the Indian country, chased the raiding Mexicans back across the Rio Grande, and generally exceeded the call of duty.

Bandera Pass had been the site of many skirmishes and battles through the centuries. More than a hundred years before the rangers fought the Comanches there, the Spaniards and the Apaches fought it out in the pass. This area had previously been occupied mainly by the Apaches. That tribe had lived in the vicinity of the pass in the early eighteenth century during the Spanish occupation of Texas. Indeed, the Apache hunting grounds had extended from San Antonio to Santa Fe, and by 1732 their chief village was in the vicinity of what soon became known as Bandera Pass. From there they made frequent forays into San Antonio and even across the Rio Grande.

Tradition has it—and there is some evidence of truth to sustain the tale—that prior to 1732 the Indians made a treaty with the Spaniards by the terms of which the former agreed to forego raids south of the pass, and the Spaniards agreed not to encroach on the hunting grounds beyond that dividing range. Flags may have been planted on mountain peaks to mark this line.

But despite the peace-making arrangements, the Indians continued their forays into settlements around San Antonio where missions had been established. Thirteen new families and two single men had arrived from the Canary Islands to strengthen the San Antonio colony, and that village was spreading out a bit. This made it more inviting for moonlight raiders.

Depredations were so persistent that the settlers are said to have appealed to the King of Spain for protection; whereupon in 1732 Spanish troops were sent into the Bandera range. A showdown battle took place at Bandera Pass. It lasted three days and resulted in the complete rout of the Apaches. Thus placed on the defensive, and badgered by the encroachment of the fighting Comanches from the Texas plains, the Apaches gradually retreated westward and eventually settled in what is now New Mexico and Arizona.

3. BATTLE OF BANDERA PASS

O. CLARK FISHER

One of the most celebrated Indian fights on the Texas frontier took place in 1841 in Bandera Pass between forty Texas Rangers under the command of Captain John Coffee (Jack) Hays and a contingent of from three to six hundred Comanches.

Just how the pass got its name is a subject of conjecture among historians. Tradition has it that a General Bandera commanded Spanish troops who had engaged the Apaches at that site more than a century earlier. This explanation, discounted by the noted historian, the late J. Marvin Hunter, whose research found no such person in command of Spanish troops in San Antonio, is probably not as valid as the "flag" theory, frequently referred to. Bandera is a Spanish word meaning "banner" or "flag," and it is said the Spaniards hoisted flags on mountaintops near the pass after their victory over the Apaches, as a reminder of their determination to cope with any recurrence of Indian devilment.

This deep gorge, about 500 yards long and 125 feet wide, cut through the hills which separate the Medina and Guadalupe valleys, was used for centuries as a passageway by Indians, prospectors, homesteaders, missionaries, stage coaches, United States troopers, wagon trains, and even camel caravans. It was a natural pass, with hills on each side about 250 feet high. Old Camp Verde, located just two miles north of Bandera Pass, on Camp Verde Creek, was the only camel post to be established in the United States.

The fight followed by one year the famous Battle of Plum Creek, in which Hays also figured, and the two events marked a crushing blow to the warring Comanche in Texas.

After much service under Captains Deaf Smith and Henry W. Karnes, Hays, at the age of twenty-three, was in 1840 appointed Captain of a company of rangers, with headquarters at San Antonio. He served continuously until after the Mexican War. The Comanches were enraged over their defeat at Plum Creek and the loss of the loot, including between two and three thousand horses and mules, many of which had served as pack animals to carry their plunder from an earlier raid on Linnville. They came in small bands, raiding isolated ranches, stealing horses, killing women and children, and generally harassing the frontier. When the enlistment period of the men in Hays' company was about up, the citizens of San Antonio petitioned the Texas President (Houston had replaced Lamar) to continue the company in service. This request was granted and Hays and his rangers renewed their efforts to defend the frontier. A few weeks before the fight at Bandera Pass, Hays, singlehanded while his rangers stood guard, wiped out a dozen raiding Comanches in a thicket in Uvalde Canyon. The main scouting ground of the rangers was in the mountains northwest, west, and southwest of San Antonio, up the Guadalupe, Medina, Sabinal, and Nueces rivers.

In the spring of 1841 Hays took a contingent of forty rangers (from their camp on Leon Creek seven miles west of the Alamo city) northwest on a scouting mission. They pitched camp at night at a site which is now the center of the town of Bandera. The following morning they moved north en route to the Guadalupe valley. As they were traversing the famous Bandera Pass they found themselves surrounded by a large force of Comanches.

Evidently Indian scouts had detected the approach and the Comanche chief had arranged an ambush in the pass. Historians say it was the first time Captain Hays had ever been trapped. He and his men had routed the Comanches in several frontier engagements, notably in the battles of Nueces Canyon, Pina Trail Crossing, and Enchanted Rock. For a moment it looked as if he had at last been outsmarted.

The pass is about ten miles north of the present town of Bandera and some fifty miles west of San Antonio. With its steep, rock-studded sides rising sharply fifty to seventy-five feet, and with cover provided by thick brush and rock, it posed a perfect setting for an ambush. The Indians hid their horses in the hills north of the pass and were in well-concealed positions when the Rangers entered from the south.

When they were a third of the way through the pass, the first intimation of the presence of danger came; the terrible war whoop of Comanches on the warpath resounded through the gorge, accompanied by flying arrows and violent gunfire, with hundreds of redskins rushing pell-mell into the fray.

Several rangers fell, killed or wounded. Unruly horses plunged and reared, wounded and scared. Thus, with the rangers surrounded and overwhelmed, the surprise advantage set the stage for a possible major disaster. But the confusion was quelled split seconds later when Hays, cool and collected, yelled out above the tumult:

"Steady, there boys; dismount and tie your horses; we can whip them, no doubt about it!"

Those words were quoted by one of the surviving rangers, Ben Highsmith, years later, in an interview with historian A. J. Sowell.

Soon the Indians were falling and giving way before deadly rifle and pistol fire. They came again. Hand-to-hand fighting ensued. "Fighting was raging and the pass was full of Indians," reports Sowell. The Comanche chief attacked Sergeant Kit Ackland and wounded him. Ackland wounded the chief with a pistol, and then they clinched and both went down. Both were large, powerful men, according to Highsmith, and the combat was terrific. Both had out their long knives and rolled over and over on the ground, each trying to avoid the thrust and himself give the deadly wound. The ranger was finally victorious. The chief lay dead, "literally cut to pieces."

That left the rangers masters of the situation. The Indians again fell back, retreating to the north end of the pass. Rangers Highsmith, Ackland, Tom Galbreath, James (Red) Dunn, Sam Luckey, and Peter Fohr were wounded.

The dead and wounded rangers were taken back to the south entrance where there was a large water hole, and there the rangers spent the night. Five had been killed and six wounded. The dead were buried and the wounded cared for. The Comanches removed their dead and wounded; hence their exact losses were never determined, but it is believed that a total of about sixty warriors were either killed or wounded.

Thus ended a frontier battle of major importance. The gallantry and skill displayed by Hays and his men at Bandera Pass contributed much to the world-wide reputation of the Texas Rangers. Indian raids in that area were thereafter reduced appreciably.

Sowell reports that Jack Hays never had a better crowd of fighting men than was with him in that fight. They included Sam Walker, Kit Ackland, Peter Hansborough Bell, Ben McCulloch, Ad Gillespie, Sam Luckey, Tom Galbreath, James Dunn, George Neill, Mike Chevaille (sometimes spelled Chevallier) and Creed Taylor.

Later Walker was a lieutenant colonel in the Mexican War of 1846 and was killed in the Battle of Humantla. Gillespie commanded a company also and was killed at the storming of Monterrey. Ben McCulloch commanded a company and also served as a Confederate general in the Civil War, losing his life in the Battle of Elkhorn. George Neill was the son of Colonel James Neill, who commanded the artillery at the storming of San Antonio. Chevaille was a captain in the Mexican war, as was also Ackland. Sam Luckey was a famous humorist, singer, and storyteller around campfires. Bell was afterwards Governor of Texas.

Ben Highsmith took part in eighteen battles, and was the last man to carry a dispatch from Travis at the Alamo.

Captain Hays, "whose bravery bordered closely on rashness," continued to distinguish himself on the Texas frontier and later moved to California where he became the first sheriff of San Francisco, Federal surveyor general, and founder of Oakland.

Now—for a parting glance at the scene of that celebrated Battle of Bandera Pass—in 1900 Sowell, after his interview with Highsmith, concluded:

"The Comanches buried their chief at the upper end of the Pass, and the spot can still be pointed out by some rocks that are over the grave." The State of Texas erected a monument at Bandera Pass in 1936.

PART III

Fighting in the Far West 1858-60

Introduction

There was much unrest due to Indian activities east of the Cascade Mountains in Washington Territory in the late 1850s. It had been hoped that the Treaties of 1855, negotiated by Governor Isaac I. Stephens, would bring peace to the area, but the relief from tension was only temporary. The ink was hardly dry on the joint treaty with the Yakima and neighboring tribes when prominent Yakima chiefs, including Kamiakin, Owhi, and Qualchan, started to incite open rebellion by the Indians against its terms. There followed numerous incidents of killing, thievery, and general hostility. In fact, in 1856 there was an active military campaign against the Yakimas. At its conclusion, Kamiakin moved east of the Columbia River but continued to sow seeds of discontent.

The Indians were dissatisfied with the assigned reservations, and settlers were encroaching on the lands set aside for them in the Treaties of 1855. Eastern Washington, north of the Snake River, was closed to settlement, but with the discovery of gold at Colville and Okanogan it became impossible to keep the miners out. The Indians accused the settlers of permitting their cattle to graze tribal lands and stoutly maintained that it was not stealing for them to kill and eat such cattle. The Indians particularly resented the establishment of Fort Walla Walla by the Army in 1856. An occasional expedition by the Army into the lands east of the Columbia was one thing, but the establishment of a permanent Army post and the rapid growth of a settlement around it, so close to their tribal lands, was another.

47

*Major (Brevet Lieutenant Colonel) William Jenner Steptoe,
Ninth Infantry, was in charge of building Fort Walla Walla. He
had graduated from the United States Military Academy in 1837,
and had been breveted twice for gallantry and meritorious conduct during the Mexican War. He had served in the Third Artillery from the time of his graduation from West Point until March
3, 1855, when he had been transferred to the Ninth Infantry with
a permanent rank of major.*

*Early in 1858 Major Steptoe, commanding officer at Fort Walla
Walla, received a petition for military assistance from some forty
white persons living at Colville, some miles north of the Spokane
River and many miles north of the fort. The petition stated that
the signers were afraid for their lives and property because of the
behavior of the neighboring Indians. The Palouse Indians had
recently raided the Walla Walla Valley, almost to within sight of
the fort, and stolen a number of cattle belonging both to the military and to civilian residents. A report reached the fort that the
Indians had killed two miners en route to the Colville gold mines.
The tension was building up.*

*Meanwhile, some hundreds of miles south in Nevada, then a
part of Utah Territory, much the same situation was developing.
Nevada had been on the route of many, many California emigrants and there had been some, but relatively little, trouble with
the Paiutes (Pah-Ute was the spelling used by most early writers,
however, Pay-Ute, Pih-Ute, Paiute, and Piute were also used).*

*The finding of gold and silver at Gold Hill, Virginia City, and
Silver City caused a squeezing of the Indians from their favorite
spots. The white men were killing their game, cutting and burning their pine-nut trees, and occupying their favorite water holes
and camping sites. The Paiutes had accustomed themselves to
many of the azure-skied and rugged mountain valleys or parks.
They considered the mysterious solitudes of the rolling plains and
desert wastes theirs. They resented being pushed around.*

*The winter of 1859–60 was one of unprecedented severity. The
Indians in the Truckee meadows were starving and freezing. In
desperation they raided the isolated ranches for food. In January,
1860, Dexter E. Deming was brutally murdered by the Paiutes at
his ranch in Willow Creek Valley.*

Troops were requested by Isaac Roop, convention-elected Governor of Nevada Territory (Nevada was made a Territory by Congress in 1861), of General Clark, Commander of the Department of the Pacific. No troops were sent. The accumulated hostility between the whites and Indians had reached a point by the spring of 1860 where only a spark might cause a flaming war.

4. THE INDIANS HAVE AN INNING: TO-HOTO-NIM-ME

JACK DODD

Major Steptoe informed his Headquarters, Department of the Pacific, by letter dated April 17, 1858, that he planned to lead an expedition from Fort Walla Walla to Colville to try to develop an understanding between the miner-settlers there and the Indians. En route he stated he would take corrective action against the Palouse Indians for the cattle-stealing raid in the Walla Walla Valley and that he would try to locate and capture the murderers of the two miners. The general situation being what it was, the Department of the Pacific offered no objections to Steptoe's proposed expedition.

On Thursday morning, May 6, 1858, Steptoe's command left Fort Walla Walla with a strength of 152 enlisted men and five company officers. Included were C, E, and H Companies, First Dragoons, and a 25-man mounted detachment from E Company, Ninth Infantry, the latter to man the two twelve-pound mountain howitzers. Additional personnel were Assistant Surgeon John Field Randolph; First Lieutenant Hugh Brady Fleming, the commissary officer; civilian packers, and several Nez Perce Indian scouts.

Departure had been delayed because the assembled baggage was too heavy a load for the pack animals. When the adjustments had been made the amount of ammunition was reduced to about forty rounds per man. This limited amount was to be a significant matter several days later, and also the single subject of censure of Steptoe's leadership of the expedition by Winfield Scott, Lieutenant General of the Armies.

The command did not head directly north for Colville but proceeded in a northeasterly direction for the Red Wolf crossing of the Snake River, located at the mouth of Alpowa Creek, because the hostile Palouses were reported to be gathered in this locality. Chief Timothy, a long-time friend of the whites and owner of a fleet of canoes, was camped with his band of Nez Perces at this crossing. The location of the hostiles, as well as the canoes, probably influenced Steptoe's decision to cross the Snake here.

The Palouses moved northward when the troops approached the Snake. Timothy's canoes were used to ferry the soldiers and their baggage across the river, and his people swam the horses to the other side. After the crossing, the command proceeded downriver several miles to the mouth of Skalassams Creek, now named Steptoe Creek, and, by following a route up this stream, reached the plateau north of the Snake. The retreating Palouses were then pursued in a leisurely manner over what is believed to be the old Indian trail betwene Lapwai and Colville.

While Steptoe was camping on the Palouse River eight days out of Fort Walla Walla, some friendly Indians advised him that the Spokanes would resist any movement of troops into their country. This warning was unexpected but was not considered

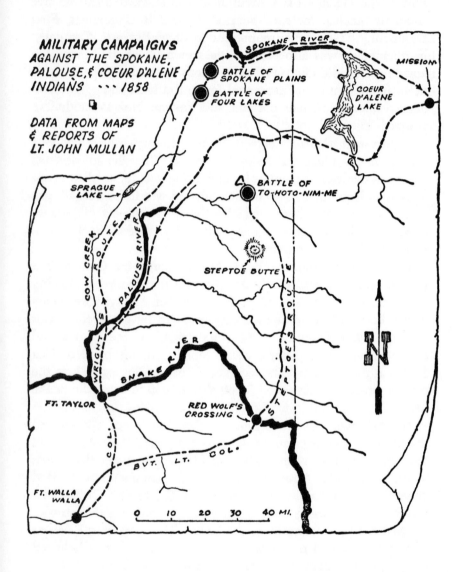

MILITARY CAMPAIGNS
AGAINST THE SPOKANE,
PALOUSE, & COEUR D'ALENE
INDIANS ··· 1858

DATA FROM MAPS
& REPORTS OF
LT. JOHN MULLAN

SPOKANE RIVER

BATTLE OF
SPOKANE PLAINS

MISSION

BATTLE OF
FOUR LAKES

COEUR
D'ALENE
LAKE

SPRAGUE
LAKE →

BATTLE OF
TO-HOTO-NIM-ME

STEPTOE BUTTE

COW CREEK

WRIGHT'S ROUTE

PALOUSE RIVER

STEPTOE'S ROUTE

SNAKE RIVER

N

FT. TAYLOR

RED WOLF'S
CROSSING

COL.

BVT.   LT.   COL.

FT. WALLA
WALLA

0   10   20   30   40 MI.

serious enough to cause any deviations from the northward route because the Spokanes had been friendly to the whites in the past.

An uneventful night was spent on May 15 at a camp on To-hoto-nim-me Creek near the present town of Rosalia, Washington. This creek was also called Ingossomen Creek and today is named Pine Creek. On May 16 the troops continued their march but at about 11 A.M. an estimated force of a thousand to twelve hundred Spokane, Coeur d'Alene, and Yakima Indians suddenly appeared. They did not attack, but from their threatening actions, war paint, and attire, it was obvious they were not friendly. Major Steptoe halted his troops at about a hundred yards' distance from the massed Indians. He told the Indians he wished to parley, and several spokesmen came forward to tell him they had been informed the soldiers had come to make war, and if so, they were ready to fight. The major replied that his mission was peaceful, as he was going to Colville to bring about a better understanding between the whites and their Indian neighbors. His answer somewhat satisfied the Indians, but they said they would not allow him to cross the Spokane River. The parley was dismissed when Steptoe saw that little was to be gained by continuing the discussion. He advised his officers to be alert, for a fight was possible.

At this location the terrain was not suited for a small force to battle an overwhelming number of warriors. Steptoe decided to move on up the trail to find a more favorable site, but cautioned his command not to fire until an order had been given. The advance was slow because of the crowding Indians. Steptoe had to abandon the trail when it entered a gulch surrounded by hills that were thronged with Indians. They jeered and taunted the soldiers when the detour was made. The troops reached a small lake about a mile away and halted with the water at their backs. They remained mounted and alert.

The Indians wished to resume the parley and, when the discussions began, sought to explain their hostile manner. They asked Steptoe why had he taken such an indirect route to Colville, and why had he brought the two howitzers with him. They considered these to be evidences of hostile intent. They reiterated that there would be no canoes available for him at the

Spokane River, and they threatened to destroy the canoes on the Snake to prevent his return to Fort Walla Walla. The Indians not engaged in the conference continued to taunt and insult the troops. In the afternoon the Indians informed the soldiers there would be no fighting that day because it was Sunday, but that they would return to fight. Their respect for the Sabbath was no doubt due to the work of the missionaries who had been among them. At sunset the Indians withdrew, and by dark none could be seen.

When the Indians had left, Steptoe reviewed the critical situation his command was facing. Believing his small force had little chance of reaching Colville against such a large and determined enemy, he decided to return to Fort Walla Walla. His decision was influenced by the fact that no help could be expected in crossing the Spokane River and by the knowledge that his small supply of ammunition was inadequate for a prolonged fight. A messenger was dispatched to Fort Walla Walla to advise the garrison of the situation and of the need for assistance. But Steptoe realized that delivery of the message would not alleviate the desperate situation the command was facing.

On the morning of May 17, after an uneasy and restless night, the troops began to retrace their trail. Second Lieutenant David McMurtrie Gregg with H Company took the lead, with C Company commanded by First Lieutenant (Brevet Captain) Oliver Hazard Perry Taylor following. The infantry detachment commanded by Captain Charles Sidney Winder was third in the column, and it was followed by the pack train. Second Lieutenant William Gaston with E Company brought up the rear. The column had gone only a short distance when it was overtaken by Father John Joseph Augustine Joset, a Jesuit priest in charge of the Coeur d'Alene Mission. Some Christian Indians had informed Father Joset of the presence of the military in the country and of the contemplated opposition by the tribes. He had hurriedly ridden ninety miles at the suggestion of the Coeur d'Alene chief, Vincent, who believed Father Joset might be able to avert a disaster. Steptoe had not previously met the priest but, although it had been rumored the missionaries were supplying the Indians with powder and were encouraging their hostility toward the government, he greeted Father Joset in a kindly manner.

Father Joset asked Steptoe to confer again with the chiefs. The major agreed but insisted that all talking be done on the move because the restlessness of the pack stock would not permit halting the column. Father Joset left to bring back the chiefs, but he was able to return with only Chief Vincent and some sub-chiefs of the Coeur d'Alenes. Major Steptoe told them he was returning now to Fort Walla Walla because the presence of his command was offensive to the Spokanes and Coeur d'Alenes, and because it would not be possible to reach Colville without their help in crossing the Spokane River. Unexpectedly one of Steptoe's Nez Perce scouts stepped forward and struck Chief Vincent with a quirt and accused him of "talking with a crooked tongue." Before more could be made of the incident one of Chief Vincent's uncles rode up and warned him to leave, as the Palouses were about to open fire. With this warning Chief Vincent and his companions left, followed by Father Joset.

By 8 A.M. about three miles had been retraced but a large number of Indians had gathered about Lieutenant Gaston's company at the rear of the column. Suddenly Gaston's company was fired upon, but the dragoons obeyed orders and withheld their fire even though the Indians were sweeping back and forth, shooting at them in an irregular manner. Upon receiving no return fire the Indians became quite brave and galloped along the flanks of the column. Within about twenty minutes all of the troops were under long range fire.

The route being followed was through narrow bottom lands surrounded by rolling hills. The five hundred or more Indians recognized the advantage of holding the higher terrain. Each time it appeared that the soldiers were heading for a hill the attackers raced madly to cut them off. A large hill in advance of the column appeared to be the objective of a large group of Indians. Fire from this hill would have been disastrous to the troops. Gregg's company was ordered to occupy the hill in advance of the Indians. He succeeded, but when the Indians saw they had lost the race for this hill, they advanced to another which commanded the first. Gregg left some men on the hill he had just taken, and successfully charged the second. By this time the units of the command were widely separated. About a mile of retraced trail had been gained by short charges since the start of the attack. Each time the dragoons charged, the Indians would scatter, only to wheel about and strike back at the dragoons as they returned to the column.

Gaston's company at the rear of the column was taking the brunt of the attacks. By this time one soldier had been killed and Gaston had been wounded in the hand. Lieutenant Taylor, with C Company, was also fighting desperately, making many short and furious charges from the flanks. The gunfire and the yelling Indians terrorized the pack train, and the frightened animals required constant attention to prevent them from stampeding. About eleven o'clock Captain Winder reached the hill occupied by Gregg. The two howitzers were brought into action, causing fear but few casualties. Taylor's and Gaston's companies fought desperately in an attempt to join up with the rest of the command. To prevent this union the Indians concentrated their attack on these two companies. Gregg, from his position on the hill, saw a body of Indians in front of Gaston's company. When it was apparent Gaston's company was about to charge this group, Gregg ordered his men to charge down the hill at the same time. The Indians were caught in an angle between the lines of the two charging companies, and they suffered many wounded plus at least twelve fatalities. Chief Victor of the Coeur d'Alenes and several of his prominent tribesmen were killed in the "angle." These losses infuriated the Indians, and the combined companies had to fight vigorously to reach the hill which had been held by Winder's men. In the meantime, by many short charges, Taylor had managed to join Winder and the pack train on the hill. For the first time in three hours the entire command was united. Casualties were, so far, one man killed, several animals lost, and a number of men and animals wounded.

From the hill the troops could see large and apparently increasing groups of Indians on the surrounding heights. Some were signaling to more distant allies. Major Steptoe re-formed his command. Because water was sorely needed, his immediate objective was to reach To-hoto-nim-me (Ingossomen) Creek. Taylor's and

Gaston's companies were assigned protection of the flanks. Gregg's and Winder's units were ordered to defend the rear and to keep the pack train moving ahead. Final instructions to the men included the necessity for conserving ammunition. The movement of the troops down the slope, shortly before noon, was immediately met by Indian demonstrations on all sides. The crowding of the horde of warriors was so great the troops did not dare charge any distance from the main column for fear they would be cut off. About twelve o'clock, E Company attempted to reduce pressure from a group of attackers by charging them. Lieutenant Gaston was fatally wounded. His death demoralized his men, but some fought bravely and furiously to save his body from the elated Indians, who were inspired by the killing of a "soldier chief." These Indians, who had previously retreated from organized charges, now reversed their usual tactics and charged E Company. Their attack was so fierce that it required the combined efforts of Gregg's and Winder's companies to hold the Indians until Gaston's disorganized dragoons could be re-formed. Some of the pack animals were lost because many of the men attending them had been needed to save E Company. The command continued to fight as it moved slowly forward, using the howitzers whenever possible.

While Gaston's company had been under attack, C Company led by Lieutenant Taylor was also fighting vigorously on the other flank. About 12:30 P.M. Taylor was shot through the neck and tumbled from his horse. He was lifted back onto his mount while his men fought a gallant hand-to-hand fight with the Indians who rushed in when he fell. First Lieutenant James C. Wheeler, Jr., took over Taylor's company. Major Steptoe decided that it was not possible for a moving column to continue such a fight and that a defensive position was required. His command was now about half a mile north of the campsite used the night of May 15. Ahead and to the left was a long ridge with a high point on one end. The column moved to its summit. The horses were picketed in the center of the knoll, and the men took prone positions in a circle around the crest. One howitzer was placed with a field of fire down the slope and the other was aimed along the ridge.

The hill was completely surrounded by determined Indians who kept up a constant fire on the troops. Some of it came from warriors on distant hills and some from Indians who had crept up the slope to shoot at closer range. Organized charges by dismounted Indians were repulsed several times, but each charge taxed the limited supply of ammunition. If these attacks continued, the command knew it was but a matter of time until they would be annihilated by a frenzied charge of hostiles, who now outnumbered them eight to one. The strength of the companies was weakened by the loss of those killed and wounded; they were also suffering from lack of water; their ammunition was down to two or three rounds per man; and they were strained and fatigued. Eight hours of constant action after an almost sleepless night had left them in poor condition for more fighting. At sunset the Indians withdrew, believing they could finish off the soldiers later. The withdrawal was a relief to the besieged soldiers, but the ring of twinkling campfires reminded them of what the next day would bring forth. Surgeon Randolph attended Lieutenant Taylor and the other wounded. Unfortunately Taylor's wound was so severe that he died on the hill.

Major Steptoe discussed the almost hopeless situation with his officers. He first believed the command should remain on the hill, but decided to leave it after several of his officers convinced him that the odds for survival were better if an escape was attempted. One of the Nez Perce scouts was sent to find a way through the encirclement, and Lieutenant Gregg was assigned the duty of preparing for the evacuation. The dead that could be reached were buried. The two howitzers were dismantled and also buried. The light-colored horses were blanketed, and all loose equipment that might rattle was tied down.

The scout returned with a report of a gap in the Indian lines in the direction away from the trail. Those of the fifteen wounded who could not sit their saddles unaided were lashed to their horses. Only supplies that could be tied to the saddles were taken. Lieutenant Wheeler's dragoons, accompanied by Captain Winder's infantry and the wounded, led off about 10 P.M. All supplies, camp equipment, and extra animals were left behind. Campfires were not extinguished. The first group left so quietly that the remaining dragoons on picket duty or busy preparing for the departure did not hear them leave. Little time was wasted in the final evacuation when Surgeon Randolph, who had assisted the first group, advised Gregg that the others had left.

Father Joset wrote later that the Indians had planned to maintain a round-the-clock attack by means of reliefs. The Coeur d'Alenes had the night shift and were to be relieved in the morning by their allies. About midnight the Coeur d'Alenes were surprised to find the hill unoccupied after they had made an assault. They did not notify the other Indians of the evacuation and did not pursue the troops, because the abandoned supplies and equipment became their first interest. When the Spokanes returned in the morning they apparently decided that it would not be possible to overtake the fleeing soldiers.

It is estimated to be ninety miles from the hill beside To-hoto-nim-me Creek to Red Wolf crossing. At dawn the weary troops stopped for a brief rest after crossing the Palouse River. They had ridden at a fast pace most of the night, anticipating that the Indians would overtake them. Twenty-four hours after leaving the battlefield they arrived at Chief Timothy's camp on the Snake River. They were welcomed by the Nez Perces, who fed them and guarded the camp the remainder of the night while the soldiers slept.

The troops pushed on to Fort Walla Walla after spending most of the next morning crossing the river. An uneasy moment occurred when a large party of Indians was seen approaching. The troops deployed into a defensive formation but, as the Indians drew near, saw a large American flag in their midst. Word of the fight had reached Chief Lawyer, and he and about sixty Nez Percé warriors had come to offer their services. The offer was declined, as Steptoe's command was in no condition to fight a return engagement. The march continued to a campsite about fifteen miles from the crossing of the Snake. A welcome sight that evening was the appearance of Captain Frederick Tracy Dent with B Company, Ninth Infantry, and provisions from the fort. Steptoe's messenger, who had left the night before the fight, had reached Fort Walla Walla after a 125-mile ride. Dent had lost little time in starting out and by forced marching had met

Steptoe a little short of the midway point. Two days later the entire command reached Fort Walla Walla.

Two weeks had elapsed since the expedition had left the fort. In that time Steptoe's men had fought gallantly against a foe that outnumbered them eight to one, and had miraculously escaped from an almost certain massacre. The final losses were two officers, ten men, and three friendly Indians killed, plus ten men wounded, and 29 horses killed or lost from wounds in the "Battle of To-hoto-nim-me." The exact hostile losses are not known, but acknowledged losses were nine killed and 40 or 50 wounded.

5. THE SOLDIERS HAVE THEIRS: FOUR LAKES AND SPOKANE PLAINS

JACK DODD

Following Steptoe's defeat and the receipt of his report, the Department of the Pacific immediately initiated action for a retaliatory campaign against the Palouse, Spokane, and Coeur d'Alene Indians. Colonel George Wright, Ninth Infantry, was appointed commander of the campaign. The colonel had graduated from West Point in 1822 and during the succeeding thirty-six years had experienced a very active military career. He was a battle-tested soldier who had been breveted three times for gallantry or meritorious conduct—once during the Seminole Indian War in Florida and twice during the Mexican War. His service

61

also included campaigns against the Indians of the Pacific Northwest.

Fort Walla Walla was designated as the assembly point for the troops and supplies. Colonel Wright arrived there early in July to prepare for his expedition. Before starting northward, he entered into a mutual aid treaty with the Nez Perces in order to have friendly Indians in his rear. This treaty was signed on August 6, 1858, and was not broken until 1877, when Chief Joseph's band went on the warpath. Thirty Nez Perces were recruited to serve with Wright. They were dressed and equipped as soldiers so they could be distinguished from hostile Indians.

The Snake River was the most formidable stream to be crossed by the troops en route to the territory of the hostile tribes. Major Steptoe had recommended that a crude fort be built on the Snake for the protection of a ferry. On August 7, while his command was assembling, Colonel Wright sent Captain Erasmus Darwin Keyes, Third Artillery, to select a site and to build a fort. With Keyes was a company of dragoons and six companies of dismounted artillery with two twelve-pound howitzers and two six-pound guns. Thirty thousand rations were carried by wagons and mules. First Lieutenant John Mullan, Second Artillery, who was to gain renown as the builder of the wagon road between The Dalles, Oregon Territory, and Fort Benton, Montana Territory, was the engineer officer. The first action of this campaign occurred when road-builders near the Snake exchanged shots with Indians scouting their activities. The fort was quickly completed at the north of the Tucannon River and named Fort Taylor in honor of the Lieutenant Taylor who had been killed while serving under Major Steptoe. It was poorly located to withstand modern warfare, but the overlooking bluffs offered no tactical advantage to a foe without artillery or long range weapons.

The remaining units left Fort Walla Walla on August 15 and arrived at Fort Taylor three days later. By August 26 the command had crossed the Snake River. Several days had been taken to ferry 570 regulars, 30 Nez Perce recruits, 100 civilian employees, 800 animals, and the baggage and subsistence for 38 days. Captain (Brevet Major) Francis Octavus Wyse with D Company, Third Artillery, was left behind to man Fort Taylor and to protect the stored supplies and boats. On the morning of the twenty-seventh the march into hostile territory began. Not until the third day out of Fort Taylor were any Indians seen, although their presence was attested to by the vast areas of blackened prairie which had been fired to deprive the expedition's livestock of forage.

When first observed, the Indians were in small bands that kept their distance while moving along the flanks of the column. Gradually their numbers increased, and by 5 P.M. on that third day they were bold enough to attack the pickets. The firing was brisk, but when Colonel Wright turned out part of his command the Indians ran away. The dragoons returned to camp after they had chased the attackers for more than four miles.

The next day, August 31, the Indians were more numerous, but they did not come near the column. That evening they struck at the pack train, but the deployed rear guard and the infantry drove them away. Camp was made that night at "Four Lakes"—a distance of 123 miles from Fort Walla Walla. Thus far two brief skirmishes had been fought with no casualties. The following action of five hours' duration is listed in War Department records as the "Battle of Four Lakes."

On the morning of September 1, Indians were observed gathered on the summit of a high hill about two miles northeast of the campsite. Colonel Wright marched from camp at 9 A.M. with E and C Companies of the First Dragoons, commanded by Captain (Brevet Major) William Nicholson Grier; A, B, G, and K Companies; Third Artillery, armed with rifle muskets, commanded by Captain Keyes; one howitzer detachment under First Lieutenant James Lyon White, Third Artillery; thirty Nez Perce Indians led by First Lieutenant John Mullan; and B and E Companies, Ninth Infantry, commanded by Captain F. T. Dent. The guarding of the camp and supplies was assigned to Captain James Allen Hardie. The guard force consisted of M Company, Third Artillery, commanded by First Lieutenant Horatio Gates Gibson, assisted by Second Lieutenant George Brown Dandy, one manned howitzer and a guard of fifty-four men under Second Lieutenant Lylan Benton Lyon.

The hill that was occupied by the Indians is now named

Wright's Hill. It is about 455 feet higher than the almost level terrain surrounding its base. To the northeast is Riddle Hill, and in the valley between are Granite and Willow Lakes. Meadow Lake is located at the eastern base of Wright's Hill. West of Riddle Hill is Silver Lake. These four lakes are visible from the summit of Wright's Hill and gave the name to the campsite and battle.

When the troops approached the hill, Colonel Wright ordered Captain Grier to advance with his company of dragoons to the north and around the left base of the hill. This movement was planned to place the dragoons in position to intercept the Indians as they were driven from the hill. The colonel and the remainder of the troops marched to the right of the hill to gain a position where the ascent would be easier. This maneuver was expected to drive the Indians in the direction of Captain Grier's dragoons. Captain Keyes deployed his dismounted artillerymen as skirmishers when they were about six hundred yards from the waiting Indians. Captain Edward Otho Cresap Ord's M Company assisted by First Lieutenant Henry B. Davidson's E Company of dragoons gallantly scrambled up the slope and drove the Indians from the top of the hill. They retreated down the north slope and rallied at the base of the hill in the cover of ravines, trees, and brush.

Colonel Wright reached the hilltop and planned the next phase of his attack. The Indians at the base of the hill seemed determined to hold their position. A vast plain to the north was occupied by about five hundred mounted Indians who were riding back and forth waving their weapons, by their actions daring the troops to attack them. To the right of the base of the hill in a pine forest were more Indians. Captain Grier's dragoons had swept around the hill and were in position for the foe to be driven in their direction. While waiting for action they were being subjected to ineffective long range fire.

The colonel ordered Captain Keyes to deploy artillery Companies B, under First Lieutenant George Percy Ihrie, and G, led by First Lieutenant Dunbar Richard Ransome, along the crest of the hill. Captain Dent's infantry battalion, consisting of two companies, E under Captain C. S. Winder and B commanded by First

Lieutenant Hugh Brady Fleming, was directed to move to the right in order to deploy before the pine forest. First Lieutenant Ogden Tyler's A Company with the howitzer was moved to a lower position where they could direct its fire more effectively.

The deployment took about five minutes and then the order to advance was given. The two artillery companies moved steadily down the slope, and the infantry companies moved toward the pine forest. The Indians at the base of the slope were driven out onto the plain or into the woods at the right, and those in the forest were forced to retreat. The artillerymen passed the dragoon company waiting on the extreme left. Then Captain Grier's dragoons and those of Davidson, who had been following behind the skirmishers, suddenly charged through the gaps between the skirmishers, and struck at the Indians on the plain. Many warriors were killed or wounded by the dragoons when they cut and slashed with their sabers. In a short time the Indians had fled from the plain, but the slashing attack of the dragoons was not halted until their horses became winded after a pursuit of over a mile. Revenge was no doubt behind the fury of those dragoons who had served with Gaston and Taylor when those officers had been killed at To-hoto-nim-me Creek. The skirmishers who had come off the hill and those who had deployed in front of the pine forest were now in one continuous skirmish line. This line passed and continued to advance about six hundred yards beyond the halted dragoons. Colonel Wright halted the skirmishers when he saw there was no further opposition. Several shots fired by the howitzer drove the remaining Indians out of sight.

The battle was won, recall was sounded, and the troops returned to camp at 2 P.M. Not a single man had been killed or wounded. The Indian losses were some eighteen or twenty killed and many wounded. One reason for the lack of casualties among the military was that they had longer range weapons than did the Indians, who were armed with Hudson's Bay muskets, bows and arrows, and lances.

The troops rested at the Four Lakes campsite for three days. They broke camp early on September 5 and moved northward to fight a battle which is officially listed as the "Battle of Spokane Plains." After a five-mile march an open plain or prairie was

reached. Mounted Indians were discovered moving parallel to
the column about three miles distant from the right flank. Their
speed indicated they were attempting to intercept the column
before it reached the pine forest across the north end of the
prairie. The column, especially the long pack train, was closed
up without delaying the forward movement. The Indians were
observed setting fire to the grass at points in advance and to the
right of the column.

Three artillery companies were deployed as skirmishers to the
front and to the right of the main column. These were Ord's K
Company, Tyler's A Company, and Gibson's M Company. Captain Hardie's G Company of artillery was deployed to the left at
the same time. The two howitzers supported by E Company,
Ninth Infantry, were also advanced to the line of skirmishers.
There was a brisk interchange of fire. The entire command was
about to be enveloped by the grass fires which had spread into
a single "wall of fire." Colonel Wright ordered an advance, and
the skirmishers, the howitzer units, and Captain Grier's dragoons
moved forward through the flames. The Indians fled to the shelter
of the rocks and trees in the pine forest when they saw that the
flames had not stopped the soldiers. They retreated still farther
when shelled by the howitzer. As they retreated, they were followed by the skirmishers and the dragoons.

At this point the border of the plain had been reached. Ahead
were rocky hills and gullies covered with an open ponderosa pine
forest. The line of skirmishers was ahead of the main column
and the entire command was in a T formation. The skirmishers
formed the cross-bar and the column the stem of the T. The trail
the column had followed so far that day had led almost due
north, but now it turned sharply about seventy degrees to the
right. The main column turned to follow the trail. By this time
most of the skirmishers had already passed the turning point, and
when the column behind them changed directions, they did not.
This turning movement placed all of the skirmishers except M
Company on the left flank. Most of the Indians who had been in
front of the skirmishers were now concentrated on the left flank
as a result of this turning movement, and the moving column
was not subjected to enemy fire most of its length. The right

flank of the column faced the open plain, but no Indians were near. The skirmishers on the left flank advanced away from the column and drove the Indians ahead of them. The main body halted about two miles past the turn to permit most of the skirmishers to return to the column. Up to this time Lieutenant Gibson's M Company had protected the right flank. Later when a group of Indians formed on this flank, Captain Grier with the two dragoon companies, C and I, passed through the skirmishers of Gibson's company and charged the Indians. Two Indians were killed and three wounded.

When the march continued, Captain Ord's company remained on the extreme left of the skirmishers. His company charged when the scattered opposition consolidated, and drove them from three high table rocks where they had taken refuge. He continued to pursue them along the flanks until he overtook the main column. His company then assumed a position on the left flank, assisted by M Company and the howitzers. In the meantime B Company had kept the Indians away on the right flank.

The command continued to the Spokane River, continually driving the Indians on ahead, and meeting with little resistance. When the troops camped on the river, at a site now within the present Fort George Wright Military Reservation, they had completed a march of twenty-five miles from the previous camp. Over fourteen miles of this distance had consisted of a marching fight of seven hours' duration. Every man who had left the Four Lakes Camp arrived at the camp on the Spokane River. Not one had been killed and only one was wounded slightly. Indian losses in the Battle of Spokane Plains are not known. Two chiefs and two brothers of Chief Garry of the Spokanes are known to have been fatalities, besides many Indians of lesser note either killed or wounded. It is alleged that Chief Kamiakin of the Yakimas was wounded by the flying debris from a nearby hit of a howitzer shell.

The troops were tired from their long marching fight and rested all the next day. During this day some Indians indicated from across the river their desire to talk to Colonel Wright. Arrangements were made to meet them the following day at the ford two miles above Spokane Falls. On September 7 the command moved to the ford, where Chief Garry told Colonel Wright that he regretted that his people had fought the soldiers and that he had been unable to control his chiefs and warriors. The colonel bluntly told Garry that his people had been badly whipped in two battles in which they had suffered many losses, and that he himself had not lost a man or animal. He further advised Garry that he had come into the country of the Spokanes to fight, and if the Spokanes now wanted peace he would tell them what to do. He added if they did not want peace he would wage war until they were exterminated. He then told Garry to return to his people, and to tell them what he had said.

After Garry had left, another Spokane, Chief Polotkin, came to parley accompanied by nine warriors. The colonel kept Polotkin as a hostage because he had been active in all the recent fights. One of his warriors was taken into custody. He was suspected of being implicated in the killing of the two miners whose murder had been reported by Steptoe. This warrior was hanged several days later when his guilt was determined. The remaining warriors were told to assemble for a council with Wright.

While the command was moving up the Spokane River, a great cloud of dust was investigated, and the soldiers discovered a large herd of horses being driven away from the route of the command. It was pursued, and over eight hundred horses were captured. It was later determined that this herd was the entire wealth of Chief Tilcoax, whose band of Palouses had been guilty of hostilities for several years and were responsible for many of the horse- and cattle-stealing raids upon the Walla Walla Valley. These later crimes had been freely admitted by Tilcoax to Steptoe during the latter's expedition in May. What to do with the herd presented a problem. A board was convened. It decided that killing was the only practical way to dispose of them. During the first day of this operation the horses were killed individually, but as this proved too slow a method, the slaughtering on the second day was accomplished by massed volleys of rifle fire into the corraled herd.

While the command was disposing of the animals, a communication was received from Father Joset in which he reported that the hostiles were suing for peace. He also advised that the friendly Indians were overjoyed by the victories of the soldiers. The former had expected to be sacrificed if the hostiles won, because they had not joined them on the warpath. The colonel wrote Father Joset to gather all the Indians at his mission for a talk.

On the night of September 13 when the command arrived at the Coeur d'Alene Mission, they found most of the Coeur d'Alene tribe assembled to meet with Colonel Wright. Some of the hostiles had fled eastward with other recalcitrant chiefs, including Kamiakin and Tilcoax. The Coeur d'Alenes were repentent and most agreeable to the terms presented to them by Wright in a seven-point preliminary treaty. On September 17, 1858, this treaty was signed by eighteen chiefs and sub-chiefs representing all but six or eight bands of the Coeur d'Alenes.

In brief, the terms were: all hostilities should cease; all property of the United States should be surrendered immediately; those who had commenced the fight with Steptoe should be surrendered; one chief and four men with their families should be given as hostages; all white men should be permitted to travel in Coeur d'Alene country unmolested, and no Indian hostile to the United States should be allowed within the limits of their country; the United States would remain at peace with the Coeur d'Alenes if the terms of the treaty were observed, and would return all prisoners and hostages unharmed within one year; a permanent treaty would be made when the articles had been complied with; and the treaty should also be extended to the Nez Perce Nation, as they had been allies of the United States.

The Coeur d'Alene Mission was the farthest point east that the expedition visited. To reach it they had marched 217 miles from Fort Walla Walla. On September 18 the troops left for a camp on Latah Creek, arriving there on September 22 after a 47-mile march. The Spokanes were assembled on Latah Creek when Colonel Wright arrived. Among them were Chiefs Garry and Polotkin of the Spokanes, Chief Milkapsi of the Coeur d'Alenes, and Father Joset. Milkapsi had not been at the Coeur d'Alene Mission, and now he wanted to sue for peace. Father Joset had been working tirelessly for peace and at the conclusion of the council with the Spokanes, when he left to return to his mission, he was thanked profusely. It was reported that Kamiakin and Tilcoax had been at the camp of the Spokanes but had fled when the troops approached. Chief Garry was sent to bring them back, but returned empty-handed because they refused to return with him.

The council with the Spokanes was held on September 23, with 107 chiefs and warriors present. Terms identical with those stated to the Coeur d'Alenes were specified by Colonel Wright, and the treaty was signed by 36 chiefs and other Indians, including Milkapsi.

Owhi, the Yakima chief, came into camp the evening of the council. He had not been considered trustworthy since Wright's Yakima campaign of 1856, because during the peace settlement he had failed to return with his people after promising to do so. Owhi, when placed in custody, told Wright that his son Qualchan was camped nearby. A message was sent to Qualchan directing him to come to the camp, but he appeared before it would have been possible for the messenger to have reached him. His record was so studded with killings, robberies, and attacks on the whites that he was hanged within fifteen minutes after entering the camp. It has been suggested that Kamiakin had sent him to the camp as a negotiator, since Qualchan cursed Kamiakin and accused him of treachery before he was executed. His father, Owhi, was fatally shot a few days later while attempting to escape.

Captain Grier was sent on September 24 with three companies of dragoons to the Steptoe battlefield, which was situated about twelve miles southwest of the Latah Creek camp. The two howitzers that had been buried on the hill were recovered. The bodies of the personnel killed during the battle were found, and were removed for subsequent burial in the cemetery at Fort Walla Walla.

A large body of Palouse Indians came to the Latah Creek camp while Wright was waiting for Captain Grier to return. They had participated in the recent fights but had decided to surrender after Kamiakin and Tilcoax had fled. Fifteen of those who had left their own country to fight the troops were seized and six of the most notorious were hanged.

On the twenty-sixth the troops left Latah Creek and marched

to the mouth of the Palouse River, arriving at that point on September 29. While they were en route, Slowiarchy, a Palouse chief, came to Wright and told him that his young men had gone to war against his wishes. Slowiarchy was told to assemble his people for a meeting at the mouth of the Palouse. At the council held there, Wright denounced the Indians severely. He demanded that they should surrender the murderers of the two miners plus those guilty of stealing horses and cattle from the whites, and that all stolen property should be returned. The Palouses complied with his demands. One of the murderers was hanged. Of the known cattle thieves, two had been hanged previously at the Latah Creek camp, and one had been killed at Four Lakes. Among the prisoners were three who were Walla Wallas or Yakimas. They too were promptly hanged.

Colonel Wright was more severe with the Palouses than he had been with the other conquered tribes. He refused to sign a peace treaty with them at that time, but advised he would do so the next spring if their conduct was satisfactory. He demanded that all white men must be allowed to travel unmolested in their country, and that all thieves and murderers not then available should be turned in. As a warning he advised that he would exterminate the whole tribe if he should be forced to return.

The command arrived at Fort Taylor on October 2 and at Fort Walla Walla on October 5. The garrison at Fort Taylor accompanied Wright to Fort Walla Walla, and Fort Taylor was not used again. The expedition had been a success. The command had marched over four hundred miles; had fought two decisive battles; had lost no men in combat; had recovered stolen government property; had hanged eleven bad Indians; and had completely pacified the Palouse, Spokane, and Coeur d'Alene Indians.

Before Colonel Wright could return to garrison duty, he had one more Indian matter to settle. He met with the Walla Wallas in a council, and those who had fought in the recent battles were asked to stand up. Thirty-five stood and four of the most notorious were immediately arrested. These four were hanged without delay.

The measures that Colonel Wright used to demonstrate to the Indians that he was determined to have peace in their territory were certainly not for the faint-hearted, but they did bring complete pacification. Almost twenty years later, when both the Sioux and Nez Perce were at war with the United States, emissaries of those tribes tried to solicit alliances from among the tribes concerned, but were flatly refused because the "hatchet was buried" by the Spokane, Palouse, and Coeur d'Alene Indians when they signed the peace treaties in 1858.

6. THE BATTLE OF PYRAMID LAKE
ARTHUR W. EMERSON

Early in the spring of 1860, Paiute Indians of the region from southern Idaho to Arizona gathered at Pyramid Lake for a war council. This site was twenty-odd miles north of present-day Wadsworth, Nevada. No one knows the number assembled—several hundred or several thousand—though indications point to possibly a thousand braves with their families and hangers-on.

While the Paiutes were in council, the Williams Station (trading post) episode was the final straw that brought on the bloody Battle of Pyramid Lake and subsequent warfare.

There are several versions as to just what brought about the attack at Williams Station, with its burning of buildings and killing of whites. The generally accepted story is that two young

Bannack squaws had been captured and taken to the trading post. Their husbands and several friends, attempting to rescue them, went to the Williams Station the morning of May 7, 1860. They were met with resistance. Three white men were killed; the shanties were burned and two other white men perished in the flames. The squaws were released.

According to another version, a Paiute buck and his squaw had come into the Williams Station. The men at the station seized and tied the buck, and raped the squaw. They then turned the buck loose. He fled to the council grounds where he got the help of Little Winnemucca (Chiquito) to head a party which went to the Williams Station. This party killed five people and burned the buildings, rescuing the squaw, yet not harming a white woman at the station. This report was made on May 18, 1860 by "Tennessee," a Genoa (Carson Valley) reporter to the San Francisco *Herald*.

There are also other versions, all of them in one way or another involving Indian girls or squaws.

Back at Pyramid Lake, where the council discussions were going forward, Old Winnemucca (Poito), head medicine chief of the Paiutes, said little but at heart stood for peace. Young Winnemucca (Numaga) was called the war chief, yet he too was against war and was the only chief at Pyramid Lake who opposed making war against the white intruders in their land.

While Numaga was rendering a plea to the Pyramid Lake Council not to embark on war, an Indian messenger on a foam-flecked pony dashed up to the council grounds and reported the killings and burning at Williams Station. Numaga gave up his pleas and said, "The whites will now come. Let us prepare."

The morning of the eighth, Williams, who had been absent on the fateful seventh, returned to his station to find the burned buildings and dead men. He did not stop to bury the bodies but fled to Virginia City, where he gave the alarm. Messengers were dispatched in every direction, alerting the people as to what had happened and calling for volunteers.

Fortunately for historians, the Thompson J. West Company, in preparing their *History of Nevada*, 1881, considered Pyramid

Lake and the subsequent events as the most important Nevada Indian war. As a result, the company sent a party of writers in 1880 to examine the ground and to interview Indians and whites who might have participated in, or had knowledge of, the battle. From all the information obtained by the experienced company staff, it was possible to develop what is believed to be a reasonably accurate account of the struggle.

When word of the Williams incident was received at the several settlements, detachments were organized at once at Genoa, Carson, and Silver and Virginia Cities. They all gathered at Virginia City. On the ninth of May they poured out of town en route to Bucklands Station on the Carson River. On May 10 they arrived at the scene of the Williams episode, buried the dead, and held a tactical council. That afternoon they proceeded down the Carson and camped at what is now Wadsworth on the Truckee River.

The contingent was made up of four detachments, numbering 105 men, all mounted, and one pack mule. Each detachment had its own leader. The Genoa Rangers were under the command of Thomas F. Condon, Jr.; the Silver City Guards were led by Captain Richard G. Watkins; Captain Archie McDonald and Captain F. Johnston directed the Virginia City hearties; and Major William M. Ormsby was selected to lead the Carson City Rangers.

They went into battle without an over-all leader. For all practical purposes, Major Ormsby later on took, or was given, leadership. The troops were miners, stagemen, prospectors, hay farmers, cutthroats, professional gamblers, politicians, and others. They were poorly armed—a heterogeneous mixture of independent elements without discipline. Indications are they did not believe the Indians would fight. If they had really expected opposition, many would not have been there. They had a slogan, "An Indian for breakfast and a pony to ride." Some even had pleasurable visions of sacking Paiute villages, killing a few braves, capturing a number of squaws, and having a hell-bent outing of rollicking fun. There were, too, a number of serious, hard-thinking men who had, however, more patriotism than judgment in Indian warfare.

This quickly-assembled band of volunteers slept out their last night under stars that seemed closer than the moon, closer in the vastness of the solitudes. It seemed to some as if it were a time when each man's soul drew near to his Creator. They awoke on the morning of the twelfth to a view of green and hazy Nevada landscape. Their advance continued north along the Truckee River, following the trail left by the Indians who had been assembling at Pyramid Lake.

No resistance was met during the morning. Shortly after noon the volunteers came out on a plateau elevated above the river bottom. They saw a number of Indians in the bottom land, on a grassy meadow. These disappeared into the sagebrush when the white men hove into sight.

The grassy meadow narrowed on each side of the river at the south end, facing the rising ground to the south. A narrow trail on the east side of the river led down into the green valley below. "Abe" Elliott objected to going down this trail. He said it was suicide. But the Indians stayed quiet, allowing the white men to descend into a battlefield of the Indians' choosing. Shortly after the troops, at Major Ormsby's command, had gathered in this geological kettle, Abe Elliott, who had a telesight rifle, tried a shot at an Indian in the distance with no effect. Almost at once arrows and a few pistol bullets began flying from the higher ground—from behind rocks and sagebrush clumps.

Ormsby quickly gathered his leaders about him and held a council of war. They decided to go after a band of Indians which had suddenly appeared on an elevated bench directly in front of them to the north. Orders were given for all men to tighten saddle cinches and prepare to mount. At the command the men flew to their saddles and, whooping wildly, some thirty to fifty of the whites dashed up a ravine onto the plateau. This was about 4 P.M.

They found that the Indians had again melted from sight. But as subsequent action proved, the Indians' right wing rested on an elevated point at the margin of the valley, with their forces deployed in a half circle around to the east and south. Thus Ormsby's men had charged right out into an Indian corral with an Indian behind every sagebrush and rock.

Then the heavens burst open with the bloodcurdling yells of

the Indians and a discharge of guns and arrows. This left a horse or two without a rider. The battle was lost right here, if indeed there ever had been a chance of victory.

The volunteers had traveled all day without water and with little rest for their weary horses, whose condition was matched by that of many of the men not accustomed to the trail. With no Indians in sight, part of the company halted when they gained the elevated battlefield. Many who had lagged behind suddenly saw their comrades ahead falling and their horses running wild as the Indians opened fire. Dan Drumheller, in his narrative, says there were "three charges—each time a few fell, and yet no Indians in sight but plenty of boys unsaddled."

By this time many horses became unmanageable, riders were losing their firearms and gear, and a number of the men were retreating. The volunteers who had made the charges stayed about ten minutes on the plateau, trying to control their horses and decide what to do. They then started a retreat in an attempt to join their comrades who had stayed behind on the lower ground.

First they tried to get to the bottom land to the west along the river, where a string of cottonwoods grew. This was a mistake, because Chiquito's band was hiding there. The Indians now had the whites all but surrounded. An Indian contingent then moved south onto the higher ground—a second plateau—and shot down into the whites with pistols and bows and arrows.

Numaga rode out from the cottonwoods between the whites and the Indians as the Indians were pushing out from the timber. He tried to stop the fight and hold a council with Chiquito, who refused to listen and with a group of braves rushed past Numaga. The whites fell back from the Indian charge and formed again about a hundred yards to the rear. Again and again the retreating whites tried to make a stand. The Indians on horseback had pushed in, leaving only a narrow corridor between themselves and the stream. The whites attempted to run the gauntlet. When a horse was shot from under one man, Eugene Angel, he fell to the ground and was at once riddled with arrows and bullets. Another rally was attempted three quarters of a mile further south near the river. A man named Meredith was killed here in a grove of cottonwoods.

The last stand, a desperate effort to stem the tide, was made less than a quarter of a mile from where the trail left the meadow and ascended about fifty feet to a piece of tableland above. Major Ormsby realized that if the Indians gained this eminence, all would be lost. So he ordered Condon and Watkins to take their men to that point and hold it. This they did, but as soon as they had gained the point most of their men kept right on going and left the two leaders almost alone. A sixteen-year-old boy, Anton Kauffman, in later years said, "The last I saw of the battle, and the bravest thing I ever saw, was Captain Watkins standing there on the trail, leaning on a crutch (he had only one leg), and blazing away at the Redskins."

During the time Watkins was attempting to hold the point, Condon started back to tell Ormsby of the critical situation there. During this time Chiquito had engaged a man named Headly, who was without a gun, in a horse-to-horse, man-to-man struggle. Headly pushed Chiquito back into his own Indian group but himself fell, riddled by arrows and bullets. Chiquito then pushed out toward Ormsby, only to have his own horse shot from under him. Therefore, Chiquito had nothing to do with the massacre that finally took place on the narrow trail leading out of the meadow, along the cliff, and up a ravine. This ravine was swarming with Indians sending arrows and bullets down into the retreating whites.

The Indians pushed on behind the whites as they now tried to hurry up the narrow trail to the higher country. They were continually being jostled from the sides and caught from behind by the exhilarated Indians. The Indians began yelling and whooping in exultation. Soon the volunteers were in complete panic. The trail was narrow—they actually hindered each other in their haste. Those in the rear were picked off by the victors—by gunshot, by arrow, or by hand. When a mount was shot out from under a white, the luckless man was pounced upon by the Indians.

By the time the volunteers reached the first piece of higher ground, probably eight whites had actually been killed on the trail. But now it was every man for himself—pushing to the limit the tired, thirsty horses. With fresher horses, the Paiutes were having such sport chasing the whites that it soon became a veritable game. An Indian would ride up to white, leap from his horse to the back of a volunteer, and push him to the ground. Or he would ride up beside the volunteer, wrestle him from his horse, and throw him to the ground to be ridden over by the pursuing braves. One Indian was met by a pistol in his ribs when he grasped a falling horseman. Both rolled to the ground, where, after a deadly struggle, William Spears was sacrificed on the battlefield.

About seven or eight miles south of the scene of battle, Major Ormsby had left a small contingent to protect the narrow neck of level land where the trail went again down to a meadow along the river and then rose to the higher open country to the south. This was in order to secure a line of retreat for the main body of men, if necessary, and to provide a more or less protected spot for a last stand. But when the first flying volunteers came roaring back from the battlefield, the rear guard took off with them. And as Ormsby's men came to the narrow trail in retreat, they were jammed in together, hindering their own progress. The Indians again overtook them here, rode into the floundering rear guard, and assailed them with clubs, arrows, and bullets. Some would push on through, leaving white men strewn along the trail to be dealt with by the slower-moving braves. The whites were apparently putting up little, if any, fight here. It was a jamming, jostling group trying to escape, throwing their guns aside, and begging the Indians not to slaughter them. Five volunteers were laid low by a volley of gunfire as they crowded along the Truckee River bank.

Major Ormsby was killed between the battlefield and the narrow strip of meadow to the south. His horse had been shot from under him at the edge of the meadow, and he tried to ride out on a mule. He was wounded in both arms and blood was streaming from his mouth. Captain Watkins attempted to help Ormsby but soon saw that little could be done, as Ormsby's mule was slow and wounded.

As Watkins himself said later, "The thought of self 'conquered valor,'" and in the next moment, after a few parting words to Ormsby "I was off to Carson." According to the Indians, the major finally reached the last rise near the narrow meadow and started up the ravine. His saddle turned on the mule and he went to the ground. He rose to his feet, thought he saw an Indian he knew, and called out to him, "I am your friend." The Indian said, "Too late now," and put an arrow into him. By this time most of the rear guard had passed him and gone on as fast as their jaded horses could carry them.

Probably the last victims were three men named McLeod, Jones, and McCarthy. They were overtaken after they had gained the open country. They must have put up a good fight, since the Indians put on an impromptu war dance after the killings. The pursuit stopped at about what is now Wadsworth because it was getting dark and the Indians could no longer see the whites, who were fanning out and away from the trail to hide and to work their way back to the settlements.

Later reports indicated 42 whites killed, 30 missing, and 33 reporting back to their towns. The Indians claimed 46 whites killed and admitted to only three warriors wounded and two horses killed.

By the morning of May 15, 1860, men on horseback began arriving at Carson and Virginia Cities and Dayton and other villages. Those on foot were drifting into Buckland Station, and panic overcame the people of the valley. Exaggerated reports were sent over the wires to California. Women and children were hustled into barricaded buildings and sentinels posted. At Silver City a rock fort was built, but no Indians showed up. A party was formed to go and seek assistance from a cavalry unit supposed to be at Honey Lake Valley. In the next few days the trails to California were crowded. Those who stayed were probably so frightened they could have offered little resistance.

Colonel Jack Hays, Texas Ranger, First Sheriff of San Francisco, and United States Surveyor General for California (see Chap. 3), arrived in Carson Valley "on private business" on May 11. When the word of the defeat reached the valley the leading citizens asked Hays to take command of a new force of volunteers which they agreed to form. Hays accepted the command and led the 550 volunteers (many from California), and by mutual consent the 200 regulars sent from California (under the command of Captain Joseph Stewart), in pursuit of the Paiutes. They pushed out from Virginia City on May 24. On the twenty-eighth they were camped near the site of the burned Williams Station buildings. By June 2 they reached the big bend of the Truckee River. At Pinnacle Mount between there and Pyramid Lake they met and defeated the Indians, who lost some 46 of their number. The whites' loss was eleven killed and wounded. Hays continued to harass the Paiutes until they broke up into small bands and scattered.

This was the final real stand of the Paiute Indians as a nation in Nevada, though they did continue to harry the overland stages, pony express stations, and immigrant caravans. After this so-called clean-up of the Paiutes, many of the white citizens who had fled in panic to California started back over the trail, drawn by the lush promise of a gold and silver boom.

Again in April 1861, the Paiutes assembled some fifteen hundred braves at the mouth of the Walker River, where they intended to make a final desperate attempt to throw out the intruding whites. But Governor James Warren Nye, recently appointed by President Lincoln as Territorial Governor, dispatched a unit of soldiers which broke up the attempt.

After continuous isolated raids on settlers and small settlements, a severe Paiute outbreak took place in eastern Nevada. This led to the establishment of Fort Riley, and the Paiutes fled to the desert, where many starved.

The Battle of Pyramid Lake and the immediate after-effects signaled the opening of a decade in Nevada history which outshone the fantasy of Aladdin's lamp. Nevada became a seething melting pot of lust and lush gains—never before experienced and never again to be equaled. Vast were the spoils—easily gained and easily lost—fanning the glowing embers of adventure and greed.

PART IV

The Civil War Plus
1861–65

Introduction

The fighting in the war years of 1861–1865 was by no means confined to that between the North and South. There were many bloody battles with the Indians in this period.

While there is no reason to believe that the Confederacy tried to stir up a general revolt by all the tribes, there seems to be considerable evidence that the Indians between the Mississippi and the Rocky Mountains planned simultaneous attacks on all white settlements in that vast stretch of country in 1862. This, however, was Indian planning and Indian strategy and not the work of Confederate agents. Nor were the planned attacks to be confined to the settlements loyal to the Union.

Indians up and down the frontier watched the experienced soldiers march away to the Potomac front. In a number of cases all the soldiers were withdrawn, and in others only a skeleton force was left to man the frontier forts and posts. As the tempo of the war in the East increased, more and more of the young, able-bodied men were called and the Indians observed the ever-weakening manpower on the western frontier. Many settlements had, literally, only old men and boys left to defend them.

The Indians, dissatisfied with the treaties, with the lands allotted to them, and with the government rations and goods supplied them, were quick to seize the opportunity. President Lincoln in his message to Congress in 1861 mentioned the unrest in New Mexico and the fact that all the Indian country south of Kansas was already in the hands of "insurgents from Texas and Arkansas."

In 1862 the President's message pointed out that there were "open hostilities" at several points along the frontier. These were to get worse before 1862 was over, for that was the year of the terrible Sioux uprising in Minnesota.

The Confederacy's Texas border settlements also suffered. Within days after the surrender of Union forces at San Antonio and Camp Verde at the beginning of the Civil War, the Comanches were on the warpath—raiding, killing, and stealing cattle and horses. Many of the German families in the hill country northwest of San Antonio were loyal to the Union and sent their sons of fighting age to Mexico to avoid service in the Confederate army. Others joined companies of the Texas Frontier Troops or ranger companies, on the assurance that they would not have to fight the Union but would be used solely to defend the border against the Indians. There were many minor yet bloody battles with the Indians on the Texas frontier during 1861–65.

The fighting during these years was not confined to the territory east of the Rockies. The Paiutes and the Shoshones were harassing the mail and stage routes through western Utah and Nevada and swooping down on isolated ranches, farms, and mines. Colonel Patrick E. Connor and his 300 California-Nevada Volunteers put an end to most of this trouble at Bear River in 1863. Connor lost 14 men and had 49 wounded, whereas he officially reported that "we found 224 bodies (Indians) on the field." The Mormon settlers called this a massacre.

Flour was $45 a sack in Denver in the summer of 1864—freighting from the East was at a standstill and prices skyrocketed in the Colorado settlements. The Sioux and the Comanches plus some bands of the fighting Cheyennes were on the warpath in the Eastern Plains country. In the fall and winter of 1863 and on into the summer of 1864 the Indians were raiding constantly. The murder of the Hungate family of four only thirty miles from Denver finally aroused the citizens of that pioneer city. They quickly formed the Third Colorado Volunteer Cavalry and at dawn on November 29, 1864, the Third under Colonel John Chivington surprised and wiped out a sleeping village of Cheyennes and Arapahoes on Sand Creek. This affair has commonly been called "The Sand Creek Massacre" and is one of the most controversial incidents in Colorado history.

The second war in the period 1861–65, The Indian War, was fought almost entirely with volunteer troops under state or territorial leadership. Neither the North nor the South could spare "regulars" or even enough experienced officers to lead the volunteers against the Indians. These citizen-soldiers, enlisted for periods of three to six months, did a good job—they had to if they were not to lose their wives, children, homes, and livestock to the raiding Indians.

7. THE BATTLE OF WOOD LAKE

NOEL M. LOOMIS

The Battle of Wood Lake, Minnesota, in 1862, is not always called that. Colonel H. H. Sibley himself referred to it as a skirmish. Some writers have called it a massacre. The forces involved were not large by the usual standards but they did represent, on each side, a strong concentration of forces of two warring nations: the United States and the Sioux Indians.

Wood Lake was the turning-point of the great Sioux uprising, during which the Indians terrorized western Minnesota, northwestern Iowa, and eastern Dakota for over a month. They destroyed thousands of acres of crops, burned hundreds of homes, took some two hundred girls and women into captivity and subjected many of them to the most savage and brutal forms of rape, and killed hundreds of whites of all ages, male and female.

It was not a planned uprising, as many have said. Had it been, the Sioux should have wiped out the settlers, for Little Crow was able to command some six thousand Indian warriors. The elements of revolt had been present for some time, but the immediate cause was the finding of a nest of hen-eggs by four young Sioux braves. Technically, the eggs belonged to a white settler, and one brave warned another that he dare not take them. He dared and this led to boasting and finally to the murder of some whites in a farmhouse. That incident inflamed the entire Sioux Nation.

The background, as usual, is a sorry one on both sides. By treaties as late as 1858 the United States had taken land claimed by the Indians and had promised to pay for it at so much an acre, the payments to be spread out over a long period of years. These payments, which became known as the annuity payments, were theoretically supposed to compensate the Indians for the loss of their hunting lands. In 1862 they amounted to about $15 a year per head among the Sioux at the Yellow Medicine and Redwood Falls Agencies in western Minnesota. As usual, too, the payments were somewhat irregular, but this was not all the fault of the government.

In this case, the Indian agent had, in late 1861, given the Sioux an extra payment of about $2.50 per head to save trouble. This had been taken from the 1862 annuity payment fund, not then appropriated by Congress. The Indian Department, on unstable ground because of the $2.50 payment, dared not send more money until Congress made the actual appropriation.

In the summer of 1862 Congress was more than occupied with the Civil War, and the annuity payments got little priority. The payments were ordinarily made in June, but in 1862 the money did not arrive until the middle of August. Meanwhile the traders and storekeepers in the Indian country began to refuse credit to the Indians. Cutworms had ruined what corn the Sioux had planted, and they were desperate for food. (A white woman, cared for by a family of non-combatant Sioux, reported they had no bread, but corn and potatoes, sometimes beef, sometimes dog, occasionally coffee and sugar.)

The Indians were plagued with many factions. Five bands of Sioux were represented on this reservation. There were two headquarters, each headed by a white agent, called the Upper and Lower Agencies (only a few miles apart). In addition there was distrust between the two agencies. Then there were Farmer Indians (those who were trying to adopt the ways of the white man), and Blanket Indians (those who were recalcitrants).

A Soliders' Lodge was formed in one band shortly before the outbreak, to take up problems that were not being handled satisfactorily by the various chiefs and spokesmen. A strong element in this was Little Crow, the third hereditary chief to bear that name. Little Crow, known to be rebellious, had been forced into an election for the chieftainship and had lost to Traveling Hail. Up to the very time of the outbreak, however, Little Crow, though unhappy about the Sioux' treatment by the whites, continued to advise caution because he had a fair knowledge of the resources of the whites.

The Indians were plagued also with a horde of gamblers, liquor-sellers, and other whites and half-breeds who took full advantage of the red man's lack of experience.

Thousands of Indians at the two agencies barely existed through the winter of 1861–62 although Major Galbraith, the Indian agent, made every effort to feed them. In July, 1862, they were in dire need from the failure of their crops. They muttered and talked, and finally a large group of warriors went to the agency and demanded food. They pointed out that the traders' warehouses were filled with food, and demanded to know why they could not have enough to feed their families. Andrew Myrick, one of the store-owners, said they could eat grass as far as he was concerned. (This incident and its aftermath sound sensational but appear to be well supported.)

Then the four young braves found the eggs and began the series of incitements that led to the massacre of white settlers. This was on Sunday, August 17, 1862.

They told their tribal leaders what had happened, and Chief Skakopee, another recalcitrant, sized up the situation: "We have shed white blood," he said, "and they will stop the payment entirely. We have killed white women, and we cannot expect them to have any mercy on us. They will kill Indians indiscriminately."

He promptly sent runners to other leaders, calling for a council. This was at the Lower Agency.

They got Little Crow out of bed, and he, inspired partly by the opportunity of regaining his standing, agreed there was only one thing left to do: kill and burn. The whites would be after them, and this was their chance. Besides, he pointed out, recent half-breed deserters from Renville's Rangers, a sort of home guard unit for Minnesota, had reported that the whites were engaged in a great war among themselves, and that all the able-bodied men had gone to fight, leaving the frontier practically undefended.

The western frontier broke out in flames the next day. By noon a hundred whites lay dead and buildings had been burned. Myrick was found slain with grass in his mouth. Little Crow laid siege to Fort Ridgely and could have taken it if his Sioux had been willing to make a charge.

The long-repressed Sioux rose up in vindictive hatred at Spirit Lake in Iowa, at Lake Shetek in Minnesota, and as far southwest as Sioux Falls in Dakota; they attacked Norwegian Grove near what is now Henderson; they raided Breckenridge, burned Hutchinson, attacked Forest City, Hilo, and Butternut Valley.

These raids were deadly and vicious; all the savage resentment of the Sioux—especially of the younger warriors—burst forth in this orgy of violence. Families were massacred, food (which the Indians needed so badly) destroyed, buildings burned, children killed, and women taken captive. These latter usually were raped, held or staked down for as many as twenty repeated offenses, and afterward often killed, mutilated, and scalped. Girls ten years old were treated the same, and many died.

The center of violence was about the two agencies, and spread rapidly down the Minnesota River. St. Peter's and Mankato and Madelia for several days were defenseless. New Ulm was deserted. Fear was felt even in the capital of Minnesota; in St. Paul, families deserted the outskirts and moved in closer together.

Colonel Sibley was sent to Mankato and told to organize a

force and drive up the river, back to the agencies; he was to
defeat the Indians, recover the captives, and bring back for
punishment all Sioux who had taken part in the uprising.

He began to gather various units—men who could bear arms,
and especially those who had arms to bear, for the whites, settled down to farming, appear to have had a minimum supply of
rifles. Most of the defenders of New Ulm used shotguns.

After the first few days of killing and plunder, the Indians
began to realize that the whites had not fallen like ripe wheat
before the wind. True enough, the Sioux had wrought terrible
devastation, but now Sibley, seemingly unafraid, was coming
after them. The word went out: Sibley was coming up the Minnesota with a cannon, a howitzer, and sixteen hundred men—
and some of these were battle-trained troops.

The Sioux began to fight among themselves. The Upper Sioux
blamed the Lower Sioux for starting a war without consulting
them.

Most of the women and girl captives were gathered in Little
Crow's camp, and the friendly Indians were fearful that, on any
pretext at all, Little Crow and his fighting chiefs would decide to
cut the throats of all captives. A decisive whipping by Sibley—
anything—might touch it off.

Sibley, in the meantime, marched slowly up the valley. He was
under great pressure to hurry from the public in St. Paul, but it
would seem he handled his forces well.

After rescuing a detachment from the almost-disastrous battle
of Birch Coulee, Sibley left a note on a stake for Little Crow,
and this was delivered when Little Crow returned from the
Hutchinson raid. In answer Little Crow sent what may be one
of the clearest statements of the massacre:

*Yellow Medicine, September 7th, 1862. Dear Sir,—For
what reason we have commenced this war I will tell
you. It is on account of Major Galbraith. We made a
treaty with the government, and beg for what we do get,
and can't get that till our children are dying with hunger.
It is the traders who commenced it. Mr. A. J. Myrick told
the Indians that they would eat grass or dirt. Then Mr.*

Forbes told the Lower Sioux that they were no men. Then Roberts was working with his friends to defraud us out of our moneys. If the young braves have pushed the white men, I have done this myself. So I want you to let Governor Ramsey know this. I have a great many prisoners, women and children. It ain't all our fault. The Winnebagoes were in the engagement, and two of them were killed. I want you to give me an answer by the bearer. All at present. Yours truly,

his
Friend Little x Crow
mark

Sibley continued to advance. He camped in the vicinity of Wood Lake (actually nearer Lonetree Lake), two miles from the Yellow Medicine River, on September 22. He had then about eight hundred men.

With Sibley were three hundred of the Third Minnesota Infantry (this regiment had been surrendered to the Confederates at Murfreesboro and paroled except for the officers), several companies of the Sixth, several companies of the Seventh, some twenty-five cavalrymen, an artillery battery, and a small group of Renville Rangers, with perhaps a few other scattered units represented.

Sibley had been informed that Little Crow would not attack until Sibley passed the Yellow Medicine River, but Little Crow was up most of that night arguing with the other chiefs; Little Crow wanted to attack that night, but they overruled him. He agreed to wait until Sibley's entire force was strung out and indefensible the next morning.

But food was not plentiful with the soldiers, and some of the Third, wanting to show their ability as foragers, learned in Tennessee, took a wagon or wagons and started out ahead. Sioux braves fired on them, and this brought the entire Indian force into sudden action. The Third, under Major Welch, sprang to the defense and fought its way forward half a mile. Sibley ordered them to retreat on the main force. Welch answered that he could hold the Indians—which was precisely what the Sioux wanted:

to keep the force broken up. The Sioux began to spread out fan-shaped to envelop the Third. Sibley sent a firm order to retreat, and Welch obeyed.

Sibley had chosen a good camping place, with the lake on his left, a ravine on his right, and a small stream of fresh water before him; and he had capably disposed his forces—the Third in front, the Sixth on the left, the Seventh on the right. The wagons and artillery were in this partially enclosed area. The Renville Rangers were on the right front.

The Sioux, after the Third regiment retreated and got away from them, attacked the main force on both sides. The Sioux had about eight hundred men. Sibley held half of his force in reserve.

The Third held fast along the front. A considerable force of Sioux attacked on the left flank, and two companies of the Sixth under Major McLaren fought them back.

A party of Sioux tried to infiltrate through the ravine on the right, but Lieutenant Colonel Marshall with the Seventh regiment fought them off. The Renville Rangers under Captain Gorman fought with both the Third at the front and the Seventh on the right, and seem to have had the most action of any unit. Eventually the six-pounder gun cleared the Sioux from the ravine, and from that time on only desultory firing occurred. After two hours the Sioux withdrew abruptly.

The whites lost nine killed, fifty wounded. The Sioux left sixteen dead on the battlefield; Sibley refused Little Crow permission to take off the bodies.

The Indians were broken. They retreated north. Sibley killed time for two days, then walked into the Sioux camp and announced that he had come for the captives. He got them. By declining to press his pursuit, he allowed the Indians time to quarrel and a chance to become fully discouraged; he also avoided the fatal spark that would have precipitated a wholesale slaughter of the captives.

It was the first time the Midwest Indians had chosen open warfare with organized troops—and they were defeated. They would try it again at the Little Big Horn with more success.

Little Crow with four thousand Sioux went to Devil's Lake,

(now) North Dakota, from where the Sioux raided on a small scale until a further expedition was sent against them in 1863. But the back of their resistance was broken at Wood Lake.

In the next five weeks a military commission tried 425 Indians and sentenced 303 to death; President Lincoln commuted many of these sentences, and on December 26, 1862, at Mankato, only 38 were hanged.

It is customary to say, of the usual Indian battle against whites, that the Indian casualties were very heavy, the whites' light. Lieutenant Heard, who was recorder for the trial commission, gives these figures after very careful questioning: in the Sioux uprising there were 737 whites killed and 42 Indians.

On Monday, August 18, the annuity money from Washington had arrived at Fort Ridgely—$71,000 in gold coin. If it had been a few hours earlier the Indians' hunger would have been assuaged and the uprising probably avoided.

8. CANYON DE CHELLY

CLINTON P. ANDERSON

A new era in Southwestern Indian history emerged from the Navajo campaign of 1863–64. When the first of Colonel Kit Carson's New Mexico Volunteers maneuvered past famous Window Rock, moving toward the eastern entrance of the ancient Navajo fortress of Canyon de Chelly, Arizona, the end of organized Navajo warfare was in sight.

Until the final surrender to the Volunteers in 1864, the Navajos had been continuously engaged in hot and cold wars with the inhabitants of New Mexico and Arizona. With the acquisition of the territory in 1846, the United States inherited from Mexico that recurring menace. The Navajos had always exhibited a burning hatred toward the Mexicans, which was displayed in their unceasing raids upon the scattered villages and rancheros. Of course, the attacks were not at all one-sided affairs. The Navajos were well aware of the eager market for their captured women and children in the slave channels, both above and below the border.

Over the years the Americans had presented six treaties to the Navajo chieftains, and all had been broken before final ratification. One instance of the folly of trusting to the effectiveness of the signed treaties occurred in 1849. Colonel John M. Washington succeeded in obtaining the presence of Navajo chiefs for a big powwow in the Canyon de Chelly. There he got them to sign a "peace" treaty. Before the colonel and his troops could return to Santa Fe, some of the Navajos who had been present at the conference beat him back and carried out a successful raid, during which they captured and drove off livestock almost within gunshot range of the Governor's Palace. It was surely an uneasy peace.

In 1863 General James H. Carleton, military commander of the Territory of New Mexico, formulated plans which he hoped would result in ending the Navajo trouble once and for all. General Carleton was an experienced soldier with a reputation for being hard and persistent, but fair. He had led the famous California Column into New Mexico after the Confederate invasion and brief occupation. When it became necessary for the South to concentrate her resources and military strength against the Army of the Potomac, this column of the Army of the Pacific discovered that its primary function in New Mexico would be to fight Indians instead of men in gray. However, with the fierce Apache roaming the south and the Navajo to the west, this was no small assignment.

Taking maximum advantage of the preoccupation of the American troops with the dreaded Apache warriors and the possible return of the Texans, the Navajos were quite active in 1863. They completed several daring and successful raids, replenishing their livestock herds at the expense of the terrified ranchers. Dauntingly, they rode all the way from their stronghold in the west to the Rio Grande. They collected the fruits of their journey from Santa Fe in the north to Socorro in the south, attacking and ransacking the river settlements and ranches along the way.

In 1860 General Edward Canby had waged a campaign against the Navajos. He had defeated the Indians in isolated battles but, as events quickly unfolded, no war had been won. In an effort to bring the campaign to a successful close, General Canby met to parley with the chiefs at their request. They asked for peace and accepted the terms of a treaty which the general presented to them. Shortly after this the troops were withdrawn from the area.

Many explanations have been offered as to why the Navajo treaties were not dependable and could not be enforced. This was not necessarily due to the bad faith of the leaders on both sides. One reason given for the failure on the part of the Indians, which might have some merit, was the lack of any central authority due to the scattered condition of the Navajo Nation. There were many family-type groups which conducted themselves as individual tribes. They acted independently during the normal events of their lives. The negotiations of war and peace by their leaders seemed to make little difference. Therefore, a chief of one band could make a treaty of peace which would have little effect on the depredations being carried out by another sub-tribe.

For whatever reason, the hostilities continued as before General Canby's expeditions. General Carleton was determined not to settle for a false peace based upon worthless treaties. He issued a public proclamation and warning, General Order No. 15, which read:

Headquarters, Department of
New Mexico,
Santa Fe, New Mexico,
June 15, 1863.

1. For a long time past the Navajo Indians have mur-dered and robbed the people of New Mexico. Last win-ter, when eighteen of their chiefs came to Santa Fe to have a talk, they were warned, and were told to inform their people that, for these murders and robberies, the tribe must be punished, unless some binding guarantees should be given that in the future these outrages should cease. No such guarantees have been given; but, on the

> *contrary, additional murders and additional robberies*
> *have been perpetrated upon the persons and property of*
> *our unoffending citizens. It is therefore ordered that*
> *Colonel Christopher Carson, with a proper military force,*
> *proceed without delay to a point in the Navajo country*
> *known as Pueblo Colorado, and there establish a defensi-*
> *ble depot for his supplies and hospital, and thence to*
> *prosecute a vigorous war upon the men of the tribe until*
> *it is considered, at this headquarters, that they have been*
> *effectually punished for their long-continued atrocities.*

Actually, preparations for the campaign had already begun.
The master plan roughly was for Carson to strike out toward the
heart of the Navajo country. He was to kill all male resisters and
capture all women and children. All prisoners were to be routed
across the territory some 350 miles to the Bosque Redondo on
the Pecos River. The site is in the vicinity of what is now Fort
Sumner, New Mexico.

By the middle of April, 1863, the First Regiment, New Mexico
Volunteers, under Kit Carson's command, was well along in
preparing to move to the west. The rallying point for his widely
dispersed forces was Los Pinos, about twenty-five miles south
of Albuquerque near Los Lunas. Although his command con-
tained some of the Californians who had travelled east with the
column, the majority of troops were recruited from the territory.
They were confident of success and proud to serve under the
famous mountain man of Taos. Carson had already created a
legend for his feats as a hunter, trapper, guide, and Indian
fighter. He had proved himself a capable soldier at the battle of
Valverde, and this was his first independent command.

The Volunteer force consisted of 27 officers, 476 mounted men,
and 260 unmounted men. All were well acquainted with the
dangerous nature of their assignment. Most were seasoned veterans with much experience and a keen appreciation of their
adversary. The unit was well officered. Many had seen duty at
Valverde and almost all had experienced the rugged frontier
duty which was facing them in this Navajo round-up effort.

The chief quartermaster was Captain Asa B. Carey, a brilliant young West Pointer who may have rendered more than a little advice on formal military procedure to the renowned Taosan who was his commander.

Captain Albert Pfeiffer, Commanding Officer, H Company, was the first to negotiate the Gibraltar of the Navajo Nation, the Canyon de Chelly. Captain Pfeiffer was a skilled veteran and a bearer of painful and bitter memories. Once while he and a small party were bathing in hot springs south of Fort McCrae, they were attacked by a band of Apaches. Pfeiffer escaped death himself, though badly wounded, but he witnessed the death of his wife by an Apache lance. Needless to say, his heart was heavy with hatred for all Indians, and he anticipated this new assignment with a vengeful purpose.

Carson's force left the point of departure on the Rio Grande on July 7, 1863. They arrived on July 14 at Fort Wingate, near what is now the uranium capital of Grants, New Mexico, on Highway 66. After a brief stop to check equipment and supplies, they launched into the heart of the Navajo country, arriving at Fort Defiance, Arizona, July 20. At Defiance Carson was joined by a band of Ute Indians, who were procured to serve as scouts and guides against their long-hated enemy, the Navajos. A special request to the War Department had been required before the Utes could be employed. They were excellent trailers and good marksmen. Carson was anxious to utilize them in his command. He had formerly served as agent for the Ute Tribe and was well acquainted with their hunting talents, whether for game or for men. However, many of the Utes quit their jobs when they found out that they were not able to keep all the booty from the Navajos they captured. They were perfectly willing to kill the men, but they were disappointed when they discovered they could not keep the captured women and children for slaves. General Carleton had ordered all captives to Bosque Redondo. Colonel Carson, although perhaps not in complete agreement, complied.

If the Utes were not allowed to gain from their human booty, they were able to benefit from the prize money offered by General Carleton to offset their disappointment. For every sound and serviceable horse or mule captured from the Navajos, a money bonus of $20 was offered. For every sheep, they were paid $1.00.

Through the last days of July, the campaign was on in earnest. Carson's troops were in the field making reconnaisance of the apprehensive Navajos. As messages spiraled upward from the smoking mountain ranges, Carson established his supply depot still deeper within the homeland of his enemy. This base of operations was named Fort Canby in honor of the former military commander of the area. Carson found that the crops were fair that year, and it was his mission to insure that they should not be harvested for the use of their planters. The Navajos were not able to muster a large force for any single decisive battle, so this whole operation was to be fought in various small skirmishes. It was a hide-and-seek type of campaign, with the Volunteers roaming the country, destroying the crops and capturing the livestock of the Indians. Then it was not long before the plan of Ahdilohee, the Rope-thrower, as the Navajos called Kit Carson, became evident. He intended to starve them out if he could not kill or capture them. Should they be able to survive the autumn on berries, piñon nuts, and what game they could kill, the leaders of the tribe knew what lay in store for them during the dread wintertime. The Navajos fought back in bands, and made several successful raids against the soldiers. Once they even drove off the favorite horse of Ahdilohee.

But the odds were against the poorly-supplied Indians in their effort to remain in their homeland. They had appeared successful in some of their raids, but as they witnessed the increasing strength of the white man as he destroyed and captured, slowly their morale and will to fight began to weaken. Some efforts on their part to achieve another peace were made, but Carleton would not have a repetition of the 1860 debacle. To emphasize his stand and to sum up the attitude of the government as to the purpose of this expedition, we have only to read General Carleton's letter of September 19 to Colonel Carson:

> *If any Indians desire to give themselves up, they will be received and sent to Fort Wingate, with a request from that post that they be sent to Los Pinos. No Navajo Indians of either sex, or of any age, will be retained at*

Fort Canby, as servants, or in any capacity whatever; all must go to Bosque Redondo. You are right in believing that I do not wish to have those destroyed who are willing to come in. Nor will you permit an Indian prisoner once fairly in our custody to be killed, unless he is endeavoring to make his escape. There is to be no alternative but this: Say to them, "Go to the Bosque Redondo, or we will pursue and destroy you. We will not make any peace with you on any other terms. You have deceived us too often, and robbed and murdered our people too long, to trust you again at large in your own country. This way shall be pursued against you if it takes years, now that we have begun, until you cease to exist or move. There can be no other talk on this subject."

As winter approaches, you will have better luck.

So now we have a picture of the "long walk" which was facing the proud rulers of a beautiful and rugged land. Even in the face of the oncoming avalanche of fighting men and materials, it is no surprise that the brave warriors fled to their beloved canyon rather than succumb to the humiliating journey.

As winter closed in on the land of the Navajo, their freedom to roam and live unrestricted appeared to be rapidly coming to an end. The leaders retreated to the mountain walls within the Canyon, taking with them the able-bodied. The Canyon de Chelly is approximately thirty miles long, running east and west. Daily more and more bedraggled Navajos straggled into Colonel Carson's camps, choosing prison rather than starvation. Long streams of the once proud people wound their way eastward toward the unfamiliar land of the Bosque Redondo.

Eventually it fell to Captain Albert Pfeiffer and his company of New Mexican Volunteers actually to conquer the formidable Canyon. But there was not much resistance to their march from the eastern entrance to the western outlet. As they dug and plodded their way through the two feet of snow on the canyon floor, the fleeing Navajos cursed down at them from the high walls above. The soldiers burned the hogans and destroyed the orchards which lined the canyon in many places. Because they had nothing left to eat but the carcasses of dead horses, and no wood to build fires, the will of the Navajo braves was crushed at last. Colonel Carson made his encampment at the western end of the canyon, forming a net into which the remaining tribesmen were driven. When the Indians saw that the ones who surrendered were treated well and given food, they began to come in by droves.

At last the long walk really got under way. The remaining Navajos who still had not surrendered were sought by their fellow tribesmen who rode with promises of Kit Carson for their safety and welfare. The era of Navajo hostilities had ended. As General Carleton wrote to the Adjutant General in Washington, in February, 1864, " . . . you have doubtless seen the last of the Navajo War—a war that has been continued with but few intermissions for one hundred and eighty years."

An interesting postscript to the story of the Navajo Tribe is the narrative of their return to their beloved country. After four years of failure at the Bosque Redondo, it was decided to remove the Navajos once more. Their crops had failed, and the government soon recognized the futility of trying to keep the Navajo and the Mescalero Apache on the same reservation in peace.

President Grant dispatched General Sherman to Fort Sumner to make another treaty with the Navajos. General Sherman came with one intent—to remove the Navajos to the Indian territory to the east. He had many conferences with the chiefs, and they stubbornly refused the idea of moving anywhere except back to the area around their Canyon. Finally the famous Civil War General relented and agreed that the Navajos should return to their homeland.

9. THE FIRST BATTLE OF ADOBE WALLS

LAWRENCE V. COMPTON

As the Civil War progressed, less attention and fewer troops were directed at keeping the Plains Indians under control. With greater freedom of movement and less fear of retaliation, the Kiowas and Comanches became steadily bolder. In the autumn of 1862 Comanches destroyed the Wichita agency, and in 1863 they attacked many Texas border settlements. The spring and summer of 1864 brought widespread depredations in Colorado, New Mexico, and Texas by Cheyennes, Comanches, and Kiowas. Wagon trains were attacked, frontier ranches burned, livestock stolen, and settlers killed. The Santa Fe Trail was the life line of New Mexico. Over it moved the military supplies for the California and New Mexico volunteers plus the necessities for the civilian population.

Many of the depredations occurred along the New Mexico portion of the Santa Fe Trail, and finally General James H. Carleton, who commanded the Department of New Mexico, decided to put a stop to them. He believed that the Comanches and Kiowas were in winter quarters south of the Canadian River and in October 1864 issued orders directing a campaign against them. This called for the assembling of a force under the command of Colonel Christopher (Kit) Carson at Fort Bascom, on the Canadian River near the Texas line.

From several different military posts in the Territory of New Mexico, 14 officers and 321 men were gathered. They comprised five companies of cavalry and two of infantry, and almost all were either California or New Mexico volunteers. There were 27 supply wagons and one ambulance. Company K of the First California Infantry had two twelve-pound mountain howitzers and these played a key role in the fighting that eventually occurred. In addition to the soldiers, the expedition included 72 Indians. These were Utes and Apaches that Carson persuaded to join up by the promise of a chance to fight their old enemies, the Comanches and Kiowas, and of plunder.

Carson and his command left Fort Bascom on the sixth of November, crossed the Canadian River, and proceeded east along its north side. By the afternoon of the twenty-fourth, they had reached Mule Spring in the Texas Panhandle. In the two weeks of marching there had been no evidence of hostile Indians, but late in the afternoon the Indian scouts returned to the Mule Spring camp with the news that ten miles ahead they had found the fresh trail of a large body of Indians with many head of horses and cattle. This exciting knowledge threw the camp into frenzied action. Carson ordered his five companies of cavalry and the section of howitzers to prepare to move out. The infantry company was directed to remain with the supply train and follow the cavalry in the morning. As the sun was setting, all was in readiness and the marching order was given. By midnight the command was back in the valley of the Canadian River and had found the fresh trail of the Indians they were seeking. Carson thought the Indian camp was nearby and to avoid blundering into it ordered a halt until daylight. This was a long, cold wait, with each man standing by his horse, holding its bridle rein. There was no talking, no smoking, and very little movement as a heavy frost chilled all.

When dawn finally arrived, the command was mounted and moved quietly along the trail found during the night. At the head of the column was Kit Carson and his seventy-odd Utes and Apaches perched on their horses and wrapped in buffalo robes. Following them was part of the cavalry force, then the howitzers, and the remainder of the cavalry at the rear. It was soon after the march had gotten under way that the first contact was made with the enemy—a picket of three mounted Indians on the opposite side of the Canadian River. Almost immediately, Carson's band of Utes and Apaches shucked their buffalo robes, forded the river, and were in whooping pursuit of the fleeing pickets. They were followed by two companies of cavalry designated by Carson.

It was now apparent that quick action would be required if the attack upon the Indian village was to be accomplished with any degree of surprise. To this end, Carson ordered his remaining three companies of cavalry to proceed as rapidly as they could. Carson himself and a detachment of cavalry remained to escort the howitzer battery. Although the two mountain howitzers were on prairie carriages, these were so small that the cannoneers could not ride on them. Thus the battery was unable to keep up with the rest of the command in its advance. Also contributing to its slow progress were the low wheels and narrow tracking of the carriages, which caused frequent upsets and delays.

The advance cavalry elements soon came upon the Kiowa village—about 150 lodges made of whitened buffalo skins—and took it somewhat by surprise. The Kiowa warriors put up a stiff resistance but withdrew down the river about four miles to a point near an old adobe building known as Adobe Walls.

This was probably the first trading post in the Texas Panhandle. It was built on the north side of the South Canadian River, in present-day Hutchinson County, by William Bent in about 1843. Bent, of the famous trading family, hoped to wean the Kiowas and Comanches from their habit of trading only with the Comancheros, or Mexican traders. Bent thought that if the Indians had a permanent place at which to trade, his company would reap the profits that were enriching many of the caravan traders from Old and New Mexico. The original post, sometimes called Adobe Fort, had thick adobe walls. The Kiowas and Comanches, however, continued to rendezvous with the Mexican traders on the plains and feared that a white settlement would grow up around the post. The hostility of the Indians, the distance that Bent had to bring his goods, and the small amount of trade led him to abandon the post.

The Indians were reinforced and made their stand near the old trading post. When Carson arrived with the battery he found his cavalry dismounted and deployed as skirmishers, with their horses corralled in the Adobe Walls ruins. Confronting them were about two hundred mounted enemy warriors charging back and forth, shouting war cries and sporadically firing. Behind these, a thousand or more fighters were assembled and preparing to charge the soldiers. And a mile away and clearly in sight was a huge Indian village of about five hundred lodges. Already several wounded cavalrymen were being treated inside the Adobe Walls.

The two howitzers were quickly put into position on a small rise near the ruins and started firing. The roar and explosion of the first shot stopped every Indian in his tracks and started a tumultuous retreat to the village. By the fourth shot, not one Indian was within range of the howitzers. While the Indians were reorganizing, the cavalrymen used the short respite to eat and to water and graze their horses. But the enemy was soon back in the field and the battle resumed.

As the afternoon progressed, the Indians were continually reinforced by warriors from other encampments of Kiowas and Comanches farther down the Canadian River. At the same time large parties could be seen going upstream in the direction of the Kiowa village from which the cavalry had routed them in the morning. Carson now found himself in a situation verging on the desperate. Instead of facing a few hundred warriors he was opposed by perhaps one to three thousand. His supply train, advancing from Mule Spring, was in danger of being captured by the large number of Indians that were going to the rear. Yet his orders were to punish the marauding Kiowas and Comanches, and an excellent opportunity lay before him to destroy the five hundred lodges that were in sight just a mile away. But the odds were too great and in the middle of the afternoon he ordered the return march.

This was an orderly but difficult retreat—much of it was done on foot. The horses were assembled in fours with one man to lead and handle each group of four. At the rear of the column were the howitzers. All men not thus occupied were used as skirmishers in front and rear and on both flanks. The Indians resisted the march frantically, attacking from all sides and setting fire to the tall dry grass through which the column had to pass.

Carson reached the Kiowa village shortly before sunset. He found it filled with Indians trying to save their property from the destruction they knew was planned. The howitzers were again brought into action. A couple of shots followed by a cavalry charge drove the Kiowas into the far side of their village. Then its systematic looting and destruction began. Half the command was detailed to hold the Indians back, the other half to set fire to the lodges. The village was the winter headquarters for its occupants and the lodges were found to be filled with food and ammunition. There were hundreds of fine buffalo robes and every man took one or more of these. The remainder were burned with the lodges.

Destruction of the village was quickly accomplished. One hundred and seventy-six buffalo skin lodges were burned, and along with them went all the winter provisions and clothing of the Indian families who lived in the village. With this accomplished, the cavalry was re-formed, and moved out in darkness in search of the supply wagons. These were found within a few hours and, after thirty hours of marching and fighting, Carson's force was reunited. Following a day of uneasy rest, with the enemy in view but not attacking, the return to Fort Bascom started on the morning of November 27. No further contacts were made with the Indians.

Carson had narrowly avoided a catastrophe at the Adobe Walls. His force was tremendously outnumbered and the Indians fought furiously. Without his howitzers and their explosive shells he might have been annihilated. The surprise and destruction from the artillery caused enough uncertainty among the Indians to permit his successful retreat. The battle cost the Army two killed and twenty-one wounded. The loss to the Indians was reported as sixty killed and wounded. Only one of the several Indian villages was destroyed.

Although the Battle of Adobe Walls did not inflict the punishment General Carleton had hoped for, it did materially reduce the Indian raids on the wagon trains on the Santa Fe Trail. The Kiowas and Comanches moved eastward to a new winter camp on the Cimarron in Indian Territory (now Oklahoma). Furthermore, Carson's expedition to their remote winter quarters convinced the Indians that they could not avoid Army reprisals. The Kiowas, Comanches, and Apaches signed a treaty with the United States late in 1864 under which they agreed "to cease all acts of violence or injury to the frontier settlements, and to travelers on the Santa Fe road, or other lines of travel, and to remain at peace." Although the Army continued to escort the wagon trains on the Santa Fe Trail until the end of the war, there was little or no Indian trouble on it. The first battle of Adobe Walls took place after the treaty was signed (neither Carson nor the Indians knew that it had been signed). Carson's howitzers and the fierce winter raids by the volunteers convinced the Indians that this was one treaty that it would be wise for them to keep.

PART V

Action on the Bozeman Trail
1866–67

Introduction

*The Bozeman Trail was known also as the Virginia City Road,
the Bighorn Road, and by several other names. The name which
eventually gained common acceptance, and which is used today
in referring to this first wagon road through virgin Indian country north of the Oregon Trail in the present States of Wyoming
and Montana, derived from the man who first traveled over and
established it as a feasible wagon route, John M. Bozeman.*

*In the spring of 1862 Bozeman was working in the gold fields
of Colorado. That spring he and eleven other young men left the
diggings there and started for Montana, where James and Gran-
ville Stuart had discovered gold in 1860–61. He arrived safely
in the Virginia City-Bannack gold camps after some stirring adventures. During that winter of 1862 he and John M. Jacobs left
Bannack intent on finding a wagon road from the Montana gold
fields to the North Platte River, and hence east to the Missouri
River. Such a road would shorten by several hundred miles the
journey and freighting of supplies over the existing roads by way
of the Fort Hall and Salt Lake roads. Bozeman and Jacobs set
their course from the Yellowstone south along the east side of the
Big Horn Mountains. This was then the unmolested hunting
grounds of Sioux and Crow Indians. There the Sioux stripped
Bozeman and Jacobs of their clothes and arms, took their horses,
and set them off afoot. After many hardships the two men gained
the settlements.*

*That spring of 1863 Bozeman guided a train of freighters from
the Missouri River up the North Platte River. When he tried to*

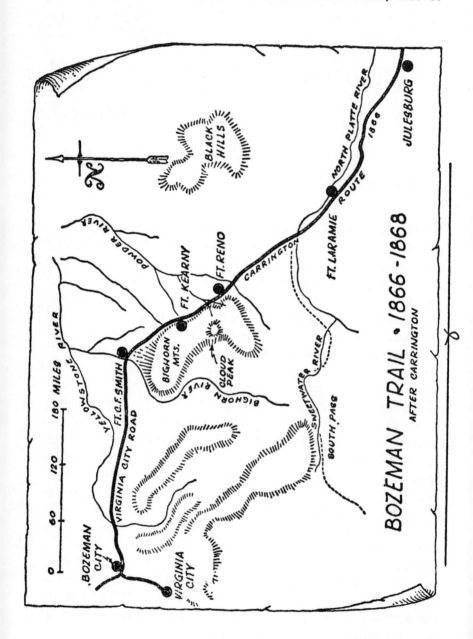

*take it north along the route he had traveled a few months earlier,
Sioux met them and drove the train back. Bozeman and nine men,
traveling by night and hiding by day, went north through the Big
Horn country and crossed the Belt Mountains between the Galla-
tin and Yellowstone Rivers at the pass that has since borne his
name. The next year, 1864, Bozeman succeeded in bringing a
freight train through from the Missouri to the Montana gold fields
over his route, and several others followed. By the end of 1865
it had become the favorite road to the Montana gold fields from
the Missouri River country.*

*This led to a clamor for official protection of the road, since
the Sioux were exceedingly hostile to all white men who came
into their hunting grounds. These Indians wanted to keep all
white men out of the Big Horn country north of the Oregon Trail.
In response to the demand for officially opening and protecting
the new road to the Montana gold fields, Congress on March 3,
1865, passed an act to provide for the construction of certain
wagon roads in the Territories of Idaho, Montana, Dakota, and
Nebraska. The road over the Bozeman Trail was one of those
authorized. Colonel James A. Sawyer of the United States Army
rendered a report to the Congress on this route with a detailed
survey by Lewis H. Smith, the engineer of the expedition.*

*Coincident with this action, Brigadier General (Brevet Major
General) Patrick Edward Connor in 1865 undertook a three-way
campaign into the heart of the Indian country to pacify the In-
dians and bring to a halt their depredations along the Bozeman
Trail. This expedition, commonly known as the Powder River
Expedition, failed in its purpose, and was compelled to turn back.*

*The next spring, in 1866, the Indian Bureau sent Mr. E. B.
Taylor to Fort Laramie to negotiate a new treaty with the Sioux
which would allow a safe passage along the Bozeman Trail. Taylor was engaged in a conclave with the Sioux for this purpose
when Colonel Henry B. Carrington's column arrived at Fort
Laramie, about fifty miles northwest of present Scottsbluff, Nebraska, and twenty miles west of the present Nebraska-Wyoming
line. Carrington was en route to the Powder River country for
the purpose of establishing a series of forts for the protection of
the road through the Indian country. Learning the purpose of*

Carrington's troops, most of the Indians left in anger, declaring that they would never give up the Big Horn country to the whites nor allow them passage through it. Chief Red Cloud of the Oglala Sioux was the leader of the hostile faction, and most of the several Sioux tribes unflinchingly supported him. Chief Spotted Tail of the Brule tribe, however, favored peace and white travel over the Bozeman Road. Nevertheless, in the months that followed, most of the young Brule warriors joined Red Cloud's war party.

Although the Indians had declared their hostility to this undertaking, there is reason to believe that Taylor misrepresented the situation to the authorities back East; they expected no trouble. Lieutenant General William T. Sherman, commanding the Department of the Missouri, had visited Carrington's command at Fort Kearny, Nebraska, in May. He so little expected trouble along the Montana road that he allowed wives and children of several of the officers and some of the enlisted men to accompany the expedition.

On May 17, 1866, Colonel Carrington's force departed Fort Kearny, Nebraska, and marched off into the Indian country. It comprised about 700 soldiers, including a band of more than 30 pieces, 260 non-combatants including several women and children, and 226 mule teams.[1] Most of the troops belonged to the Eighteenth Infantry Regiment, of which Colonel Carrington was commanding officer. The command had obtained 200 horses at

---

[1] In no case known to the writer is there in print a narrative of the subject treated here where the official rank held at the time and the full names of the principal persons involved are given uniformly. Often the brevet rank of an officer is given, or the rank held at an earlier or a later date. Often the rank of general or colonel is given without indicating what grade of general or whether a lieutenant colonel. In the case of the military personnel involved in the three fights associated with the Bozeman Trail and discussed here the ranks and full names are those carried in the official manuscript rosters and post returns of the Army for the period, which the author has personally examined. He has used also both official Army printed and manuscript documents and reports, especially those of the posts principally concerned, Forts Phil Kearny and C. F. Smith.

Fort Kearny from two regiments of volunteer cavalry that were passing through eastward to be mustered out of service. According to Mrs. Carrington, who accompanied her husband, the command, after stopping at Fort Laramie briefly, departed that place on June 17. Old Jim Bridger served as guide. Approximately 135 miles west of Fort Laramie Carrington's command left the old Oregon Trail and headed north along the Bozeman Road.

Carrington's men had their first glimpse of the Big Horn Mountains on June 27 at a distance of 80 miles. The morning sun on that bright, clear day outlined distant Cloud Peak in blue shadow. The next day the command arrived at the previously established Fort Reno (formerly Fort Connor) on the Dry Fork of Powder River. Carrington halted here almost two weeks while he made preparations to abandon that post and build a new Fort Reno. This proving impracticable, Carrington left behind a force to rebuild and garrison the fort, and on July 9 continued northward. At eleven o'clock on the morning of July 13 he encamped on Big Piney Fork, a tributary of Powder River, just east of where the Bozeman Road crossed the stream. The base of the Big Horn Mountains lay six or seven miles to the westward.

Jim Bridger told Carrington there were better places for a fort eastward on Powder River, or at Goose Creek. On the fourteenth, however, Carrington and some of his officers made a reconnaissance of the region round about and decided, for what appears to have been sound reasons, to locate the new fort on a little bench of land they had passed the day before just prior to making camp. On the morning of June 15 Colonel Carrington and Captain Tenedor Ten Eyck, together with the engineers, staked out the new fort according to plans that had been drawn at Fort Kearny in the spring. A mowing machine was brought to the little bench and the tall grass cut from the plot that was staked out for a parade ground. Walks were laid out at once.

The fort was six hundred by eight hundred feet in dimensions with strong palisade posts enclosing six acres of ground. The men dug a trench three feet deep and into this set eleven-foot posts, approximately sixteen inches in diameter, tamped in gravel. The stockade posts, standing eight feet above ground with their tops sharpened, were hewn on two sides so as to fit snugly against each other. Portholes were cut into the palisades every few feet. These pine stockade posts and other timbers used in its construction were cut at two "pineries," about half a mile apart at the foot of the Big Horns, six miles west of the fort site. Fort Phil Kearny stood near what is now the little village of Story, Wyoming, just west of present U. S. 82, eighteen miles south of Sheridan.

The new fort was called variously in the days and years that followed: Fort Philip Kearney, Phil Kearney, and Philip or Phil Kearny. In this narrative it will be called Phil Kearny because this spelling of Kearny is the correct one for the man for whom it was named. Also, the official order directing its establishment supports that spelling. In General Order No. 7 of the Department of the Platte, dated at Omaha, June 28, 1866, Brigadier General Philip St. George Cooke directed that a new fort be established about eighty miles north of Fort Reno, on the new route to Virginia City, Montana. This order stated that the post was to be known as Fort Philip Kearny. It was named in honor of Major General Philip Kearny, commander of the First Infantry Division of the red diamond shoulder patch, the first shoulder patch used in the United States Army. Kearny was killed in action at Chantilly, Virginia, on September 1, 1862. The Secretary of War has ruled that, since there was no subsequent official authority for changing the name or its spelling, the spelling given in General Cooke's order is still the official designation of the fort. Strangely enough, most of the official army correspondence of the period when the fort was active uses the spelling "Kearney," and that usage, erroneously, has become generally accepted. A typical dispatch from the post carries the heading, "Fort Philip Kearney, D.T., Piney Forks." The D.T. stood for Dakota Territory, which at that time embraced this area.

At the time of the fort's establishment, Carrington had about 640 men in his command. A dispatch of his on July 30 speaks of "my 8 companies of 80 effective men each." He gives further interesting information in saying that "560 of them [are] new recruits."

Fort Phil Kearny was 223 miles from Fort Laramie. In the first part of August, Carrington sent Captain (Brevet Lieutenant Colonel) N. C. Kinney with two companies of infantry from Fort

Phil Kearny to establish a third fort on the Bozeman Road 91 miles northwestward, on the Bighorn River where the road curved around the northern end of the Big Horn Mountains. Virginia City, in the Montana gold fields, lay 281 miles northwest of this new fort, which Kinney named Fort C. F. Smith. Thus, Forts Phil Kearny and C. F. Smith were roughly in the middle of the vast stretch of 600 miles of wild Indian country that lay between Fort Laramie and the Montana gold diggings. The Big Horn country and the areas east of it, including the Tongue and Powder River valleys, were the very heart of the Sioux' most prized hunting grounds. They would never voluntarily give these up.

Indian forays became almost a daily occurrence near Fort Phil Kearny. There were fifty-one skirmishes and fights with the Indians from the time the fort was started to the end of the year, six and a half months later. The Indians attacked many small parties caught away from the fort, and almost every group and wagon train traveling the Bozeman Trail came under attack. Soon they held the fort on the Pineys virtually in a state of siege. To the Indians, Fort Phil Kearny became "the hated fort on the Piney." In the latter half of 1866, the Sioux, under Chief Red Cloud, killed 154 soldiers and citizens on the Bozeman Trail. They drove off 306 cattle (most of them oxen), 304 mules, and 161 horses.

More fights and encounters with hostile Indians took place around Fort Phil Kearny in the little more than two years of its existence than near any other Army post in the while history of the western frontier. Our purpose is to tell the main known facts about the three most famous of them. One has come down to us by the name of the Fetterman Massacre. This, however, is a misnomer; it was not a massacre. It was a fight, a small battle in which there were no white survivors.

There had been plenty of warning of what might happen if the men became careless and dared too much. As recently as December 6 a relief party had sallied from the fort to help a wood train party that had come under Indian attack while cutting wood. In pursuing the Indians too far, and separating from the main force, two men were killed and five wounded. One of the killed was a young lieutenant. Only the timely arrival of Colonel Carrington with a second force saved the first one from further casualties. This affair took place north of the fort on Peno Creek. On the nineteenth, Captain (Brevet Major) James W. Powell, a veteran soldier, calm and capable, with a relief force succeeded in rescuing another wood train under attack without incurring any casualties. He did not pursue the Indians. That night it snowed.

The next day Colonel Carrington himself accompanied the wood train over the snow-covered ground to the "pinery" on Piney Island where the wood party cut trees. There he supervised the building of a bridge to Piney Island as a means of speeding up the operation of the wood train. Only one more trip was planned; another trainload of logs was needed to complete a hospital. To get this load, the wood train left the fort on the morning of December 21. After that final load of logs had been obtained, the garrison would stay in the relative comfort of the fort during the cold, snowbound winter that was at hand. As luck would have it, that twenty-first of December was to be fateful.

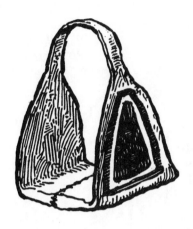

10. THE FETTERMAN FIGHT

ROY E. APPLEMAN

During the autumn of 1866 the various tribes of Sioux had gathered on Tongue River, about forty miles to the northeast of Fort Phil Kearny. Their villages stretched along that stream for perhaps twenty miles, and held a great aggregation of fighting men. In December the Sioux received important allies when several hundred Northern Cheyennes joined them. In the great Sioux camp there were also some Arapahoes. The Cheyennes had professed neutrality, but the constant insults of the Sioux and their promptings to help in driving the white man from the country finally had its effect. An important part of this conversion very likely lay in the fact that the men at the fort fired on Cheyenne parties and disbelieved their statements of friendship. The Chey-

117

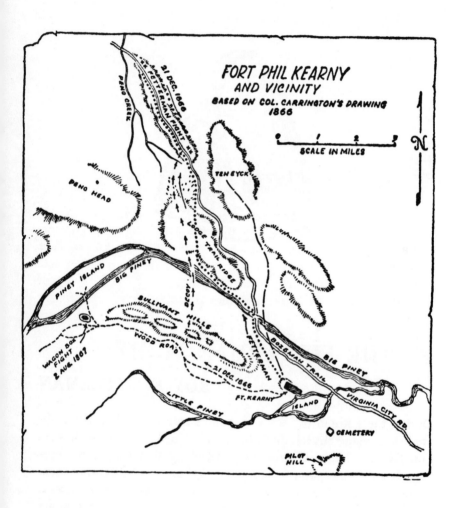

FORT PHIL KEARNY
AND VICINITY
BASED ON COL. CARRINGTON'S DRAWING
1866

SCALE IN MILES

enne chief, Two Moons, and a small party of his warriors, however, recently had been admitted to the fort. In the opinion of Colonel Carrington and Jim Bridger their purpose was to spy out its strength and dispositions and report their observations to the Sioux. The soldiers took care to make the fort appear impregnable, showing off the cannon mounted at strategic points.

Meanwhile, the Sioux chiefs formed a simple plan of attack. In their numerous attacks on the wood train the Indians had succeeded many times in drawing off pursuers to the north over Lodge Trail Ridge and into the valley of Peno Creek, five or six miles from the fort. Once quarry and pursuers had crossed over Lodge Trail Ridge, observers at the fort and pickets stationed at Pilot Hill (southward across Little Piney Fork) and other high observation posts near the fort could not see what happened beyond. The Sioux scheme was to attack a wood train just as they had done before—so often that it had become a common thing for a relief party to sally forth and drive off the Indians. The warriors who attacked the wood party would act as decoys to bring out the relief party, and when attacked by it they would retreat and attempt to draw it into pursuing them over Lodge Trail Ridge toward Peno Creek into an ambush. The great Sioux and Cheyenne war party would be hidden just beyond Lodge Trail Ridge on either side of a long spur ridge that extended northward from it. The Bozeman Trail angled up the east slope of Lodge Trail Ridge from Big Piney Fork toward this spur ridge. At a little saddle which separated this spur from the east side of Lodge Trail Ridge the road bent slightly to the right and north along the crest of the spur for something more than a mile. At its northern tip the road dropped down off the nose of the spur into the valley of Peno Creek.

According to George Bird Grinnell, who received the story from his friends the Cheyennes many years later, the Sioux and their Cheyenne and Arapaho allies rehearsed the ambush. They journeyed to the planned scene of ambush five miles north of the fort, and out of sight of it. There they marked out their places of concealment in the brush along the bases on either side of the spur ridge and sent a decoy to Lodge Trail Ridge to simulate signaling the approach of soldiers. The chiefs made the decoy, who apparently was a Minneconjou half man and half woman (presumably a hermaphrodite), return several times to his starting point, each time requiring him to announce a larger number of soldiers. Their point in doing this was to emphasize to the assembled warriors that they were not to fire on a few soldiers—that they must wait for *many*. After this rehearsal of their plan the Indians returned to their camp on Tongue River, apparently near the mouth of Goose Creek in the vicinity of the present town of Acme, Wyoming, about thirty miles north of the fort.

According to the Cheyenne story, the chiefs on the night of December 20 sent out ten warriors to reach the vicinity of the fort and play the part of the initial decoy. Two of them were Cheyennes, two more were Arapahoes, and six were Sioux. Others must have joined these decoys in the attack on the wood train the next morning. At daybreak on the twenty-first the mass of warriors left camp and followed the decoys to the ambush site. Once there, the Sioux gave the Cheyennes their choice of where they would fight. Together with the Arapahoes they took the west side of the spur ridge. The Sioux then secreted themselves on the east side. Hidden from view, the Indians waited for their decoys to lead soldiers into the trap. Most of the warriors were armed with bows and arrows, war clubs, and lances. Only a few of them had firearms.

At this time Colonel Carrington had at Fort Phil Kearny five companies of the Eighteenth Infantry and one company of the Second Battalion, U. S. Cavalry—about 398 men, including those sick, absent, or under arrest. Of this number he reported only 308 fit for duty, seven of them officers. He had 37 serviceable horses at the fort, 13 others were unserviceable. He had three mountain howitzers and one field twelve-pounder howitzer. The cavalry was armed with the new Spencer carbine. The infantry still used the old Civil War Springfield muzzle-loading musket rifle.

At between 10:15 to 10:30 the morning of the twenty-first, the wood train left Fort Phil Kearny for the last load of logs. Counting its escort and the armed woodcutters and teamsters, there were about eighty men in the wood train. Its course was westward from the fort along the south side of Sullivant's Hills toward

Courtesy National Park Service

TRAPPERS ENROUTE TO RENDEZVOUS *by Paul Rockwood*
(CHAPTER 2)

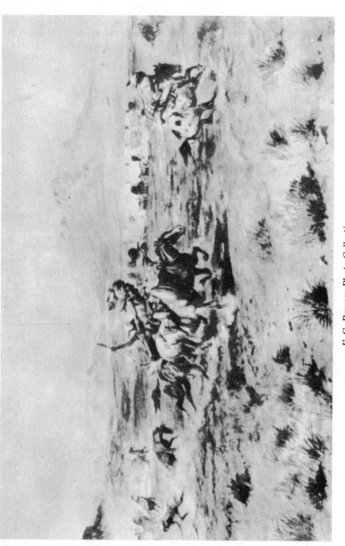

F. G. Renner Photo Collection

GUNPOWDER AND ARROWS *by Charles M. Russell*

Indian attacks on the wagon supply trains skyrocketed the price of flour to $45 a sack in Denver in 1864. (PART IV, INTRODUCTION)

LIEUTENANT GRUMMOND'S EVEN CHANCE *by Charles Schreyvogel*

Later in the day Grummond, Fetterman, and all their soldiers were killed. (CHAPTER 10)

INDIAN CHARGE *by Charles Schreyvogel*

The Indians made many such attacks during the Hayfield fight.
(CHAPTER 11)

Courtesy National Park Service

DIORAMA OF THE WAGON BOX FIGHT
(CHAPTER 12)

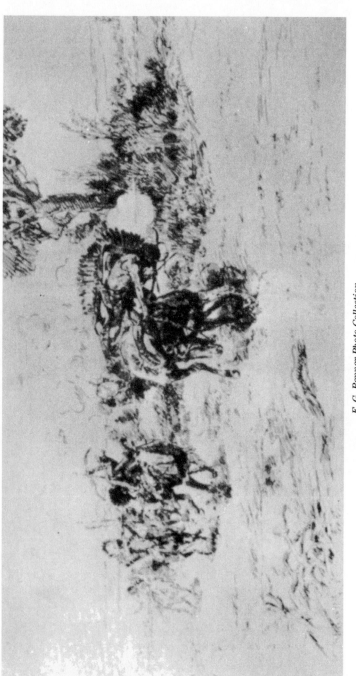

THE DEATH OF ROMAN NOSE *by Charles M. Russell*

The wily old warrior felt that he was doomed to die if he joined in the attack. (CHAPTER 13)

FORSYTH'S FIGHT ON THE ARICKAREE *by Frederic Remington*
(CHAPTER 13)

CAVALRY CHARGE *by Frederic Remington*
(CHAPTER 14)

F. G. Renner Photo Collection

THE BATTLE OF THE LAVA BEDS *by Charles M. Russell*
(CHAPTER 16)

Courtesy Potomac Corral of the Westerners

MACKENZIE'S SCOUT FINDS THE WINTER CAMP
by William Loechel

the pinery. About eleven o'clock the picket on Pilot Hill, south of the fort, reported that the wood train had corralled about a mile and a half westward and was under Indian attack. A few shots were heard from that direction. Colonel Carrington immediately ordered a relief party to go to its rescue. He indicated that Captain (Brevet Major) James Powell would command this force, just as he had done two days earlier. But Captain (Brevet Lieutenant Colonel) William J. Fetterman, commander of A Company, Eighteenth Infantry, claimed by virtue of his senior rank the privilege of commanding the relief force. Colonel Carrington acquiesced in this request and gave him men of his own company that were available for duty, and some others. Second Lieutenant George W. Grummond asked to be allowed to take out the cavalry. This, too, Carrington granted.

The relief party as finally told off included Captain Fetterman, Lieutenant Grummond, and 76 enlisted men—48 of them from the Eighteenth Infantry, one unassigned, and 27 from the Second Battalion, Second Cavalry. In some manner, Captain Frederick H. Brown, until recently the regimental quartermaster but now on the point of leaving Fort Phil Kearny for reassignment, joined the group without orders. He rode out on Calico, a pet paint pony. Two civilians, James S. Wheatley and Isaac Fisher (sometimes spelled Fischer), accompanied the party, making 81 men in all.

Colonel Carrington gave to Captain Fetterman the following order as the latter made ready to depart: "Support the wood train, relieve it, and report to me. Do not engage or pursue Indians at its expense. Under no circumstances pursue over the ridge [Lodge Trail Ridge]." To Lieutenant Grummond, Carrington gave orders to "report to Brevet Lt. Col. Fetterman, implicitly obey his orders, and not leave him." Before the command left, Carrington instructed Lieutenant A. H. Wands, the acting regimental adjutant, to repeat the orders, and he did so. Colonel Carrington knew, as did everyone at the fort, that Fetterman had a rather contemptuous attitude toward the Indians and not long before had asked, along with Captain Brown, to lead a hundred mounted men against the whole Sioux Nation. Carrington, of course, denied this request. Brown, whom Carrington at this point did not know was with the party, was a ringleader at the fort among those who thought Colonel Carrington's attitude toward the Indians was too cautious and that he should have led them out in a campaign against the red men. Brown apparently slipped away to accompany the relief party in the hope of having an engagement and killing an Indian before he left the Big Horn country. Conscious of the over-zealous disposition of Fetterman, and fearing rash action despite his orders, Carrington crossed the parade ground as the last of the party was leaving, mounted a sentry platform, halted the cavalry which was passing outside the fort, and again repeated his orders.

As the relief party started out, five Indians came out of the brush east of the fort at the point where the Bozeman Road crossed Big Piney. A case shot from one of the howitzers unhorsed one of them and flushed about thirty more from the nearby trees and bushes. All scampered away to the hills northward.

Fetterman led his infantry out of the fort to the road crossing of Big Piney, where Grummond's cavalry, which had saddled quickly, joined him. The combined party then moved around the east end of Sullivant's Hill, immediately north of the fort, apparently intent on going west on the north side of it in the hope of intercepting the Indians attacking the wood train on its south side, or of coming in on their rear. When last seen from the fort, Fetterman's command was moving up Big Piney and the southern, lower slopes of Lodge Trail Ridge, with skirmishers out. Big Piney Creek passes on a northwest-southeast axis between Sullivant's Hill and Lodge Trail Ridge. Accordingly, in traveling up Big Piney westward in the direction of the corralled wood train, Fetterman had Lodge Trail Ridge on his right, or to the north of him. It is considerably higher than Sullivant's Hill. Half an hour after Fetterman's relief party left the fort a picket reported to Colonel Carrington that the wood train had broken corral and was continuing on its way to Piney Island. It was now about 11:40 in the morning.

Earlier, shortly after Fetterman had disappeared around the end of Sullivant's Hill, Colonel Carrington realized that the party did not have a surgeon with it, and he sent Assistant Post Surgeon C. M. Hines, a civilian, with an escort of four men to catch up with Fetterman and accompany him. Hines returned before long and said the wood train had gone on before he arrived at the place where it had corralled, that in trying to find Fetterman, he had found the country in the direction of Peno Creek full of Indians, that they were swarming around Lodge Trail Ridge, and that he had seen nothing of Fetterman's command.

About noon, men in the fort heard firing towards Peno Creek. This stream lay mostly to the west and north of Lodge Trail Ridge but had one of its sources in the saddle between Lodge Trail and the spur ridge which ran northeast from it, and along which passed the Bozeman Road. The first few shots were followed by constant firing. Carrington immediately dispatched Captain Tenodor Ten Eyck (name variously spelled Tenedore and Theodore, but official post returns spell it Tenedor) with a force of fifty-four men to join Fetterman. They left the fort on a run. Soon Carrington sent forty more men to join with them. Ten Eyck had with him two wagons. He did not follow the Bozeman Road straight to the scene of the firing. Instead, he soon bore off to the right and gained the high ridge to the east of the road. He reached its crest in about half an hour, at a distance of perhaps four miles from the fort, and just as the sound of firing ceased in the direction of Peno Creek. From this high point, Ten Eyck sent an orderly riding pell-mell back to the fort to report to Carrington that he could see nothing of Fetterman, but that a large body of Indians, numbering several hundred, were on the Bozeman Road below him, challenging him to come down and fight. Beyond them and for miles around in the valleys he could see other large bodies of Indians.

For several hours Colonel Carrington and the 119 men he had retained in the fort to guard it and the women and children waited in ignorance of what had happened, but they feared the worst. Carrington was down to so low a point in manpower now, with the wood train and its escort, the Fetterman party, and the Ten Eyck force away from the fort, that he released prisoners from the guard house and organized all the quartermaster employees and civilians in the fort for its defense in the event of an Indian attack. After receiving the report of Captain Ten Eyck's

messenger, Colonel Carrington sent riders to recall the wood train
and its escort from the pinery. Fortunately, all these men returned
safely to the fort.

The lapse of time from the beginning to the end of firing indi-
cates that the action lasted in all about one half hour, from
approximately 12:00 noon to 12:30 P.M. Just what happened to
Fetterman and his men can never be known in full detail or with
complete accuracy. Much, however, has been learned from Indian
sources, and the evidence on the field of battle disclosed the
principal calamitous facts. This evidence pretty well substantiates
the Indian story; taken together they permit reconstructing a
fairly reliable account of the disaster.

Resuming the Cheyenne account as given to Grinnell by a warrior who took part in it when he was eighteen or nineteen years
old and who, as an old man, forty-eight years later, guided Grinnell around the field pointing out specific spots where key incidents happened, the story tells how well the decoys succeeded
in their mission. As soon as the decoys saw the large force under
Fetterman leave the fort, they in turn ended their demonstration
against the wood train and rode back in the direction of Lodge
Trail Ridge and the Peno. Therefore, instead of intercepting
them, Fetterman was himself intercepted and led into a chase
up the slope of Lodge Trail Ridge. From the crest the decoys
rode down to the Bozeman Road and northward on it along the
spur ridge. Fetterman halted his command on the crest of Lodge
Trail Ridge, apparently mindful of Carrington's orders not to
pursue beyond it.

Seeing that failure threatened their plan, one of the Cheyenne
decoys charged back and, to the warriors who were watching
him from concealment, seemed literally to ride in among the
soldiers on the crest of Lodge Trail. This bold sally worked, for
some troops started down off the ridge after the daring warrior,
and soon the whole command was trailing along the Bozeman
Road on the spur ridge, chasing the decoys northward. The
cavalry detachment led; the infantry followed behind on foot. It
appears that Fetterman's force was somewhat strung out at this
point. To all appearances they were safe enough; the only In-

dians in sight were the small group fleeing ahead northward down the Bozeman Trail.

The decoys dropped off the northern end of the spur ridge to the little valley of Peno Creek, crossed it, and then on the other side of the creek split into two parts, half of them turning to the right and half to the left. In the meantime, the mounted foremost of Fetterman's command had reached the northern end of the spur ridge where the ground dropped off to Peno Creek, a full mile from the slope of Lodge Trail Ridge where U. S. Highway 87 now passes through the saddle between it and the open ridge in a deep cut, and where the Fetterman Monument now stands high above the road on its east side. They had started down the slope toward Peno Creek when the decoys split in two parts and, turning to left and right, rode their horses back across the creek. This apparently was the signal for springing the trap.

Warriors hidden in the tall grass south of Peno Creek now rose up in front of the soldiers and began to fight. Captain Brown must have been in the vanguard of the pursuers, for the body of the calico pony he rode that day was found later on the northwest slope of this spur ridge where it slanted down to the Peno, and apparently where the attack began. By this time the entire Fetterman force was on the spur ridge below Lodge Trail Ridge. The multitude of Indians hidden on either side of the spur ridge rushed from their places of concealment and cut off the soldiers from Lodge Trail, filling the road behind them where it curved off the slope of that ridge to the spur. Fetterman's whole command was in the trap.

Early in the fight, Wheatley and Fisher took a covered position behind rocks near the northern end of the spur ridge and gave a good account of themselves before they were killed. They were the best armed of Fetterman's group. They had recently purchased Henry sixteen-shot repeating rifles and had been anxious to try them out. A few of the more experienced soldiers took positions near Wheatley and Fisher. The cavalry for a time fell back in good order under Grummond; in the rear part of the column the infantry tried to turn back. According to the Indian account, some of the soldiers were so horrified and unnerved

when they saw they were surrounded by the countless horde of
warriors that they were overcome without offering resistance.

A Cheyenne named Two Moons, who was in the fight, said
later that Fetterman dismounted his mounted men and that in
a very short time thereafter the horses either broke away or were
turned loose. Lieutenant Grummond, Sergeant Lang, and a few
others made a courageous fight, according to the Indians; while
he lived Grummond held his men together and they fought as a
unit about half a mile beyond, or north of, the main body of
soldiers. Behind them on the spur ridge, near the base of Lodge
Trail Ridge, the bulk of the infantry had by this time huddled
together in a small area among some large sandstone boulders
that offered partial protection. Captains Fetterman and Brown
apparently joined them there.

At this time, Indian sentries on Lodge Trail Ridge signaled to
those below that another relief force had left the fort and was
coming in their direction. This was the Ten Eyck column. The
Indians thereupon charged in on the surviving soldiers and killed
or captured them all. Exceptions probably were Fetterman and
Brown, who, to avoid capture, apparently killed each other with
revolver shots in the temple. It would appear that by this time
most of Fetterman's men had expended all their ammunition.

A short time later the Indians attempted to lure Ten Eyck from
the hill where he remained on the defensive against the two
thousand warriors he estimated were within view. Apparently
not wishing to push their good fortune too far, the Sioux and
Cheyennes in the afternoon gradually disappeared from the scene
of the fight. It is believed they thought one of the wagons Ten
Eyck had with him pulled a cannon, and they feared to face it.

After the Indians had disappeared, Ten Eyck near dusk led
his force cautiously down to the Bozeman Road. When he
reached the point where the large body of Indians had been congregated he found the bodies of forty-nine soldiers. In this group
were Fetterman and Brown. The bullet holes in their left temples
had powder burns around them, indicating that revolver muzzles
must have been pressed against their heads, or nearly so. Their
bodies lay side by side. It appeared that they had stood face to
face and shot each other as the Indians charged. Ten Eyck did

not go beyond this spot. He placed the bodies of the dead men in the wagons and returned to the fort.

At the fort it was expected that the large Indian force would attack during the night or the next morning. Sometime after dark two men, one of them leading a horse, approached the sentry at the "water gate" inside the fort. The two men were Colonel Carrington and John (Portugee) Phillips. The horse was the best one at Fort Phil Kearny, the colonel's own Kentucky thoroughbred. Out into the night and a thousand dangers from severe weather and savage Indians rode Phillips. He had volunteered to try to get a message for help to Fort Laramie, 236 miles away. It appears that the plight of the pregnant Mrs. Grummond, widow of the young officer killed that day, was one of the factors that caused Phillips, a civilian, to volunteer for what seemed a ninety-nine per cent chance of death. But Phillips got through the blizzard-swept and Indian-infested country.

At ten o'clock in the morning on Christmas Day he arrived at Horseshoe Station and there filed two dispatches, one to the Army departmental commander at Omaha and the other to the post commander at Fort Laramie. Not taking any chances that the messages would fail to get through on telegraph, Phillips continued toward Fort Laramie. He arrived there in a state of collapse at eleven o'clock that night and delivered Carrington's dispatch before a Christmas levee that was in full swing at "Bedlam"—a large building and the Post headquarters where such festivities were held (Old Bedlam is still standing at Fort Laramie National Monument). Outside, Colonel Carrington's Kentucky thoroughbred sank to the ground and died.

At Fort Phil Kearny, Saturday December 22, the day after the Fetterman fight, was bitterly cold and a storm threatened. Carrington said he was going out to get the bodies of the rest of Fetterman's men. His officers tried to dissuade him, saying that he would meet the same fate. He quietly excused them from accompanying him, and prepared to make the venture. But when it was apparent that he was really going, he did not lack for volunteers. Accompanied by Captain Tenedor Ten Eyck, Second Lieutenant Winfield S. Matson, Dr. Elisha R. Ould (a civilian surgeon in Army pay), and eighty men, Carrington set out in the early afternoon with wagons along the Bozeman Road toward the scene of the ambush. He left behind as he proceeded a string of pickets and lookouts to advise him of any action in his rear or against the fort, and to maintain signal communications with sentries at the fort.

He passed the place where Ten Eyck the previous evening had found the bodies of the forty-nine men, in the vicinity of where the Fetterman Monument now stands. He continued north down the spur ridge, and himself has said, "The scene of action told its own story." About halfway down the ridge he found the body of Lieutenant Grummond and some of the cavalry in a little group. Pools of dried and frozen blood on the road and the sloping sides of the spur ridge showed where Indians had fallen (apparently snow from the fall of two nights before covered at least parts of this ridge). Within ten feet of Grummond's body Carrington saw three pools of blood. Along the ridge he found the bodies of eleven cavalry horses and nine Indian ponies. The heads of all the cavalry horses pointed in the direction of the fort. In the valleys around the ridge Carrington could see some abandoned, crippled horses.

At the northern tip of the spur ridge Carrington came upon the bodies of Wheatley and Fisher and a few soldiers. Scattered around the body of one of the civilians, apparently Wheatley, were 50 expended cartridge shells from his Henry repeating rifle. Wheatley's body had 105 arrows in it. In this vicinity Carrington counted 65 bloody spots in the space of an acre. This told of the execution wrought on the Indians in this one corner of the battlefield by Wheatley and Fisher with their new rifles, and by the few veteran soldiers who fought with them. There, apparently, fell most of the Indians who were killed or wounded in the fight. There were no Indian bodies found. The Sioux and their allies, true to their custom, had taken away all with them. It was ten o'clock that night before Carrington returned to the fort. Only just before dark had he found the bodies of the last men. Nearly all the bodies had been stripped of their clothing and horribly mutilated.

That night the temperature dropped to twenty degrees below zero, and a snow blizzard built up in the Big Horn country. The garrison at Fort Phil Kearny spent the next five days in preparing the eighty-one mutilated bodies for burial, in carefully identifying each man, and in digging graves in the deeply frozen ground. The dead, each in its pine case, were buried on Wednesday, December 26, in two graves east of the fort in a cemetery at the foot of Pilot Hill. In one were placed the bodies of Captains Fetterman and Brown and Lieutenant Grummond. In the second, a large common grave fifty feet long and seven feet deep, the others were buried.

Here these men, with the exception of Grummond, rested until June 1896, when they were removed and re-interred at Custer Battlefield National Cemetery on the twenty-fourth of that month. There they rest today, along with many other victims of the Indian wars. Grummond's body rested in its grave at Fort Phil Kearny only a few weeks. When Colonel Carrington and his party and Mrs. Grummond departed the fort in January, 1867, they took his body with them.

On January 3, 1867, thirteen days after the Fetterman fight, Colonel Carrington wrote an official report of the sad affair, which he dispatched to the Department of the Platte headquarters at Omaha. This report was first published in 1887, twenty years after it was written, when Congress by Senate resolution requested the War Department to submit to it papers relating to the incident. A few passages from this report will disclose a little of the terribly mutilated condition of the bodies. Carrington concluded this report by stating, "I give you some of the facts as to my men, whose bodies I found just at dark, resolved to bring all in . . . " Mutilations: eyes torn out and laid on the rocks; brains taken out and laid on rocks, with members of the body; hands and feet cut off; arms taken from sockets; skulls severed in every form from chin to crown; punctures upon every sensitive part of the body. Some of the more indecent forms of mutilation listed by Carrington need not be stated explicitly here.

After enumerating the forms of mutilation, Colonel Carrington's report continued: "All this does not approximate the whole truth. Every medical officer was faithfully aided by a large force of men and all were not buried until Wednesday after the fight.

"The great real fact is," he said, "that these Indians take alive when possible, and slowly torture. It is the opinion of Dr. S. M. Horton, post surgeon, that not more than six were killed by balls. Of course, the whole arrows, hundreds of which were removed from the naked bodies, were all used after the removal of clothing." (Carrington apparently means the men were captured and shot full of arrows while still living.)

We know that 81 white men were killed in the Fetterman fight. We do not know how many Indians lost their lives or were wounded. The only direct evidence on this point is Carrington's statement that he counted more than 65 places where great splotches of blood showed on the ground near his fallen men. According to Cheyenne accounts given to Grinnell many years later, only two Cheyennes were killed but about 50 or 60 Sioux lost their lives. Another Indian account states that one Arapaho, two Cheyennes, and 11 Sioux were killed. Captain James H. Cook, who became friendly with Red Cloud in the chief's later life when he was living peacefully on a reservation, asked the Indian how many of his warriors lost their lives in the fight. Red Cloud replied that he thought only 11 were killed outright, but that a number of others had been wounded so badly that they died in camp later. Although the matter is controversial, the weight of evidence seems to support the claim that Chief Red Cloud of the Oglala Sioux was present at the Fetterman fight, although he may not have been in personal command of the warriors.

When word of the Fetterman disaster reached the Department of the Platte, the commanding general, Brigadier General (Brevet Major General) Philip St. George Cooke, at once ordered the relief of Colonel Carrington. The latter appears to have been blameless in the affair and had done everything possible to avoid a catastrophe. He has long since been vindicated.

Lieutenant Colonel (Brevet Brigadier General) Henry W. Wessels, in a desperate march in bitter weather, arrived at Fort Phil Kearny on January 17 with reinforcements—two companies of the Second Cavalry and three companies of the Eighteenth Infantry. He took over the command from Colonel Carrington, who, six days later on January 23, departed the post with which his name will always be associated. Carrington took with him his headquarters staff and the regimental band, and the wives and children of these soldiers who had accompanied them into the Indian wilderness. A detail of sixty men escorted Carrington's party. The ordeal of this group's journey in reaching the North Platte River in temperatures as low as forty degrees below zero, and in deep snow, cannot be told here.

Today as motorists speed past the site of Fort Phil Kearny, perhaps not one in fifty knows that he is passing the place where so much drama was enacted in a bygone day. Possibly many do not even know that a Fort Phil Kearny ever existed. And still fewer know any of the details of the stirring events enacted there less than a hundred years ago, when this beautiful country was a howling wilderness. But this enchanting spot in the shadows of the Big Horns can speak eloquently to those who have taken the trouble to learn its history.

11. THE HAYFIELD FIGHT

ROY E. APPLEMAN

Just as soon as Colonel Carrington had the construction of Fort Phil Kearny well under way he acted on his orders to establish another fort along the Bozeman Trail at the northern end of the Big Horn Mountains. In early August, 1866, he issued instructions for this purpose to Captain (Brevet Lieutenant Colonel) N. C. Kinney of the Eighteenth Infantry Regiment, whom he had selected for the undertaking. According to the new fort's first Post Returns, Captain Kinney started from Fort Phil Kearny on August 4, 1866, with D and G Companies of the Second Battalion, Eighteenth Infantry Regiment, and by a series of marches arrived at the Bighorn River on August 10. On the way, Indians made an effort to run off his mules one evening, but the courageous efforts of the wagon master foiled their attempt. Two days after arriving at the Bighorn River, Kinney moved on August 12 from his temporary camp to the site he had selected for the new post. He began on that day construction of this new fort, which he named C. F. Smith in honor of Colonel (Brevet Major General) Charles F. Smith, commanding the Third U. S. Infantry Regiment.

In his own words, written on Fort C. F. Smith's first Post Returns, for the month of August, 1866, Captain Kinney described the site as follows: "The site selected for the fort is on an elevated plateau, 300 yards from the River Bank, 8 miles above the mouth of Rotten Grass Creek and 2 miles below the debouchment of the River from the mountains. The ferry, by which all trains cross the river, is within 800 yards of the Fort."

The road from Phil Kearny approached the new fort from the southeast, dropping off the hill line to the wide valley and bench land about eight miles away. It passed the fort on the west, descending a natural, shallow draw on that side that slanted slightly northwest to the river. On the north side of the river the road continued northwest over broken ground toward the distant Montana settlements.

Fort C. F. Smith was placed at the edge of the benchland, perhaps a hundred feet above the flood plain of the river that it overlooked immediately to the northward. From the fort there was a spectacular view of the surrounding country. To the northeast a wide prairie extended along the east bank of the Bighorn River. To the south and west the Big Horn Mountains rose majestically. Through them the Bighorn River had cut its way in a hundred-mile long canyon, emerging from it to the high prairies only a mile or two upstream from the fort site.

Captain Kinney built a square fort, about 125 yards on a side. It was built much like Phil Kearny; logs cut from the nearby Big Horns were placed on end in a trench and the earth then packed around them. There is some evidence that adobe bricks were used for some parts of the fort, perhaps after the initial construction. At the southeast corner there was an observation tower. If men on duty there were vigilant it was impossible for anyone to come within a mile of the post in daylight from any direction without being seen, and in most quarters the visibility of the intervening ground extended several miles. At the southeast and northwest corners of the fort two small cannons were emplaced in special protruding, window-like embrasures so that they could sweep the ground along the four walls of the fort. A good spring of water was near the fort. The river at its closest point was three hundred yards away. Inside the palisade, log houses were built for the garrison.

Fort Smith was the most isolated of the posts guarding the Bozeman Trail. After the closing down of winter weather and the tragedy of the Fetterman Fight near Phil Kearny in December, there was no communication with Fort C. F. Smith for a long time during the harsh months that followed. The Phil Kearny Post Returns disclose that five times in January 1867 the commanding officer there made efforts to establish communications with Fort C. F. Smith but each time Indians, deep snow, or bitter weather turned back his messengers. This post, like Phil Kearny, was held virtually in a state of siege by the Sioux and their allies from the time of its establishment until its abandonment.

Fort C. F. Smith stood on traditional Crow Indian hunting grounds. The Sioux, however, for many years had been pressing the Crows westward. Sioux warriors roamed north of the Big Horns in the hunt and on the warpath. With the coming of soldiers to the Bozeman Trail, the Sioux for the time being patched up a truce with the Crows so that they could concentrate their efforts against the white man. North and west of the fort raiding Blackfeet might be encountered at any time.

Captain Kinney was anxious to establish a good relationship with the Crow Indians, and when they did not show up soon after the fort was established he decided to send a messenger to them. As it chanced, the famous mountain man, James P. Beckwourth, a mulatto who had lived with the Crows in the 1820s and 1830s for ten years and had risen to be one of their chiefs, was at the fort. He was now an old man. He had been forced to flee the Crows for his life because they believed he was responsible for a great misfortune that overtook them. Despite the fact that he feared the Crows would kill him, Beckwourth volunteered to go out to find them and try to bring them in. He selected a lone companion for the effort, Private James W. Thompson. Beckwourth set out for Pryor's Creek, which he knew to be a favorite haunt of the Crows. On the way he became very ill, and he instructed Thompson to go without him. Thompson found the Crows where Beckwourth thought they would be. When they returned with him to where he had left Beckwourth the latter was dead.

Some time later the Crows, having finished their hunt, came to Fort C. F. Smith with Thompson. Kinney was able to establish friendly relations with them, and they pitched their camp opposite the fort on the north side of the Bighorn River and remained there for a part of the autumn and winter. Because the Crows were now at peace with the Sioux, some of their young men visited in the Sioux camp from time to time, and brought to Fort C. F. Smith intelligence of the hostile camp.

News that came in this way was their first knowledge of the Fetterman Fight. The Crows said there was much weeping in the Sioux lodges from losses in that affair. After this news, Captain Kinney increased vigilance and reduced drastically the number of Crows allowed inside the fort at any one time. Rations ran low during the winter and, according to one of the soldiers stationed there, the men had to convert grain for the mules and horses to food for themselves. As soon as the passing of winter permitted, a supply wagon train came from Fort Phil Kearny.

The coming of spring, 1867, to Fort C. F. Smith brought also the death of John Bozeman, who had given his name to the Bozeman Trail. He was killed in April by a band of marauding Blackfeet while on his way to the fort from the Montana settlements.

During the summer a supply of hay and wood had to be procured for the coming winter. Soon after establishing the fort the previous year, Corporal Abraham Staples and Private Thomas Fitzpatrick had been killed by Indians in the hay-cutting. It was a dangerous activity, subject to almost daily raids and attacks by the ever-present Sioux. The best hayfields lay two and a half miles northeast of the fort where tall, natural grass grew profusely around the mouth of Warrior Creek (later known as Battle Creek), where it emptied into the Bighorn River. It was there that Mr. A. C. Leighton, the sutler and freighter of Army supplies, who had entered into a contract for the purpose, de-

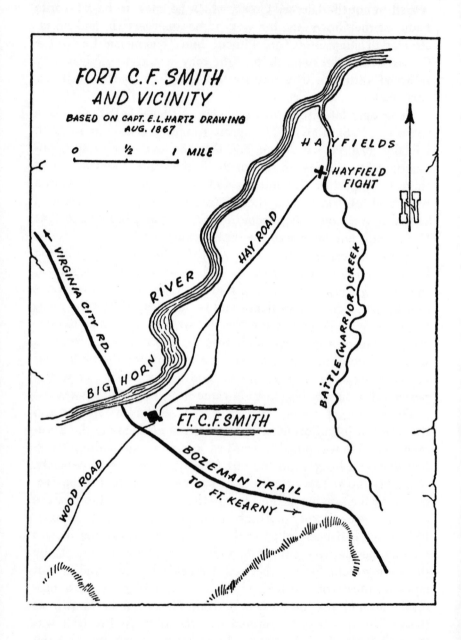

FORT C.F. SMITH
AND VICINITY

BASED ON CAPT. E.L. HARTZ DRAWING
AUG. 1867

0   ½   1   MILE

HAYFIELDS

HAYFIELD
FIGHT

N

VIRGINIA CITY RD.

RIVER

HAY ROAD

BATTLE (WARRIOR) CREEK

BIG HORN

FT. C.F. SMITH

WOOD ROAD

BOZEMAN TRAIL

TO FT. KEARNY →

cided to cut the hay for Fort C. F. Smith. The post commander was to provide a military guard for the civilian haymaking party. It was in connection with this haymaking that the remarkable fight of a small group of white men against an overwhelming number of Indians occurred on August 1, 1867. It has been known ever since as the Hayfield Fight.

It will be well to mention one or two things that occurred at Fort C. F. Smith just before the fight which had a bearing on it.

Captain Kinney relinquished command of Fort C. F. Smith in June 1867 and returned to Fort Phil Kearny in accordance with orders. For an interval thereafter, Captain Thomas B. Burrows commanded the post. On July 23, 1867, Captain Burrows signed a special report which stated that on that day Lieutenant Colonel (Brevet Brigadier General) L. P. Bradley had arrived at the post with H and I Companies of the Twenty-seventh Infantry, comprising about three hundred officers and men for duty. It will be noted that Colonel Bradley arrived at Fort C. F. Smith only a week before the Hayfield Fight. He brought with him the new Allin modified Springfield breech-loading fifty caliber rifle. This weapon was immediately issued to all the troops who had been at the fort throughout the winter.

The wagon train that brought reinforcements, supplies, and the new rifles also brought some new mowing machines. Mr. Leighton moved the mowers and his civilian haymakers to a camp two and a half miles northeast of the fort in the latter part of June, apparently about the twenty-second or twenty-third, and began the task of putting up the year's supply of hay for the fort's livestock. The first task was to build a corral for the protection of the mules at night and a place of defense for the men in case of attack. The workers and their military escort remained in the corral overnight and did not return to the fort at the end of each day's work.

A square about a hundred feet on the side was marked out and upright posts placed in pairs at intervals of about six feet. Logs were laid on the ground between these posts. Along the logs heavy pole stringers were fastened to the posts about halfway to the top and at the top another row of pole stringers were fastened. Between the stringers green willow branches were interlaced, with their foliage left on them. When finished, this enclosure was a good corral and a reasonably good defensive position. There was an opening at the south side. Across it a wagon's running gear was placed, and at night the wheels were chained to the entrance posts. Inside the corral on the west side, a row of four wagon boxes with their bows and canvas tops on them were set on the ground; also on that side, north of the wagon boxes, three soldiers' tents were erected. A picket line to which the animals were tied at night ran the length of the corral on a north-south axis, fifteen feet off the center line, but whether to the east or west of it is not clear. A kitchen tent stood just outside the corral at its southwest corner. The corral was situated on the west side of Battle Creek, which curved around its south and east sides. At its southern side, the corral in one place was within forty feet of the creek. A dense growth of willows grew along the creek and came closest to the corral at its southwest corner. Trenches were dug at designated points outside the corral.

After the haymaking party and its military escort set up their camp at the meadows they were daily under hostile Indian observation and minor attacks. The Indians generally let the workers cut the hay unmolested, but when it was dry and ready to rake up and load on the wagons, they would drive the workers to the corral and burn the hay. Crow Indians came around almost daily, also, and the impression grew among the workers that they did not like to see the hay cut.

On these visits the Crows warned that the Sioux were near and planned attacks to wipe out the hay party. The men heard such tales so often that they gave little attention to the stories, believing that the Crows were prone to exaggeration and were trying to scare them. It was known, however, that the Sioux and their allies were in a great camp fifteen or twenty miles eastward in the valley of the Little Bighorn River.

On the last day of July a band of about twenty Crows stopped at the hayfield and told the men there that the Sioux were preparing to attack them the next day in great strength. They said that at a big powwow in the Sioux camp there had been an argument about how to destroy the forts along the Bozeman Trail. Red Cloud had urged that the entire force first attack Fort

Phil Kearny, and that after it had been destroyed they should return and destroy Fort C. F. Smith. Others, including a Minneconjou chief, argued that Fort C. F. Smith should be destroyed first. This argument grew bitter and was finally resolved by the Indian camp dividing into two forces, one behind Red Cloud which was to go to Fort Phil Kearny, ninety-five miles away, and the other to attack Fort C. F. Smith, close at hand. The Crows said the attack would come on the morrow and if the workers did not immediately go to the fort they would be killed. The men at the meadows laughed off the story. The Crows went to the fort and repeated their story there. Apparently it was received there also with disbelief.

On the morning of August 1, 1867, there were nineteen men, nine of them civilians, at the hayfield corral according to Finn Burnett, one of the civilian workers. The Fort C. F. Smith Post Return for the day, however, states that there were nineteen soldiers and six civilians there. Another participant, a soldier who has left an account of the affair, states that the civilian workers were provided a guard of twenty-one soldiers. He does not say how many civilian workers were there. The Post Return for the day is the only contemporary and official record. The statements of the two participants are from memory and made many years later. It is accepted here, therefore, that there were twenty-five white men present at the Hayfield Fight, nineteen soldiers and six civilian workers.

The soldiers were armed with the newly issued fifty caliber Springfield rifle and had plenty of ammunition. They also had revolvers. The civilians were even better armed. Most of them had either Spencer or Henry repeating rifles, and also revolvers. One, however, Zeke Colvin, a veteran of the Confederate Army, still clung to a favorite Enfield muzzle-loading musket he had picked up on the battlefield of Wilson's Creek in Missouri and used thereafter throughout the Civil War.

Our knowledge of the Hayfield Fight rests on meager evidence. There is a brief mention of it in the Fort C. F. Smith Post Return for the day, and no other official Army report of it has yet come to light. This may be because the only commissioned officer present in the fight was killed in the action. Otherwise, the account of the fight rests on the stories of it given many years later by the two participants, one a civilian and the other a private soldier. These two accounts generally agree, but differ on several details. Based on the available evidence and a personal knowledge of the terrain involved, the present writer believes the main events to have been as follows:

On the morning of August 1 the civilians, after breakfast, went out to the hay meadows with their machines while pickets took their usual posts as lookouts. Most of the soldiers in the escort detail lolled around the camp. About 9:30 a few shots were heard from the direction of the hayfield where the machines were at work. Soon the mule teams pulling the mowers came in at a run. Bands of mounted Indians chased the mule teams and fired occasional shots at them. It would seem that for a brief time small bands of warriors tried to draw the men out of the corral with the intention of leading them into an ambush, but this did not work. Soon a large force of mounted warriors appeared in the valley to the northeast and approached the corral. There were hundreds of them.

Second Lieutenant Sigmund Sternberg of G Company, Twenty-seventh Infantry, was the commanding officer of the little military detachment assigned to protect the hay party. According to one report he had intended to fight from the trenches outside the corral but a large force of Indians was at hand, leaving him no time to get his men in position there. All the men took places inside the corral, spaced pretty evenly around the little perimeter, soldiers and civilians intermixed. Most of the men lay prone on the ground behind the big lower log and fired over the top of it. Lieutenant Sternberg stationed himself at the southern entrance, standing erect. He believed a soldier should fight in that posture.

At the beginning of the attack a warrior on a black horse galloped toward the stockade with a fire brand of burning hay. He had ridden to within a few feet of the corral when a shot by Zeke Colvin brought the horse crashing down against the stockade. The daring warrior was pinned momentarily between the falling horse and the logs. In a few seconds he freed himself and started toward the willows for safety. A bullet brought him down only a few feet from his horse. In the intense fight that now developed, with the Indians riding back and forth close to the corral and sending showers of arrows and many bullets into the place, Lieutenant Sternberg was killed by a bullet through the head.

One of the civilian haymakers, D. A. (Al) Colvin, a brother of Zeke, now assumed command. He had been a captain in the Union Army during the Civil War, and was a cool and determined fighter. He also appears to have been a dead shot. Colvin ordered everyone to keep down on the ground and to fight from behind the lower log. He carried a Henry sixteen-shot repeating rifle and had a thousand rounds of ammunition for it. Burnett says that Colvin fired about three hundred rounds during the day and no one knew of a shot missing its mark. Although this may be an exaggeration of Al Colvin's performance that day, there seems no reason to doubt that he gave courageous leadership to the little band of white men and that he did fearful execution with his Henry rifle. This was the same kind of weapon that Fisher and Wheatley had at the Fetterman Fight and which apparently caused most of the Indian casualties there.

After the first rush had failed, the Indians withdrew for a time and the men in the corral had a brief respite. Soon the Indians began to take up positions from which they could snipe at the corral. A bluff a few hundred yards to the west gave some protected positions in that direction and the willow thickets along Warrior or Battle Creek afforded other positions on the south and east. They began to shoot fire arrows into the corral, hoping to set the dry willow wickerwork ablaze. They also began to shoot at the string of thirty-one mules and one horse tied to the picket line and visible to them. They soon killed or wounded every animal save one mule and the horse.

There was some hay to the west of the corral and the Indians set fire to it. According to one of the participants in the fight, a great wall of flame flared up thirty to forty feet above this burning hay. The wind had brought it to within twenty feet of the enclosure when suddenly the flame subsided and was followed by a dense smoke that drifted back into the faces of the Indians. Several fires were started in the grass at other points around the corral, but the men inside put out every fire that reached the stockade. In the intervals when the Indians gave them brief respite the men scooped out shallow pits and trenches behind the logs for better protection.

After Lieutenant Sternberg fell, the Indians made another major attack, thinking the white men leaderless. This time they pressed the attack and some are said to have reached, and tried to break through, the corral before they were killed. When this short but threatening attack had been repulsed, the men found that another soldier had been killed, one wounded, and a civilian named Hollister badly wounded in the abdomen. The wounded soldier, an unnamed sergeant, had a big hole in his shoulder. He was placed in one of the tents out of the hot sun, but in every subsequent Indian attack during the day he staggered out to the firing line with a revolver and joined in the fray.

Not so courageous were two others. One, a big civilian teamster who was a bully and had been generally feared, barricaded himself behind a heap of harness and boxes and lay there crying, taking no part in the fight. Another, a soldier, went to pieces and threatened to commit suicide so that the Indians could not capture him alive for torture. Al Colvin took this man's gun away from him and told him to go and grovel in a hole some dogs had dug in the corral the day before.

In the second general attack the Indians had suffered so many losses that they adopted a safer method of carrying on the fight. They took up sniping positions around the corral wherever the terrain and the willow growth would provide any cover or concealment. The fighting died down about noon and the men then had time to become aware of their thirst. A party was organized to go to the nearby creek with buckets and pans while the others prepared to cover them. Strangely, the water party dashed the short distance to the creek and back several times without drawing a single shot. Apparently the Indians had withdrawn a short distance for a breather, or perhaps to eat some food.

The warriors soon returned to the scene, however, for it was not long before they resumed the sniping. A chief on a sorrel horse rode up on the east side of the creek and stopped within rifle range, peering at the corral. A well-directed shot dropped him into the water, where he lay struggling, badly wounded, until he drowned.

Now the Indians made a lively attack from the west, swooping down on their ponies from the bluffs that lay a few hundred yards off in that direction. They rode back and forth in swift passages along the west side of the corral. A chief, or possibly a medicine man, thought to be a Cheyenne, led this assault. One of the civilians, named Duncan, brought him down with a shot from his new Winchester rifle. Other warriors now swooped in on the dead run and lifted the fallen chief from the ground and carried him to the bluffs. Watchers from the corral saw him rise there to a sitting position, stunned, but apparently not badly hurt.

The last big Indian effort came against the south side of the corral. It was a foot attack. A chief, said to be a Minneconjou Sioux, led it. In attacking from this direction the Indians had to cross the creek, dash through the willows, and cross a few yards of open ground to reach the enclosure. Al Colvin guessed an attack was to be made there and concentrated most of the men on that side. He ordered his men not to fire until he should fire. The mass of Indians plunged down the far bank with the chief in the lead. The latter was the first to reach the open and dash for the corral. Colvin fired, and simultaneously a volley rang out from the others. The big chief went down and never moved afterward. The rapid and heavy fire from the south side of the corral sent many of the racing warriors sprawling. Before they reached the enclosure, the mass of Indians turned and retreated back across the creek. The more daring of the warriors returned and made several attempts to recover the body of their chief, but he lay so close to the enclosure that none succeeded and several lost their lives in the attempts. This last major effort virtually ended the fight, except for some scattered sniping from long range. Large groups of Indians could be seen a little later far down the valley of the Bighorn riding away eastward.

After most of the Indians had departed, Al Colvin allowed one of the soldiers, who had many times asked to do so, to carry a message to the fort. A bulge north of the benchland between the fort and the hayfield corral intervened in the line of sight and prevented visual contact between them. Although the men in

the corral knew that those in the fort could not see them, they
were pretty sure that the firing could be heard and they wondered why help had not been sent. Colvin allowed the volunteer
to mount the horse, which was unhurt, and wrote out a message
for Colonel Bradley, the post commander, describing the situation. He stated that he had some dead and wounded, that the
Indians except for a few snipers had left, and asked for a relief
party from the fort. The soldier buckled on two revolvers and
rode quietly toward the point of bluff that hid the fort from
view. Before he had gone far a group of perhaps thirty Indians
rode out to intercept him. They caught up with the rider at a
ravine which opened to the river within a few hundred yards
of the fort. Two accounts of how the messenger escaped differ,
but he did so with the help of a strong covering fire from the
fort, where the soldiers saw his predicament. Colonel Bradley
then ordered out two companies as a relief party.

On the way to the corral, the column came under fire from
some hidden Indians, and the lead company stopped. A lieutenant in command of the second company went forward and
said he was going through. At that the relief party continued
and arrived at the corral without difficulty.

Colvin and his men were able to find a few mules able to
pull wagons despite their wounds. Two teams were made up,
the dead and wounded placed on the wagons, and the whole
party returned to the fort, apparently just before sundown.
Although the Post Return says the action lasted only three or
four hours, it does not give the time it started or ended. The
participant accounts indicate that the fight started about 9:30
in the morning and continued until well in the afternoon, perhaps
as late as four or five o'clock. It is believed their version is the
more nearly correct in this particular.

After the hayfield party returned to the fort they found that
their predicament had been known to the post commander and
others there earlier in the day. Captain (Brevet Major) Edward
S. Hartz, commanding officer of I Company, Twenty-seventh Infantry, saw the fight in progress from the slopes of the Big Horn
Mountains, where he had gone that morning with a wood party.
He watched it briefly through field glasses and then galloped

ahead to the fort and asked the post commander for permission to take troops to the relief of the haymaking party. The post commander refused this request and ordered the gates closed and all men confined to the fort. Apparently he was afraid that if he allowed a column to go to the relief of the hay party it would meet the same fate as the Fetterman group the previous winter, and felt that his duty was to protect the fort and the main body of his troops. It would appear that he chose to leave the small party of haymakers and their escort to their fate. When it became clear that this party had defeated the Indians, he then allowed two companies to leave the fort and go to it.

The evidence extant is not in full agreement as to the number of men killed and wounded in the Hayfield Fight. Burnett says three of the defenders were killed and four wounded. He lists Lieutenant Sternberg and an unnamed sergeant as the soldiers killed; J. C. Hollister, the teamster, died of his wounds. The four wounded, he says, included three soldiers, one of them a sergeant, and one civilian. The Fort C. F. Smith Post Return, however, states that casualties were Lieutenant Sternberg, Private Thomas Navins, and one civilian, killed; and one sergeant and two privates wounded, for a total of six casualties. A stone monument was erected the next summer, June 1868, at Fort C. F. Smith, over the burial place of these men. It is from that marker that the author obtained the full name of Navins and Hollister. This marker, surely one of the oldest to be placed as a memorial over more than a solitary grave commemorating men who fell in the Indian wars of the West, is now in the national cemetery at Custer Battlefield National Monument, Montana, where those buried in the Fort C. F. Smith cemetery were re-interred many years later in their final resting place.

The number of Indian casualties cannot be given with any accuracy, any more than can be the number of Indians engaged in the fight. The only Fort C. F. Smith record mentioning the fight that the author has seen states that the Indian loss was estimated at eight killed and thirty wounded, and that all these except one were carried off the field by their fellow warriors during, or at the end of, the fight. Burnett, on the other hand, believes that Al Colvin alone must have killed or wounded 150

Indians! The truth probably lies somewhere between these two extremes. According to Burnett, a newly arrived cavalry contingent went out to a sandstone ledge two miles east of the Hayfield Fight ground the second day after the fight, led there by Crow Indians, and found 50 bodies of dead Sioux. The Crows said another mass burial place two miles farther on held still more Sioux dead. The party did not go on to verify this second burial place because of the known presence of a large party of the enemy. Crows who entered the Sioux camp after the fight said the Indian losses were very great. But their idea of what constituted a great loss would be hard to define; and, also, the Sioux camp would have been mourning its losses in both the Hayfield and Wagon Box Fights at the time the observation was made.

Burnett's account estimates the Sioux and their allies at the Hayfield Fight numbered 2500. The other participant who has left an account of his recollections (he was a Union veteran of the Civil War) stated that a "band of five or six hundred" made the initial attack, and were eventually joined by twice as many more. The Fort C. F. Smith entry on the subject in the Post Return states that the number of Indians was "variously estimated at from 500 to 800." It seems unlikely that the Indian force attacking the hayfield party was much more than 1000 warriors. When the Indian conclave split at their big encampment eastward, the larger part accompanied Red Cloud to attack Phil Kearny. Allowing 1000 Indians as the attacking force would give it a numerical superiority over the defenders of 40 to 1. It must be remembered, however, that only a relatively small number of the Indians had firearms; the great majority of them had nothing better than bow and arrows, lances, and war clubs.

Two days after the fight at the hayfield, about August 3, a full company of infantry with a twelve-pound howitzer accompanied a haymaking party back to the meadows. This time they built a solid cottonwood log corral and stacked sod around the logs. This new corral was half a mile northeast of the old one and out in the flat of the river bottom where Indians would find no cover and concealment close to it. Although the hostile Sioux kept parties at hand constantly and made almost daily forays trying to run off the stock and to burn the hay, they never made an attack on the new corral. Despite this harassment the haymaking went on and a supply was brought in for the winter.

Though never publicized like the Wagon Box Fight near Fort Phil Kearny the next day, the Hayfield Fight at Fort C. F. Smith on August 1 was very much like it. In both instances the attacking forces of hostile Sioux and their allies met work details from the two forts, and engaged them, expecting an easy victory before continuing on to the forts themselves. In each case the two small forces of white men fought from behind barricades and, with the help of the new Springfield rifle, inflicted on the Indians losses so heavy as to discourage further attacks on the forts themselves.

12. THE WAGON BOX FIGHT

ROY E. APPLEMAN

The winter of 1866–1867 was a severe one in the Big Horn country and snow piled up eight feet high around Fort Phil Kearny, reaching at times to the top of the palisades. The cold was intense, the mercury falling far below zero much of the time during January and February. In these conditions neither Indian nor white man moved much along the Bozeman Trail.

With the coming of spring, however, the Indians resumed their hostile actions along the road. As spring passed into summer they watched the old Bozeman Trail so closely that all traffic over it came to a halt except the heavily guarded military convoys the Army sent into the country to provision the forts. The Indians did not directly attack the forts, but they made many demonstrations in sight of them. The men in the posts kept close to the relative security of their fortifications. To roam very far from them was to court disaster.

This was the situation when it came time, in the midsummer of 1867, to replenish the Fort Phil Kearny wood fuel supply for the coming winter. A civilian contractor, J. R. Porter of the Gilmore & Proctor firm, arrived at Phil Kearny in June with a bull train of supplies. Porter had the contract from the Quartermaster Department to supply wood for the fort. He was to do this under the protection of the military. Porter's train brought seven hundred new breech-loading Springfield rifles and a hundred thousand rounds of ammunition for them. These new weapons were issued to the troops on July 10, pursuant to an order of Colonel (Brevet Major General) John E. Smith, commanding at Fort Phil Kearny.

Early in July the wood contractors established a base of operations about six miles west of the fort, and a short distance east of the pineries from which they would take the wood. The escort for the contractor's party during the month of July was A Company, Twenty-seventh Infantry. At the end of the month, C Company, under the command of Captain James W. Powell, relieved A Company in the escort duty and moved from Fort Phil Kearny to the contractor's corral to carry out its assignment for the month of August.

Upon arriving at Piney Island, Powell found that the contractor had divided his men into two groups. One party was felling trees and cutting them into cordwood. This group made camp in a pine woods on Piney Island at the foot of the mountains and across Big Piney Fork from the main camp. The other party made its camp on a bare, relatively level expanse of ground a mile southeast of the woodcutters' camp and that much closer to Fort Phil Kearny. Here the mules grazed and were corralled at night, and here fourteen wagon boxes had been set off the running gears of the wagons used to haul the cordwood to the fort. Just outside the enclosure several tents were erected in which the men slept. Various supplies—forage for the animals, food for the men, and spare equipment—were placed inside the corral. Here, too, were placed seven thousand rounds of ammu-

nition for the new weapons and, it seems, some spare arms. Two
wagons with canvas tops still on their bows stood just outside the
wagon box corral, according to Sergeant Samuel Gibson, one at
the east end holding the woodchoppers' rations, and the other on
the south containing the military escort's rations. Some evidence,
however, seems to indicate that one wagon might have been at
the east and the other at the west end of the wagon box oval.

The wagon boxes of the corral were the ordinary wood wagon
beds, about four feet high, used by the Army Quartermaster
Corps at the time. With their bowed arches in place supporting
a canvas top, they were not very different from the traditional
covered wagon one sees today in Western movies. The wagon
beds resting on the ground did not have their bows and canvas
tops on them. At least some of the wagon beds had two-inch
auger holes bored in the sides facing the outside of the corral,
a foot or two from the bottom, forming a loophole for firing. The
wagon beds were not lined with iron sheeting, as is sometimes
alleged. Logs, sacks of grain, ox-yokes, kegs, and miscellaneous
supplies were at hand and some bags of beans and other supplies
were placed inside the wagon boxes against the side facing out
when the attack became imminent. This means of strengthening
the thin board sides of the boxes, together with blankets thrown
over the tops of the wagons to hide the exact location of most of
the men from the Indians, provided the best protection for the
men in the corral.

The division of forces among the woodcutters made it necessary for Captain Powell to divide his men for guard duty.
Captain Powell had fifty-three men in C Company including
himself. To the woodcutting camp in the pine woods he sent a
non-commissioned officer and twelve men. He provided another
non-commissioned officer and thirteen men to escort the wood
train to and from the fort. Powell and First Lieutenant John C.
Jenness with the remaining twenty-six men posted themselves in
the open area at the wagon box corral. There they were centrally
located to guard the livestock and the several parts of the wood-
cutting operation.

Captain Powell was a soldier of nineteen years' experience.
He had enlisted in the Army as a private in 1848 and had risen to

Brevet Major in the Civil War. Just two days before the Fetterman disaster in December 1866 he had distinguished himself in an Indian engagement near Fort Phil Kearny, and at other times in the Indian alarms around the fort he had earned a name for cool bravery.

It is necessary to describe rather closely some of the terrain features immediately around the wagon box corral. Certain aspects of the action there can be understood properly, and a perpetuation of some persistent misconceptions about it avoided, only if the adjacent lay of the land is clearly understood. The corral was not in the middle of the little plateau-plain, as has so often been stated. The writer has made a careful examination of the ground on foot. Only then did certain things become clear in what had appeared contradictory or unexplained evidence in the statements of participants in the fight.

Instead of being in the middle of the plain, the corral was near its northern edge, and about one half mile west of the westernmost point of Sullivant's Hill. Level ground stretched away from the corral on three sides—the west, south, and east—for perhaps half a mile or more. On one side, the north, this level bare ground extended no more than a hundred yards, in some places perhaps less, to where the ground dropped off into the valley of the Big Piney. The northern rim of the plain and a little shallow drainage trough that had eroded through it into the plain northwest of the corral proved to be the terrain features which the Indians turned to their advantage in attacking the wagon box corral. It was along the northern rim of the plain, close to the corral, that Indian snipers later caused the most trouble. From the shallow swale that led up to the plain from the valley of the Big Piney at a point only a couple of hundred yards from the corral came the large, and almost successful, foot charge of Indians. Except on the north the Indians could find no cover within gunfire range of the corral.

The close proximity of the drop-off on the north side of the corral almost certainly prevented the mounted warriors from riding around the corral on that side. To have done so would have made them perfect targets for the soldiers in the corral. It is reasonably clear, therefore, that the mounted charges were not complete circles around the corral, but must have been back and forth on the south side and sallies at the western and eastern ends, or passes on the south side and then circles back at a distance to repeat the pass. Terrain factors account for the fact that some men in the corral stated they did not experience any mounted attack, while others stress the initial mounted attack that almost overran them.

The question naturally arises as to why the corral was placed near the northern limit of the plain and not in the middle, where its defensive position would have been much stronger. A study of the relationship of the pineries where the timber-cutters were at work and the roads to them provides the answer. If the corral had been placed in the middle of the plain there would not have been visual control from it of the road to the pinery on Piney Island after it dropped off the plain, nor of the pinery itself. The location of the corral at the northern edge of the plain allowed the men in it to see the wood road all the way to Piney Island and also the road and the second pinery at the foot of the Big Horns to the southwest. In short, the wagon box corral was placed at the best available site from which to maintain visual control of the wood road to the pineries, each about a mile distant from it, and to offer protection to all who were engaged in the wood-cutting and hauling operation.

According to the Crow Indians, the decision of the chiefs in the great Sioux Indian camp on the Little Bighorn River to destroy the Bozeman Road forts in one simultaneous attack had been taken on July 31. Red Cloud and apparently most of the Sioux warriors started that day for Fort Phil Kearny, ninety miles away. The remainder stayed in camp and on August 1 went to Fort C. F. Smith to attack that place, but instead fought throughout most of the day with a party of haycutters and their escort a short distance east of the fort in the action that has been known ever since as the Hayfield Fight.

The Indian squaws and children, contrary to usual practice, accompanied the Sioux war party going to Fort Phil Kearny. This large Indian force did not arrive at the Pineys all together, but kept coming up, it appears, during the early morning of August 2. There were already some Indians in the vicinity of

Fort Phil Kearny on the first, for on that day a party of them drove off seven head of stock at the fort.

The Indians, for the most part, were still armed with the bow and arrow, lance, and war club. They had the rifles and revolvers gained in the Fetterman Fight, to be sure, but their supply of ammunition for these weapons could not have been large, and they could not have engaged in enough practice with the firearms to have become expert in their use. The Indians who had firearms at this time husbanded their ammunition for war use.

Early in the morning of August 2, R. J. Smyth, a civilian teamster, left Fort Phil Kearny with a partner to go deer-hunting in the nearby mountains. The two men had scarcely reached the foothills shortly after daylight when they saw Indian smoke signals in the hills. After watching these for a short time they decided they had better get back to the fort. Starting back, they found that Indians were between themselves and the fort, but that apparently they themselves had not been discovered. They turned toward the wagon box corral and succeeded in reaching it just in time. Hundreds of Indians were in view now on the surrounding low hills.

At the contractor's camp at the wagon box corral that morning a wagon train loaded with cordwood and logs left shortly after breakfast under military escort for Fort Phil Kearny. A second one went empty in the opposite direction to the pinery for a load of wood. It was about 7 A.M. Not more than half an hour later a picket called out an alarm. He said he saw Indians. In view were seven of them riding their ponies on a dead run. Within minutes, great numbers were in sight.

The three pickets and a herder in this outpost started for the corral, the three soldiers taking turns in covering their retreat and then running to catch up with the others ahead. As they neared the corral they were hard pressed by Indians from several directions and were making a run for it. Only the personal daring of a twenty-one-year-old recent German immigrant, Sergeant Max Littmann, saved them. Littmann ran out from the corral about a hundred yards toward them, dropped to one knee, and fired rapidly and effectively at the Indians closing in on the four running men. He toppled several of the warriors from their horses and held back others sufficiently to enable the four nearly exhausted men to enter the corral. Littmann then himself withdrew safely to the corral.

The first concerted move of the Indians was to run off the mule herd. About two hundred Indians on foot tried to drive off the animals, but the herders stood their ground. Only a few minutes passed, however, before sixty mounted warriors rode into the herd and ran it off.

At this time another force of approximately five hundred Indians attacked the wood train at the camp in the woods. The soldiers and civilians there had received warning of the Indians' approach and hurriedly decided to abandon the wagons and their camp. Beginning an orderly retreat, they kept the Sioux under fire as they moved eastward toward Fort Phil Kearny, bypassing the wagon box corral. Four civilian woodcutters apparently were killed in this phase of the fight.

In the meantime, the isolated mule herders tried to make their way to join this wood camp party, but a group of Sioux cut them off. Captain Powell, who saw the move, sallied out from the wagon box corral with part of his small force and attacked these Indians in their rear. This created enough of a diversion to enable the herders to escape and join the wood party. After this risky sortie, Powell and his men returned to the corral without loss of life. The wood party, after a running fight, succeeded in reaching Fort Phil Kearny, where they gave the alarm and reported that Captain Powell was surrounded at the wagon box corral. It is doubtful if the wood party could have gained the fort if the great bulk of the Sioux warriors had not in the meantime turned its attention to Powell's force at the corral.

In the corral Lieutenant Jenness watched the Indians assemble on the ground to the west between the Big and Little Piney rivers and eastward at the end of Sullivant's Hill. He told Captain Powell he thought Red Cloud and most of the chiefs were at the latter place. In a short time several hundred mounted warriors were dashing about on the open ground. Soon they headed for the corral. Powell is reported to have said, "Men, here they come! Take your places and shoot to kill." Apparently he spoke only rarely afterward during the fight.

There is confusion in the various accounts as to how the men in the corral fought. Some say they fired through two-inch auger holes in the wagon boxes. But we know that not all of them did. Some, from their own testimony, fired over the tops of the wagon beds. Still others were not in the wagon beds at all, but took their places behind barrels and sacks of supplies. It seems that each man took the kind of position that best suited his own instinct and from which he thought he could fight most effectively.

The civilian teamster, Smyth, who joined Powell's force at the corral with a hunting partner just before the Sioux surrounded the place, has stated that he took a place in one of the wagon boxes behind four bags of corn placed on their edge, two bags high. He had on hand two Spencer carbines and two Colt revolvers and fired through an auger hole bored where the four bags cornered. Sergeant Gibson has stated that he fired over the top of a wagon bed. Sergeant Littmann has recorded that he took a position behind a barrel of salt and fought the battle from there. The soldier next to him was behind a barrel of beans. Another soldier, Private Tommy Doyle, made a breastwork of ox-yokes from the bull train, which he piled up in the space between two of the wagon boxes, and fought from there. And so it went. Blankets were thrown over the wagon beds in at least some cases to help conceal the men's positions in the wagons and to absorb the heavy shower of arrows that fell in a nearly vertical descent.

Not all the men fired on the Indians. Some of the poorer shots were told off to load weapons for marksmen. One of the civilians was a "mountain man," a grizzled trapper, reputed to be a dead shot. According to his statement later he "kept eight guns pretty well het up for mor'n three hours." Counting the four civilians who joined Powell's party in the corral just before the fight started, there was a total of thirty-two men there to pit themselves against a vastly superior force of Indians. The number of Indians involved has never been determined with accuracy. Estimates vary from fifteen hundred to three thousand warriors. The Fort Phil Kearny Post Return gives the number as an estimated three thousand. Not all the Indians took part in the fight at any one time, and perhaps some of them did not enter it at any time. Apparently all the Sioux tribes were represented; Oglalas, Brules, Sans Arcs, Hunkpapas, Minneconjous, and perhaps many Cheyennes.

Lieutenant Jenness stationed himself at one end of the corral; Powell was at the other end. There is no unanimity of evidence on the manner in which the Indians delivered their first attack against the corral. Powell in his official report seems to say that about five hundred mounted warriors dashed for the corral in a dense body. He considered this attack, it would seem, the most critical one of all, for the Indians, according to him, came up almost to the corral, swerving away only a few yards from it. But there is no certain and clear picture in the testimony of several participants as to just how desperately the Indians pressed this mounted attack, or how close it came to the corral. Sergeant Gibson said the mounted warriors circled the corral and at times came within a hundred yards of it, that on their closest approaches they would drop out of sight on the far side of their ponies and let fly arrows over their ponies' backs. A few were particularly daring and rode up close, hurling spears at the corral. Sergeant Littmann, recalling the situation as it appeared to him from his position on the perimeter, on the other hand, said that no mounted charge came close to his position. It is the same in every tense battle; men in different positions see different things and the action is not the same everywhere.

Captain Powell was a practiced observer, a calm officer inured to danger. His report is a model of understatement. Accordingly, there is no reason to doubt that the select party of three to five hundred warriors mounted on their best war ponies did charge close to the corral at some points or on one side of its circumference in an attempt to ride over the little group. Had these warriors pressed home a mounted charge there is little doubt that the fight would have been over in a few minutes. At least a thousand reinforcements for them stood just out of range watching the event.

Dead and wounded ponies piled up outside the corral, the wounded animals screaming with pain. Dead and wounded Indians also lay out there. The wounded warriors made no sound.

In self-protection, after the mounted and circling warriors had withdrawn from close attack, the men inside the corral fired into the wounded Indians who lay disabled on the ground. It was not wise, they thought, to leave even one wounded and still danger-ous Indian so close to their position. The mounted, circling war-riors who withdrew out of range were completely baffled by the tremendous firepower they had experienced from what they be-lieved was a small number of men in the corral. On the ridge half a mile to the east, Red Cloud and his chiefs went into a conference and decided on a new mode of attack. In this lull the men in the corral resupplied themselves with ammunition from the boxes within the enclosure.

Many Indians on foot were now at the edge of the rim where the ground dropped sharply away on the north toward the Big Piney. This defiladed and protected area curved around the north side of the corral, and at its closest point was within seventy-five yards. It was perhaps two hundred yards away from the eastern end of the corral. Indians lying prone behind this lip of ground had the corral within easy range and kept it under steady fire, showing themselves only occasionally as they fired over the forked sticks on which they rested their guns. Those Indians with firearms seemed to take their places here.

After a while an attack by an estimated seven hundred war-riors, stripped of most of their clothing and on foot, developed. Up to this time no one had thought about the tents standing outside the corral on its south side. Now, with the large number of Indians approaching, a yell went up to get them down to open the field of fire. A number of men sprang from the corral. They came under fire from the Indians hidden to the northwest, but succeeded in pulling down all the tents except one—Captain Powell's. With a good, open field of fire in front of them, the men in the corral repelled several separate foot attacks.

During these attacks the Indians at the edge of and below the rim of the plateau and in the depression to the northwest of the corral kept up an effective fire. This fire killed Lieutenant Jenness at the west end of the corral. Sergeant Littmann, next to him on the left, saw Jenness fall with a bullet through his head. Two other men, Privates Henry Haggerty and Thomas Doyle, were killed on the north side of the perimeter—Doyle with a bullet through his forehead and Haggerty also shot through the head. Doyle had been fighting for two hours with a bullet through his left shoulder before he was killed.

By this time hundreds of arrows had been lofted into the little corral, many of them fire arrows tipped with burning pitch. These had set fire to loose hay within the corral, and soon the great piles of dry dung, accumulated from the livestock corralled nightly within the enclosure for almost a month, began to smolder. This set up a terrific stench. The air was at times suffocating with this smell and the heavy smoke. By this time also, the hot day had brought thirst to many of the men. The water barrel was outside the corral at the west end. Indian bullets had soon perforated it and the water leaked out. Under the covered wagon at the west end of the corral, however, were two camp kettles which the cook had filled with water on top of coffee grounds just after breakfast, before the fight began. Two men crawled outside and brought these kettles inside under heavy fire from the Indians to the north. Two bullets drilled one kettle and it lost some of its black water.

It was now afternoon and the Indians had withdrawn out of range of the corral, except those who were hidden near it on its north side. Many warriors congregated around the hill eastward, half a mile away, where Red Cloud and other chiefs watched. To the east and south on the level land of the little plain, hundreds of Indians sat on their ponies. Suddenly from the north, in the direction of the valley of the Big Piney, came a sound that swelled gradually to a chanting hum. Some men on that side of the corral stood up briefly to see what was approaching, but as yet they could see nothing. The sound shifted to the northwest, growing louder. Suddenly out of the shallow erosion break in the plain about ninety to a hundred yards from the corral hundreds of Indians, stripped naked except for a loin cloth, charged forward in the shape of a wedge, led by a warrior in a great war bonnet. It was learned later that this Indian leading the foot charge was Red Cloud's nephew. He fell at the first volley; and so densely crowded were the Indians, one upon another, that eye witnesses said a single bullet fired at that close range often went through two or three of them. A few of the Indians fell within five feet of the wagon boxes. The mounted warriors on the plain on the east and south sides of the corral made no effort to participate, staying out of range and merely watching. Just short of pressing home their charge and swarming over the wagon boxes into the corral, the Indians on the west side broke under heavy casualties and fled.

The Indians withdrew from range of the corral, except for those under cover to the north and northwest. From here these Indians kept up a harassing fire on the corral. Under cover of this fire other Indians crawled forward behind large buffalo-hide shields to their wounded. When one of them had successfully reached a wounded Indian, he fastened a rope to his body, and Indians at the other end of the long lariat would pull the man to safety while the daring warrior behind the shield retreated by crawling backward. Mounted warriors would also dash forward in a grand display of horsemanship, swooping low as their ponies on the dead run passed on either side of a wounded Indian, and, grasping the latter's arms or legs, carry him away between them. The operation of retrieving the Indian wounded went on for some time. Those lying close to the corral could not be rescued in this fashion. Most of them had been killed by this time, in any event.

Sergeant Littmann tells of a duel he had with a giant Indian who had gained a little depression about thirty feet away from his position. This Indian was armed with only a bow and arrows. He would leap suddenly from his little protected spot and, at the top of his leap, discharge an arrow at Littmann. This duel went on for some little time before Littmann was able to bring the warrior down.

From the corral the beleaguered men could see Red Cloud and his party on the point of high ground eastward. Some of them adjusted their sights carefully for long range and sent volleys in that direction. These shots were sufficiently effective to cause the Indian group to scatter.

The Sioux were still engaged in harassing fire and the retrieving of their wounded when a cry went up from the eastern end of the corral. A relief party from Fort Phil Kearny had come in sight! It was shortly after noon, perhaps about one o'clock, although testimony on this point differs. The boom of a howitzer gave the welcome news that the relief party had brought along one of the big guns and that it was firing at Indians in the valley of the Piney. At first only a line of blue-clad skirmishers came into sight; then the howitzer came in view in front of a line of about ten or twelve mule-drawn ambulances and wagons.

Major (Brevet Lieutenant Colonel) Benjamin F. Smith led this rescue party of a hundred men. The howitzer overawed the Indians, who scampered out of range. When Smith's relief force was within two hundred yards of the corral, Powell's men ran out to meet it. According to the Fort Phil Kearny Post Return they had been surrounded four and a half hours.

The soldiers in the relief party could hardly believe their eyes and ears when they learned that only a few of those in the corral had been killed or wounded; they had expected to find very few, if any, of them alive. Smith had organized his relief mission after the escaping wood-cutting party had reached the fort and reported the Indian attack. The Post Surgeon, Dr. (Captain) Samuel M. Horton, who had accompanied Smith's relief force, now gave to every one of the rescued men, with Captain Powell's consent, a drink of whiskey from a keg he had brought along in one of the ambulances.

Smith and Powell wasted no time. While the Indians watched out of range, apparently undecided what to do next, they gathered up the few wounded and dead, placed them in the ambulances, and immediately set out for the fort. The Indians did not attack them. When they reached the high point at the beginning of the ridge east of the corral, some of the men looked back. They saw a memorable sight—a long line of Indian ponies loaded with dead and wounded from the vicinity of the corral was moving off across the little plateau northwest to the adjacent hills. The next day when a party from the fort went back to the corral not a single Indian body could be found.

Powell's losses were astonishingly low. In the corral, three men lost their lives, Lieutenant Jenness and Privates Doyle and Haggerty, all to fire from the north and northwest. Two other enlisted men had been wounded. The Post Return gives the casualties in the August 2 fight as six killed and two wounded, all from Company C, Twenty-seventh Infantry. It does not list any civilian casualties. If the evidence is correct that only three men were killed in the corral, it must follow that three other soldiers were killed in other phases of the fight, presumably during the retreat of the wood-cutting party and its escort from the pinery to the fort.

The casualties listed in the Fort Phil Kearny Post Return for August 2, 1867, under the heading "Killed in Action with Indians at Pinery Aug. 2, 1867" is given as follows: First Lieutenant John C. Jenness, Privates Thomas C. Doyle, Henry Haggerty, George W. Harris, Horace Kitridge, and Herman Lange. The wounded are listed as Privates Nelson V. Deming and John L. Somers. So far as the present writer knows, only the names of the first three men have previously been included as casualties in any printed account of the Wagon Box Fight. In certain published accounts of the fight it is stated that four civilians were also killed in the initial phases of the action. While I know of no reason to doubt that statement, I simply record that I have seen no official document supporting or repeating it. If one includes the four alleged civilian casualties, the total white killed would be ten, and wounded, two.

The Indian loss is impossible to state accurately. In his brief, modest, and almost dull, matter-of-fact report, Captain Powell estimated that not less than 60 Indians had been killed and 120 severely wounded. Every other participant who has left any record of the fight says there were at least 400 killed and wounded, and some place the number as high as 700 to 800. A few months after the fight, in the autumn of that same year, an Indian chief who had been in the Wagon Box Fight told Colonel Richard I. Dodge that the Indian loss had been 1137. This larger figure can be discounted, for it is impossible to credit it. At the other extreme is the astonishing assertion of a present day partisan of Sioux history that the Sioux lost only six killed and six wounded in this fight. The figure given by the cool and valiant Powell may be accepted as a minimum figure; it may very well have been an understatement of the Indian losses.

It was a terrible fight for the Indians. They referred to it as the "Medicine Fight," attributing the amazing firepower of the whites to some bad medicine that overcame their own great bravery and sacrifice. According to the later statements of the Indians, they had given up the fight before the relief party came in sight, and were intent at that time only on rescuing their wounded. Fire from their snipers and skirmishers, they said, was simply covering this effort toward the end.

It is a peculiar fact that Lieutenant General William T. Sherman, commanding the Military Division of the Missouri, with headquarters in St. Louis, in his annual report to the War Department dated September 30, 1867, two months after the Hayfield and Wagon Box Fights, did not mention either one of them. Many other minor incidents involving Indians were mentioned and described, but not these two spectacular defensive engagements in the Big Horn country in the domain of the Sioux. The only explanation one can assume for this odd fact is that they had not been reported to his headquarters by that date, even though each of them had been outstanding in comparison with other events of the Indian frontier at that time.

PART VI

Post Civil War: Southern Plains 1868

Introduction

President Lincoln, in his message to Congress in 1864, urged a revised and more enlightened Indian policy that provided for the "welfare" of the tribesmen while protecting "the advancing settler." The Indians were not at that moment ready for the "welfare" the President asked for them—they were enjoying a freedom that they had not known for years.

The frontier events of the latter part of the Civil War, particularly those at Sand Creek and along the Bozeman Trail in 1866, further postponed the day when the Indian would accept the white man's "welfare" offer. Sand Creek (see page 84) enraged the Cheyennes and Arapahoes, who felt that they had been slaughtered for the crimes of the Sioux and Comanches. However, they admitted that a few renegades from their tribes had joined the hostiles in raiding the wagon trains that supplied Denver and other western settlements. For the most part the evidence supports their contention that the leaders and a vast majority of the warriors were "at peace" with the white man at the time of the Sand Creek affair. Chivington's attack certainly changed that—the Cheyennes and Arapahoes became implacable foes.

After Appomattox, the citizen-soldiers of the Union were anxious to return to their peacetime pursuits and Congress wanted to be rid of the heavy expense of maintaining an army no longer needed to fight the Confederacy. Demobilization was rapid, but the Union had two immediate problems on hand—the enforce-

ment of reconstruction laws in the South and the forcing of many
of the Indians to return to the reservations they had deserted
while the Union forces were battling the South. There simply
didn't seem to be enough trained troops to take care of both jobs.
Adding greatly to the reconstruction problem was the solution
tried in the South—the enlisting of the freed slaves and their use
in enforcing the laws among their former owners.

Major General Philip H. Sheridan, commanding the Department of the Missouri, used an entirely different approach. So
short did he find himself of trained troops in 1868 that late in
August he ordered George A. (Sandy) Forsyth, Major, Ninth U. S.
Cavalry, to employ without delay—"fifty first-class hardy frontiers-
men, to be used as scouts against the hostile Indians, to be commanded by yourself." General Sheridan felt this company of
scouts would be particularly effective in dealing with the war
parties of Cheyennes, Arapahoes, Kiowas, and Sioux then ravag-
ing western Kansas and eastern Colorado.

Within a few days Major Forsyth had recruited his detachment
from the civilians about the Kansas Army posts of Forts Harker
and Hays, enrolling the men as employees of the Quartermaster's
Department. Plains-wise Frederick H. Beecher, First Lieutenant,
Third U. S. Infantry, was assigned as second in command; Dr.
John H. Mooers was engaged as acting surgeon, and Abner T.
(Sharp) Grover, a well-known Indian scout, was named guide.
Most of the men were typical of the human flotsam that drifted
restlessly along the southwestern frontier. Young for the most part
and hardy enough, they would turn their hands to almost any
means of livelihood the moment offered. Approximately half of
them were veterans of the recently-ended Civil War.

13. THE FIGHT AT
BEECHER ISLAND

JAMES S. HUTCHINS

A little column of well-armed white men rode through the silence
of the Great Plains. It was a hot afternoon in September 1868
on the Arickaree Fork of the Republican River in the northeastern
corner of Colorado. Ahead and out on the flanks a few scouts
moved warily, scanning alternately the horizon and the sod under-
foot. At the head of the main body rode Major "Sandy" Forsyth.
Occasionally the thirty-one-year old officer swung around in his
saddle to survey the column behind, that it be kept closed up.
The major was, in fact, anxious about many things as he led his
small command along the first big, fresh Indian trail that he had
ever followed.

Forsyth's command was armed with the Spencer seven-shot repeating carbine and the Colt percussion army revolver, both among the finest cavalry weapons of that time. Every man carried 170 rounds of ammunition on his person and in his saddlebags. No tents were allowed. Transport consisted of four pack mules, bearing a minimum of supplies including extra coffee and salt and a reserve supply of 4,000 cartridges. The young commander, although a greenhorn at Indian campaigning, realized that to hope ever to catch the red man one must travel light.

Forsyth's detachment had taken the field from Fort Hays on August 29. On September 5, after eight days of fruitless scouting, the major had led his men into Fort Wallace. There, on the tenth, word had come that Cheyenne marauders had just attacked a wagon train near Sheridan City, a few miles east. As soon as his men had drawn seven days' rations Forsyth had hurried to the scene, found the Indians' trail and followed it north. Next morning the trail had petered out, the warriors having, as usual, scattered to forestall pursuit. Sandy Forsyth, having served as aide-de-camp to General Sheridan in Civil War days, knew well that to hard-bitten "Little Phil" all that counted in warfare was success. Therefore Forsyth, banking on his roving commission, had decided to gamble. He would march on as long as possible in the direction most probably taken by the raiders, in hopes of again picking up their tracks. North and west he had traveled for days, working always toward the headwaters of the Republican River, fine buffalo country and thus a favorite Indian camping ground. At last, recent signs of the presence of Indians had been discovered beside the Republican itself. Upstream the trail led, ever widening and freshening, turning finally up the Arickaree Fork.

Now, on the afternoon of September 16, Forsyth's brain was working fast. His effective strength was fifty-one men including himself. Rations were practically gone and the horses were tiring. The Indian trail had become a broad highway of ruts, left by hundreds of travois, and the marks of numerous ponies and camp dogs. "Sharp" Grover and the other experienced plainsmen agreed that they were drawing close to a large Indian village, or possibly several villages. Earlier in the day some of the men, concluding that they had, after all, not "lost any Indians"—at least not this many—had approached the major with a proposal to turn back. His cool reply had been that the detachment's mission was to find and fight redskins and that that was what it would do, regardless of odds. The men had assumed their places again quietly enough but Forsyth saw they were unconvinced. As he wondered to himself how this untested outfit would perform when the chips were down, the column entered a shallow, grassy valley, about two miles long and two broad, the nearly dry Arickaree coursing through its center. At midpoint in the valley Forsyth ordered a halt. Here, where grazing looked good, he would bivouac overnight. He expected to follow the trail upstream next morning and to encounter Indians in force sometime on that day.

The scouts' camp lay against the south bank of the Arickaree at a point where the river bed stretched about 140 yards across. Almost in the middle of this flat, sandy expanse and opposite the bivouac was a low, narrow island, a bit over a hundred yards long, covered with grass and tangled brush. While it was still light Grover and Simpson E. (Jack) Stillwell, only about nineteen but a frontier veteran, reconnoitered the little island. To Grover's practiced eye this looked like the only place in the vicinity suitable for making a stand if hostiles should jump the camp. Forsyth had the animals picketed close by before dark and personally posted a strong guard. Through the chilly night the weary scouts slept soundly. For Forsyth sleep came hard. Often he got up and visited the sentries. But from the blackness beyond the campfire glow drifted only the wail of the coyote. It seemed that nothing on two legs moved in the prairie night.

There were then, however, two big villages of Sioux and one of Cheyennes with a few Northern Arapahoes about twelve miles down the Arickaree, not upstream as Forsyth mistakenly supposed. Most of the warriors in the Cheyenne lodges belonged to the fierce Dog Soldier Society. Among them was the celebrated Roman Nose, a mighty leader in war, although not a chief. Early on the sixteenth a few Sioux warriors had spotted Forsyth's column and had hurried to alert their people. Around six hundred warriors had set off together from the camps that morning, riding in the direction from which the white men would probably attack

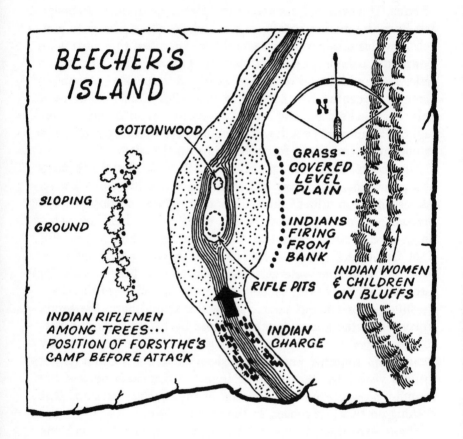

BEECHER'S ISLAND

COTTONWOOD

SLOPING GROUND

GRASS-COVERED LEVEL PLAIN

INDIANS FIRING FROM BANK

RIFLE PITS

INDIAN WOMEN & CHILDREN ON BLUFFS

INDIAN CHARGE

INDIAN RIFLEMEN AMONG TREES... POSITION OF FORSYTHE'S CAMP BEFORE ATTACK

the villages. All that day these Indians had searched in vain, not supposing that the whites were then moving in a direction away from the camps. At nightfall the great war party had halted on the prairie, but eight young braves had moved on in hopes of locating the enemy. At last, just before dawn, the youngsters spied the white men's fires and rode cautiously forward.

The restless Forsyth and one of the guards, spying movement along the faint horizon, had barely time to fire their weapons and shout, "Indians! Turn out!" as screaming riders loomed up and dashed through the herd, driving away two horses and a couple of the pack mules. Startled men grabbed their carbines and leaped to gather in the horses. Sandy Forsyth cussed out the two sleepyheads who had neglected to fasten properly their now-missing mounts and snapped the order to saddle up. In the meantime the big war party had arisen and moved out. From a distance of two or three miles the lead warriors saw the scouts' camp. The mass of Indians whipped up their ponies and, taking a very wide front, rode fast.

In the growing light Grover and others saw the red avalanche while it was still a considerable distance away and yelled the alarm. To the scouts, then standing by their horses or making coffee, the Indian onslaught was an appalling spectacle. Grover hurried to point out to Forsyth the advantages offered by the island. There they could take concealment and dig for cover while the redskins must move exposed over the river bed to finally close. On the major's orders the scouts, dragging their horses, legged it pell-mell, "like a flock of scared quail," to the island. Forsyth, concerned that the precious reserve ammunition be brought over safe, was among the last to cross. A stout two or three, Jack Stillwell among them, did not cross at this time but lay hidden in the tall grass under the river bank, anticipating good shooting.

On the island Forsyth tried hurriedly to organize a defense. Assisted by Lieutenant Beecher and other clear heads, he got most of the dazed men to tie their plunging, frightened animals in a rough circle and to take concealment inside. In the nick of time some of the scouts opened up with their Spencers, firing from beneath the horses. The Indians, now very near, had expected to swarm right over the white men, but in the face of the shots already whistling from the island their courage wavered. The terrifying charge split, thundering by the island on either side, although a few daredevils did hurl their ponies straight through the midst of the scouts. Now some of the warriors scurried on foot to take positions along both sides of the river. There they launched their arrows and fired their comparatively few guns at the island, where some of the white men could still be seen standing erect, with all their horses in plain view. Many other warriors remained mounted, circling outside of short rifle range but sometimes dashing in close.

Most of the scouts worked their carbines as fast as they could while the red men's fire raked their refuge. Now and then one slumped bleeding to the sand; some struggled up to keep on shooting. Two or three sprawled face down in the sand, shivering, and deaf to Forsyth's and Beecher's profanity. Horses, screaming and thrashing about with their wounds, were dropping fast. Through the roar of the fight a shout reached Forsyth's ears, "Don't let's stay here and be shot down like dogs!" The major, pistol out, promised to kill anyone who tried to leave the position. Forsyth and Beecher gradually got the men busy digging shallow rifle pits, heaving the loose dirt to the front for a breastwork. Forsyth continued to walk about until a bullet slammed into his right thigh. Moments later another slug shattered his left leg. Then Dr. Mooers dragged the fallen officer to the shelter of his rifle pit.

Again screeching warriors attempted a charge, but the hammering Spencers drove them back. Stillwell's little party, still hidden under the river bank, tumbled two unsuspecting Dog Soldiers from their ponies as they galloped by within a few yards' range. When another warrior was killed circling the island a chief directed the mounted men to take their ponies back to cover and fight on foot. The scouts, somewhat less excited now, lay low, shooting only when a worthwhile target presented itself. To most of them it looked like a deathtrap. Years afterward one of them remembered hearing Forsyth, his skull broken by a third bullet, cry out, "We are beyond all human aid, and if God does not help us there is none for us." The major called for someone to lead in prayer but there was no response. Instead, the final survivor among the horses crashed down and the scouts heard an Indian yell in English, "There goes the last damned horse, anyhow!"

Roman Nose had remained in camp during the opening hours of the battle. Very recently the special magic possessed by his war bonnet, which had brought him unharmed through many hard encounters, had been broken. There had been no opportunity for the lengthy ritual which might renew his headgear's power, so Roman Nose believed that if he should go into a fight he would be killed. But when news came of the losses among his fellows the warrior-instinct proved too much. In the afternoon Roman Nose went up to the battleground and stopped on a hill overlooking the place. There, sitting down among some of his friends, this man, holder of so many battle honors won in defense of the people, explained that his protective medicine was, for the time being, destroyed. But one called White Contrary, coming up, exclaimed, "Well, here is Roman Nose, the man that we depend on, sitting behind this hill," and chivied the warrior, "You do not see your men falling out there? All those people . . . feel that they belong to you . . . will do all that you tell them, and here you are behind this hill." Then Roman Nose tied his war bonnet under his chin and, in his own mind already a dead man, rode out to lead another assault. Stillwell's party heard the chargers coming and, as they swept past, one fired at the leading rider, who was very near. The big warrior's legs loosened; his body toppled over the pony's shoulders and fell heavily to the sand.

Finally night came and with it drizzling rain. Forsyth kept command despite agonizing pain. Near him Dr. Mooers lay unconscious, shot through the forehead and slowly dying. Three others of the detachment, including Lieutenant Beecher, were dead or nearly so. Nineteen were wounded, two mortally and several severely: forty-five per cent casualties since dawn among fifty-one men. While some of the men worked to improve the rifle pits, others excavated a large pit in the middle of the position. There the wounded were placed. Men dug a well and hacked meat from the dead horses. Forsyth knew that they must have aid very soon. The nearest military post was Fort Wallace, about 125 miles distant. Stillwell and old Pierre Trudeau answered the major's call for volunteers to walk to Wallace. Soon after midnight the pair glided noiselessly into the blackness.

Morning brought the red men back in force to pot at the island and to try a few half-hearted charges. The warriors were now aware of the risk involved in riding too close to the white men's holes. On this day only one of the scouts took a wound. The third day was simply a monotonous fire fight. By this time the Indians too had dug rifle pits. That night Forsyth got off two more men, John Donovan and Allison P. Pliley, bearing a written dispatch to the commander at Fort Wallace. There was no more fighting after the third day, and from the sixth day no more Indians were seen.

At the fourth dawn Dr. Mooers died. As the sun climbed high the stink from the swollen horses became almost unbearable. Moans and curses filled the air as wounded men tossed in delirium. Forsyth, in misery from the bullet in his right leg, called for his razor and himself cut out the lead. Although the battle was ended the little band had now to fight off another enemy— despair. The store of salvaged horse meat had turned rotten. An unlucky coyote and a few plums and prickly pears gave trifling nourishment but, clearly, starvation was near. Through the cold nights wolves, scenting death, howled their weird songs from the valley rim. Now and then Sandy Forsyth plucked in the dark at his throbbing leg, trying to brush away the maggots there.

On the ninth morning, September 25, Forsyth, dozing feverishly in his pit, heard one of his men yell that he could see movement on the distant hills. Soon another shouted that he saw an army ambulance among the far-off objects. Those of the scouts who could stand whirled in a crazy dance as horsemen in blue, guidon snapping overhead, raced down the slope toward the island—perfect illustration of the old cliché, "The Cavalry to the rescue."

Stillwell and Trudeau, traveling mostly at night, had reached Fort Wallace in five days. On their arrival the post commander, Lieutenant Colonel Henry C. Bankhead, had rushed a courier with the news to Captain Louis H. Carpenter and his company of the all-Negro Tenth U. S. Cavalry, then riding west from Cheyenne Wells. Carpenter had instantly turned north and set off to find the shattered detachment. En route he had run into Scout Donovan who, with Pliley, had made it to Wallace and now was on the way back to his outfit. With relief at hand Forsyth could not trust himself to the feeling inside and fumbled for a little novel that had turned up in someone's saddlebag. When Captain Carpenter came striding through the stench he found the stricken officer pretending to read *Oliver Twist*.

Next day Bankhead's column, guided by Stillwell, reached the battlefield and, as soon as it was thought safe to move the wounded, the whole force started slowly toward Fort Wallace. The bodies of Beecher, Mooers, and the rest were left buried where they had fallen in what was, by white men's standards, one of the hardest Indian fights on record. The little island was named Beecher Island in honor of the young officer who died there and, although flood waters have now obliterated the place, the name lives on. Sandy Forsyth, jolting along in an ambulance with other wounded, had two years of suffering before him but emerged a whole man, bearing the bright brevet of Brigadier General, U. S. Army.

The Indians too moved on, just one more battle behind them in a hopeless struggle to preserve their old way of life. Years later various Cheyennes who had taken part in the Beecher Island fight told George Bird Grinnell, probably the most sympathetic and best of their interpreters, that a total of nine Indians—six Cheyennes, one Arapaho, and two Sioux—had been killed there. That figure is probably very nearly exact, although Forsyth's official report claimed thirty-two. It is not remarkable that scared men, lifting their heads to the searching arrows and balls, scored but few hits among the agile figures that flitted in blurring dust.

The Cheyennes had never heard of brevets. Soon after Roman Nose's shadow-self had started along the Milky Way to *Seyan* (Happy Hunting Grounds), his mourners placed their great fighter's remains atop a lofty scaffold, among other such scaffolds, beside the Republican River and rode away. Perhaps the body of

Roman Nose was among those pulled down and stripped of their pitiful finery by the souvenir hunters among Bankhead's column when it passed that way. The human scavengers left the "good Indians'" corpses lying on the prairie. When winter came blackbirds had already picked the bones nearly clean, to bleach in the sun and rain.

14. BATTLE OF THE WASHITA

LAWRENCE FROST

At the time of the fight at Beecher Island, Brevet Major General George Armstrong Custer, Lieutenant Colonel of the Seventh Cavalry, was home in Monroe, Michigan, completing his year's suspension from rank and command resulting from a court-martial earlier in the year. Just one week after the Beecher Island fight he received a telegram.

> *Fort Hays, Kansas, September 24, 1868.*
> *General G. A. Custer, Monroe, Michigan:*
> *Generals Sherman, Sully, and myself, and nearly all the officers of your regiment, have asked for you, and I hope the applications will be successful. Can you come at*

*once? Eleven companies of your regiment will move
about the first of October against the hostile Indians,
from Medicine Lodge Creek toward the Wichita Mountains.*

P. H. Sheridan, Major General Commanding

Custer arrived at Fort Hays, Kansas, on the morning of September 30. At breakfast General Sheridan told him, "Custer, I rely on you in everything, and shall send you on the expedition without orders, leaving you to act entirely on your own judgment."

On the afternoon that he rejoined his regiment it was attacked by a band of Indians. He soon learned that this had been a daily occurrence and that the camp had been reduced almost to a state of siege. The men, though untrained and unfamiliar with Indian warfare, were rapidly becoming acquainted with their guns and horses through these daily sorties.

To catch the fleet Indian ponies with the aid of the more ponderous domestic horses of the cavalry was impossible. To follow them was equally difficult, for the ponies could maintain their strength on the grass of the plains, while grain and forage had to be carried for the cavalry horses. It was decided, at Custer's suggestion, that the best time for a campaign would be in the winter when the ponies were weakest and while the entire tribe was congregated along some stream. This plan followed that maxim of war that decreed one should do what the enemy does not expect.

For the first time the Seventh Cavalry was to serve as one body. All horses were newly shod and many fresh horses were substituted. There was a "coloring of the horses" whereby each company was given horses of one color. Once this had been completed daily target practice was ordered for all. As an incentive it was announced that out of the eight hundred men the forty best marksmen would be made into a corps of sharpshooters to march as a unit and to be exempt from guard duty.

It was determined that many of the depredating tribes camped in the winter along the Washita River. This was due south of Fort Hays, in Oklahoma, just east of the Texas Panhandle. Bases of supply would lie between Fort Dodge below Fort Hays and at Camp Supply further to the south.

The column left Camp Supply November 23 during a raging snow storm and with more than a foot of snow on the ground. Custer planned to find the winter hiding place of the hostile Indians and to administer such punishment as he was able. Though uncomfortable for the men in the cavalry column, the snow prevented the Indian villages from moving and lulled the redskins into a sense of security.

The wagon train, eleven companies of cavalry numbering nearly nine hundred men, the detachment of scouts headed by California Joe, and a delegation of friendly Osage Indians headed by Chiefs Little Beaver and Hard Rope traveled fifteen miles the first day. Because of falling snow, visibility was so poor that Custer had to use a compass to guide the column to its first night encampment on Wolf Creek.

On the fourth day out Major Joel H. Elliot, while scouting the north bank of the Canadian River, discovered the trail of a war party of 150 Indians. When informed, Custer ordered Elliot in pursuit while he detailed 80 men to accompany the wagon train. The rest of the troopers were to carry with them 100 rounds of ammunition each in addition to small amounts of coffee, hard bread, and forage for their horses. It was Custer's design to move in a direction so as to strike Elliot's trail. Scout Jack Corbin was detailed to inform Elliot accordingly. The troopers struggled on until nine o'clock that night before arriving at the point where Elliot and his three troops of cavalry had stopped. During a brief rest the Osages were consulted, and all were of the opinion that the Indian villages were not far away. All strongly advised that the pursuit be discontinued until daylight. This, Custer concluded, was the natural reluctance of the Indian to attack an unseen foe.

Orders were given to discontinue all bugle calls, and the column moved on at 10 P.M., the two Osage guides leading the way some three or four hundred yards in advance, and the cavalry about a quarter of a mile in the rear. Orders were given prohibiting speech above a whisper. No one was permitted to light a match. Soon the embers of a dying fire were discovered; then a dog was heard to bark, followed by the sound of the tinkling of a bell in a pony herd.

Though it was past midnight, the command was divided into four equal parts and so positioned as to surround the village completely and attack it at daylight. In the four-hour interval it grew intensely cold. The men were not permitted even to stamp their feet to keep warm.

Suddenly there was a shot on the far side of the village. Custer ordered the band to begin playing and immediately were heard the stirring notes of the Seventh's famous fighting song "Garry Owen." From all sides came the cheers of the men and the calls of the buglers. The Battle of the Washita had begun. The Indians quickly overcame their surprise and began a vigorous defense. Some fired from behind the nearest trees while others sprang into the waist-deep water of the Washita, using its banks as a protection from the well-directed fire of the troops. Squaws and boys in their early teens took arms against their foe. Captain Frederick W. Benteen was fired upon three times by one of these teen-age boys and, after his horse had been wounded, was forced to kill the boy to avoid being killed.

In one instance, a squaw leading a small white boy was intercepted by several troopers. When she observed that her escape had been cut off she drew a knife from her blanket and plunged it into the nearly-naked body of her unknown captive. She was quickly dispatched.

So desperate was the village defense that seventeen warriors occupying a depression in the ground could not be driven from their position. After a number of troopers had been shot down sharpshooters were employed to annihilate the Indians. In a nearby ravine the bodies of thirty-eight warriors were counted.

By 10 A.M. the fight was still in progress when a small group of Indians was observed on a knoll about a mile below the village. On inquiry from one of the captured squaws Custer was surprised to learn that they were from a series of villages extending for ten miles along the Washita and comprised of Cheyennes, Kiowas, Comanches, Arapahoes, and some Apaches. As the numbers increased there was no uncertainty in his mind that he shortly was to be attacked by superior numbers. It was time to survey the situation.

At the beginning of the attack Captain Louis McLane Hamilton, a descendant of Alexander Hamilton, had been killed. Another officer, First Lieutenant Tom Custer (Colonel Custer's brother) and two other officers had been wounded while 19 enlisted men had been killed and 11 wounded. Fifty-three squaws and children had been captured along with 875 ponies, 1100 buffalo robes, 500 pounds of powder, 1000 pounds of lead, 4000 arrows, and immense quantities of stored foods and equipment. Of the warriors under Chiefs Satanta, Little Raven, and Black Kettle, 103 had been killed including Black Kettle. Of Major Elliot and his detachment nothing had been seen since they had followed a group of retreating Indians early in the day.

The Indians increased in numbers on all sides, keeping up a continuous fire. Though completely surrounded, the soldiers fought valiantly, until suddenly quartermaster Lieutenant James M. Bell and an escort arrived with a much-needed supply of ammunition. The order was given to tear down and burn the lodges and the huge piles of captured property. Since it was impossible to take the ponies along, and since to turn them loose would provide the Indians with a means of attack and pursuit, Custer ordered all shot.

A search was made for Major Elliot and his nineteen men over an area of two miles and finally it was concluded they had been lost. (They had been surrounded and annihilated. Much controversy developed over whether Custer was justified in leaving the field without determining the fate of Elliot and his men.) It was now about an hour before nightfall, and the safety of the supply train as well as of the men was of great concern.

It was then that Custer demonstrated his tactical ability. With the band playing and guidons waving, the entire regiment, a strong force of skirmishers in advance, set out down the valley toward the remaining villages. Momentarily the Indian spectators on the surrounding hills were silent. Then, as if discerning that the troops intended continuing their destruction on the occupants of the other villages, they hastened ahead of the troops without firing a shot. This latter course was probably followed so that

Custer's Indian hostages would not be injured by stray bullets.

Long after dark the first deserted village was reached, upon which Custer countermarched his men toward the battleground, arriving there about ten o'clock. Without halting he pushed on, following the trail he had made the night before. The brisk march was continued until two o'clock in the morning and then they went into bivouac, a squadron having been sent forward to meet the supply train. At daylight they were back in the saddle, and at 10 A.M. they had the great satisfaction of meeting the train. California Joe Milner, the famous scout, was immediately sent with a dispatch to General Sheridan. He took scout Jack Corbin with him, the two of them accomplishing the errand through enemy-ridden country at night in record time.

On December 2, a mild winter day, the command began its last day's march toward Camp Supply. General Sheridan was advised by courier of the hour in the forenoon that the column would arrive at his headquarters, and that it would be their pleasure to march in review before him and his staff.

The day was bright and the ground in excellent shape as it led in a long gradual slope into the valley. The Osage guides and trailers, dressed and painted, led the column chanting their war songs and at intervals giving their war whoops or firing their guns in the air. Next came the scouts, with California Joe astride his mule. Following them were the Indian prisoners under guard, all mounted, and dressed in bright colors which were quite a contrast to the colorless clothing of the scouts ahead. Then came the band playing "Garry Owen," followed by the troops in platoons, the leading one being that of First Lieutenant William Winer Cooke's sharpshooters. As the officers gave General Sheridan the saber salute he returned it by lifting his cap. The look of pride on his face was the greatest reward he could have given them. He later stated that the scene was the most beautiful and highly interesting he had ever witnessed.

As Custer had predicted, the campaign would produce criticism no matter how it ended. Had he and his men failed to find and defeat the Indians, those who had been victims of the redskin assaults would have made extremely uncomplimentary remarks as to military efficiency and energy. As it resulted, many well-intentioned people throughout the country were distressed over the measures taken against the depredators. One group of traders and Indian agents, though well informed, charged that the Indians attacked were friendly and peaceable. Likely this was because they were growing rich from the Indians' economic ignorance and wanted no interference. Yet they knew well enough that the Indians attacked had been guilty of repeated depredations and had been caught with the evidence—white prisoners.

PART VII

Pawnee vs. Sioux

1873

Introduction

The Sioux and Pawnee had been hereditary enemies long before the coming of the first white man to the Northern Great Plains. The Pawnee were a semi-agricultural group who lived for the most part in earth-lodge villages. Like most of the more sedentary tribes, they spent a part of the year raising corn, squash, and pumpkins. Each year they went on semi-annual buffalo hunts for meat to supplement their meager existence, earned by farming.

By the early 1870s the Pawnee had already felt the impact of the white man's civilization. When Zebulon M. Pike visited them in 1806 they numbered about sixty-five hundred souls. As was the case with the other earth-lodge-dwelling groups, white man's diseases, such as smallpox, cholera, and tuberculosis, had taken a heavy toll among them. Their population was only about a third of what it had been at the beginning of the century.

The Pawnee lands had likewise been reduced. Although they lived largely along the Platte and Republican Rivers at the beginning of the century, this tribe claimed all of middle Nebraska from the Ponca lands on the north to the Kaw on the south. To the northwest was their hereditary enemy, the Sioux. With the signing of the Treaties of 1833 and 1857, the Pawnee had ceded most of their lands to invading whites. This left them with only a small reservation on the Loup River comprising the present Nance County, Nebraska.

In contrast, the Plains Sioux still remained a powerful nation up to the early 1870s. In 1868, only a few years earlier, Oglala chief Red Cloud forced the United States to abandon the Boze-

man Trail in Wyoming. His bands, together with Spotted Tail's Brule Sioux, ranged over southeastern Wyoming, western Nebraska, and western South Dakota menacing white advancements.

The Republican River was a common hunting ground for both the Sioux and the Pawnee. When the Pawnee ceded the region to the United States in 1833, the government guaranteed it as a "common hunting ground, during the pleasure of the President, for the Pawnee and other friendly Indians." By the Treaty of 1868 the United States promised the Sioux "the right to hunt on any lands north of North Platte, and on the Republican Fork of the Smoky Hill River, as long as the buffalo may range thereon in such numbers as to justify the chase."

15. THE BATTLE OF MASSACRE CANYON

RAY H. MATTISON

On a high hill overlooking the Republican Valley near Trenton, Nebraska, stands a large obelisk. This monument, erected by the Federal Government in 1930, commemorates the Battle of Massacre Canyon of August 5, 1873, the last great fight between two Indian tribes.

The war between the Sioux and the Pawnees is the story of an age-old struggle between a nomadic and sedentary people. The advantage was usually in favor of the former. White man's diseases did not wreak as much havoc among the nomadic Indians as they did among the dwellers of the damp, vermin- and disease-infested earth lodges. After at least one and a half centuries of known warfare between the two tribes, the Sioux in the early 1870s were still powerful. The Pawnees, on the other hand, had become increasingly weak.

The Sioux in the 1870s had a recent score to settle with their old enemy. In 1864, when this tribe was raiding the white settlements along the Platte, Frank and L. H. North organized the famous Pawnee Scouts. These scouts were intermittently under arms up to 1877 and served as an adjunct of the United States Army on the Plains. They were never defeated and won a number of victories over the Sioux and Cheyennes. They also served efficiently in protecting the construction crews of the Union Pacific against raiding Sioux.

Early in July 1873, about 400 Pawnees, comprising 250 men, 100 women, and 50 children started on their semi-annual buffalo hunt. They were headed by Sky Chief, one of their best chiefs. Indian Agent William Burgess selected John W. Williamson, a popular young man with the Pawnees, to accompany the party. It was Williamson's job to keep the hunting party in order so as to protect it, if possible, against both whites and hostile Indians. Another young white man, L. B. Platte, accompanied them. The Pawnee were all mounted and had about a hundred extra horses to carry the packs of dried buffalo meat and hides.

The party had a successful hunt. It first proceeded up the Platte Valley to Plum Creek; the Pawnees then turned southward to Turkey Creek where they killed forty-five buffalo. The hunters turned west to Elk Creek which they followed to the Arapaho Village on 'the Republican River and south to Beaver Creek where they killed four hundred buffalo. The Pawnee then went up the Beaver into Kansas for a few miles. There they heard a rumor that the Sioux were out. The Indians then hunted along Sappa Creek, where they killed a few buffalo, remained several days, and returned to the Beaver. From there they proceeded northward to the mouth of Frenchman's Creek on the Republican where they killed about two hundred buffalo.

At Frenchman's Creek, the Pawnees met some white buffalo hunters who warned them that a large party of Sioux was not far to the north. Williamson then advised his wards to retire down the Republican to a grove of trees so that the Pawnees would be in a good defensive position. He asserted that they were equipped to hunt buffalo and not to fight Indians. After a hot argument the hunters, instead of taking a safe trail back to their reservation down the south bank of the river, as Williamson proposed, crossed north of the Republican and on August 5 went up a ravine to a point on the plains west of Frenchman's Fork. There they found buffalo quietly feeding and pursued and killed many of them. While a part of the Pawnees were skinning the buffalo and cutting up the meat, the main body kept on the move. Suddenly they met a party of about a hundred mounted Sioux coming toward them over a bluff. Sky Chief, the Pawnee leader, was immediately shot while skinning a buffalo and thereupon scalped. Several others were also killed. The Pawnees stopped and rushed their women, children, and pack horses into a nearby ravine. The two white men, Williamson and Platte, advanced to parley with the Sioux but were fired upon and forced to move back. Platte was captured and his revolver taken from him.

The Pawnees then organized a defense line and came out and fought with the Sioux for about an hour. Suddenly a party of seven hundred to a thousand Sioux reinforcements appeared and charged the Pawnees on three sides. The defenders threw the robes and meat off their horses and endeavored to mount their women and children on them. Thirty-nine women, ten children, and a number of men were shot down while trying to mount. The Pawnees fled in terror down the ravine to the Republican River and thence down the valley to the east. After a chase of ten miles, the fleeing Pawnees managed to get south of the river. Suddenly a troop of the U. S. Cavalry who had learned too late that the Sioux were planning to attack the Pawnees, were seen approaching, and within a short time the Sioux disappeared.

When the military detachment, led by Platte, who had been released by the retreating Sioux, ascended the ravine, now known as "Massacre Canyon," they found evidence of savage brutality everywhere. Dead Pawnee women and children were lying among the dead horses. The Sioux had stripped, scalped, and mutilated the dead. They had gathered lodge poles and piled bodies on the poles and burned the dead and dying Pawnees.

Reports on Pawnee losses vary considerably. Barclay White,

Superintendent, Northern Superintendency at Omaha, reported to the Commissioner of Indian Affairs that the Pawnee casualties were 69 killed, comprising 20 men, 39 women and 10 children; 11 wounded severely; and 11 captured (these were later returned). The estimates of the Sioux losses also vary. Most contemporary witnesses stated they were small.

The Sioux responsible for this massacre were Brules from the Spotted Tail agency and Oglalas from the Red Cloud agencies. Antoine Janis, in charge of the Oglalas, disclaimed any responsibility for the outrage. Stephen T. Estes, sub-agent in charge of the Brules, first blamed the military, then Janis, and finally the Pawnees.

This massacre had a very demoralizing effect upon the Pawnees. It occurred at a time when a grasshopper plague had destroyed their crops. These disasters strengthened the influence of that segment of the Pawnee Tribe wishing to sell the Reservation and move south to the Indian Territory in present Oklahoma. The leaders of the movement fully exploited the situation and within a few weeks after the massacre they won the tribe's vote to sell out and move to Oklahoma.

PART VIII
The Modoc War
1872–73

Introduction

The Modoc War proper opened November 29, 1872 with a pistol shot by Lieutenant F. A. Boutelle, who had been sent with a party of soldiers to arrest Captain Jack and return him with his followers to the Klamath Reservation in southern Oregon. It ended June 1, 1873, with Captain Jack's surrender. There is some question whether the bloody events that took place in these six months can properly be called a "war." There is no question, however, that, considering the number of Indians involved, in lives and money it was the most costly Indian fighting in U. S. military history.

The causes of the Modoc War were the usual ones—greed for the Indians' lands, corrupt and incompetent officials, and the failure of the Federal Government to establish a firm Indian policy. Without such a policy, conflicts between its principal agents, the Army and the Bureau of Indian Affairs, were inevitable. The insecurity of the Indians was further increased by deliberate attempts to discredit their medicine men by over-zealous religious elements in the Indian Bureau. These were the same sorry conditions that had previously marked peace efforts with tribe after tribe and which were to lead to the attempt of Chief Joseph and his Nez Perces to flee to Canada and to the annihilation of Custer's command by the Sioux and their allies a few years later. In the case of the Modocs, their confinement in poverty on a reservation away from their home lands and under the domination of their traditional enemies, the Klamaths, made an outbreak almost a certainty.

The treaty with the Modocs had been signed in 1864, with

over one thousand Indians attending the ceremony. Of these, 319 were Modocs and 710 were Klamaths, which is probably a fair indication of the relative size of the two tribes. Under the terms of the treaty both bands ceded all of their lands to the government and were allowed in exchange part of the country on Upper and Middle Klamath Lakes. Since these lands were within the traditional hunting grounds of the Klamaths, that tribe was quite willing to settle on these terms. The Modocs were reported, however, to have signed "reluctantly."

Difficulties began almost as soon as the Modocs were settled on their new reservation. These were partly due to a struggle for leadership between the two chiefs of the Modocs, Old Schonchin and Captain Jack. The former was the more tractable and consequently was favored by the agency authorities. By 1865 this situation had become so intolerable to Captain Jack and his followers that they returned to their former home in the Lost River country southeast of present-day Klamath Falls, Oregon. Although the treaty had not been ratified and was not actually in force, settlers had moved into the Lost River country. Alarmed at the return of Captain Jack's band, they promptly petitioned the authorities to force him to go back to the reservation.

Captain McGregor, commanding officer at Fort Klamath, had his hands full at that time with the Paiutes, and he was reluctant to start a second front with the Modocs. Furthermore, he felt it was up to the Indian Bureau to persuade Captain Jack to return to the reservation or at least attempt to do so, before calling in the Army. The Indian officials procrastinated and it wasn't until the following year that sub-agent Lindsey Applegate journeyed to Lost River to try and prevail upon Jack to come back to the reservation. This invitation was politely but firmly refused, as was a second one by Superintendent J. W. P. Huntington in 1867. With the election of President Grant, Huntington was replaced by A. B. Meacham as Indian Superintendent for Oregon and one of his early acts was to send a messenger to Jack requesting a meeting. Jack agreed, but only on condition that the superintendent and the Indian agent come to see him.

The negotiators with their interpreters, teamsters, and a few Indians from the reservation left for Lost River in mid-December,

1869. They were accompanied also by a small body of soldiers who had been ordered to stop short of Jack's camp and await further orders from Meacham. Upon arrival at the camp, negotiations were started. These made little progress, and by nightfall of the second day the situation had become tense. At this point the soldiers, disregarding orders, charged the camp with wild yells; and the alarmed Indian leaders, thinking they had been betrayed, slipped away in the darkness. The next day, with their women and children as well as their supplies and weapons in Meacham's hands, they had no recourse but to give themselves up and agree to return to the reservation. Captain Jack did exact a promise from Meacham that they would be protected from the Klamaths and particularly from taunts that they had run away from such a small body of soldiers.

Accounts of the time suggest that Captain Jack and his followers conscientiously tried to adapt themselves to reservation life on this second attempt, but circumstances were against them. Since the reservation was on lands where the Klamaths had always hunted, they treated the Modocs as interlopers living on Klamath bounty. Demands by the Klamaths that a part of the timber the Modocs were cutting to construct winter cabins be turned over to them as tribute infuriated the self-respecting Modocs. Outnumbered and taunted by their enemies, their children prevented from gathering food, and their wives appropriated by post officers, there is little wonder that Captain Jack concluded that life under white man's rule was not for him. Appeals to the Indian agent for the protection of his people proving fruitless, and with their rations cut off in April on the grounds that Indians could find their own food, Captain Jack again led his people back to Lost River.

There were immediate recriminations between the Army and the Indian Bureau. Agent O. C. Knapp blamed the Army for inefficiency in letting the Modocs get away and Lieutenant G. A. Goodale blamed the Indian Bureau for needlessly antagonizing Captain Jack and his followers. No direct action to bring them back followed immediately, and for the next two years Jack and his band lived in relative peace with his white neighbors on Lost River.

16. BLOOD ON THE LAVA

F. G. RENNER

In the summer of 1872, Superintendent T. B. Odeneal, who had replaced Meacham, received orders from the Indian Bureau to corral Captain Jack's band of Modocs and return them to the reservation, using force if necessary. Nothing was done until late fall when Odeneal suddenly requested Major John Green, who was in command at Fort Klamath, to furnish the necessary forces. Green moved promptly and the next day, November 29, without even consulting his superiors, ordered Captain James A. Jackson and Lieutenant F. A. Boutelle with thirty-eight troopers to arrest Jack and his immediate followers.

The troopers arrived at Jack's camp of some fifteen wickiups, or huts, on Lost River at daylight and informed the surprised

Indians of their purpose. When the parley seemed to be getting nowhere, some of the Indians armed themselves. A moment later, Lieutenant Boutelle, thinking one of the Indians was about to shoot him, got off the first shot and the Modoc War was on. Firing immediately became general and for the next few minutes there was wild confusion. Despite the fact that all the shooting was at close quarters, only one Indian and one trooper were killed, although seven soldiers and a number of Indians were wounded. Both forces retreated in confusion. By the time the soldiers had rounded up their stampeded mounts and returned to the village the Modoc men had fled.

It took the Army six weeks to marshal its forces. Two companies of the Twenty-first Infantry under Major E. C. Mason were sent by boat, train, and on foot from Fort Vancouver and three troops of the First Cavalry under Captains Jackson, David Perry, and R. F. Bernard were ordered out from Fort Klamath and Camp Warner. These were augmented by three companies of citizen-volunteers, two of them from Oregon and one from California. By the middle of January the total force of between three and four hundred soldiers under the command of Lieutenant Colonel Frank Wheaton was all set to wipe out any resistance offered by the fifty-odd Modoc warriors.

The area of the Lava Beds in which the Modocs were entrenched is roughly rectangular. It is about a thousand feet wide and perhaps a half mile long, located just south of Tule Lake and near the northern boundary of Lava Beds National Monument. Wheaton's battle plan called for the main attack to be made from the west by the two companies of infantry, flanked on their left by the California volunteers and on their right by those from Oregon. On the right of the Oregonians, two troops of cavalry under Captains Perry and Jackson were to prevent the escape of any Modocs to the south. Captain Bernard with the third troop of cavalry was to attack simultaneously from the east, and it was expected that the combined forces would drive the Modocs to the unprotected shores of the lake, where they would be killed or captured.

The attack was launched early the morning of January 17, 1873, after blundering reconnaissance parties the day before had thoroughly alerted the Indians. A dense fog had settled over the area, and before the troops were within a mile or two of any Indians they began firing on imaginary Modocs. When they did get within range, many of the volunteers flatly refused to press forward and huddled behind rocks despite taunts from the Indians to come on and fight. The regulars were little better, and since the Modocs could move from point to point within their defenses to concentrate their fire, each of the attacking forces became convinced they were far outnumbered. Bernard's men might have partly relieved the situation had they advanced. Instead, they stayed safely out of range while they fired over Captain Jack's stronghold into the pinned-down infantry to the west. Twenty-four hours later what had been intended as a grand assault had turned into a shambles. In their panic, many of the soldiers had lost their rations and thrown away their weapons. Some deserted and others simply pulled back to safety. Cold, hungry, and badly beaten, the soldiers had lost their stomach for further fighting. Orders were given for the army to retire with its dead and wounded. The Modocs didn't lose a man.

General E. R. S. Canby, commanding officer of the Department of the Columbia, had been assured that the campaign would be both short and successful. When he learned that his army had been thoroughly whipped, although they outnumbered the Modocs seven to one, he promptly relieved Wheaton and replaced him with Colonel Alvin C. Gillem. Gillem's arrival from San Francisco was delayed by severe storms. It was some time before he was able to reach his field headquarters and plan the reorganization of his forces.

In the meantime, another set of events had been set in motion. Meacham, former Indian superintendent turned politician, was in Washington and proposed that a Presidential Peace Commission be appointed to negotiate for the surrender of the Modocs. The idea that a small party of civilians could successfully handle a situation that appeared to be beyond the capacity of the military was typical of the erratic actions of the Administration of the time. The Commission was duly appointed, with Meacham as its head. It promptly got off on the wrong foot. Meacham's first act was to object violently to the other commissioners recommended by the Secretary of the Interior, and after some delay men satisfactory to him were appointed. These were Jesse Applegate, a California rancher from the Modoc country, and Samuel Case, a representative of the Indian Bureau.

The commission proceeded west and on February 18 met with General Canby at John A. Fairchild's ranch, where they established headquarters. Captain Jack had learned that men from Washington were coming to talk to him but sent word that he would not meet with them except in the presence of Judge A. M. Rosborough and Elisha Steele of Yreka, white men he knew and trusted. Meacham recognized that such a concession would enhance Jack's prestige but nevertheless recommended that these men be added to the commission.

The next six weeks were a nightmare for the Commission. Repeated messengers sent to Captain Jack's camp to arrange for a meeting were, in turn, welcomed, rebuffed, and threatened, and from their conflicting reports it was impossible to determine the Indians' intentions. Some of Jack's warriors rode in to Fairchild's ranch to announce they were willing to surrender—and later changed their minds. At one point, Jack himself sent word that he was willing to lay down his arms. He even set a meeting place to make the final arrangements, but when wagons with food and blankets for "the starving Modocs" arrived at the rendezvous, no Indians appeared. Partly as a result of these frustrations, the Commission itself fell apart. Unable to agree on a course of action, Applegate, Case, and Rosborough resigned, the latter two being replaced by sub-agent L. S. Dyar of the Klamath Agency and the Reverend Eleaser Thomas, a Methodist minister from California. It was apparent, however, that something more than new faces on the Commission were needed, and shortly thereafter Secretary of the Interior Delano, without informing Meacham, placed General Canby in charge.

By the middle of March it was obvious that the Indians were deliberately stalling, and Canby decided to put on some pressure. His first move was to shift his forces closer to the Lava Beds so they would be in a position for action if the Indians decided to scatter. Colonel Gillem was ordered to move to a point about three and a half miles west of Jack's stronghold and

Mason approached still closer from the east. Since these moves were within sight of the Modoc defenses, the Indians were well aware of what was taking place. Becoming alarmed, Captain Jack first sent messengers to Canby to find out his intentions and finally met with him in person. After a number of such meetings it became clear what each side wanted, but how this was to be accomplished remained as undecided as ever.

Jack's first demand was that all soldiers be withdrawn from the Lava Beds and that certain of his men be protected from charges of murdering a number of settlers. He also wanted a reservation for his people established on Lost River, as Meacham had recommended years earlier. Canby could promise none of these things. He said only that he could accept their surrender and that the authorities would later decide what would be done with them.

The situation was further complicated by dissension between Captain Jack and his chief medicine man, Curly Headed Doctor. Jack was intelligent enough to know that he couldn't stand off the Army indefinitely and gave many indications that he was willing to surrender if assured of fair treatment. The Doctor and some of his immediate followers, on the other hand, were convinced that their medicine was stronger than that of the whites. The fact that a handful of their number had successfully evaded return to the reservation for years, had soundly defeated the Army, and had brought about delay after delay in the negotiations for peace encouraged them in this viewpoint. Consequently they were not only willing but anxious to continue the fight, and plotted to reopen hostilities by murdering Canby and other members of the Commission.

News of their intentions reached the Commission through Frank Riddle and his Modoc wife Winema (Tobey), who were serving as interpreters. Meacham knew the Modocs and was thoroughly alarmed. He urged that the Peace Commissioners go armed to the next meeting or that riflemen be concealed in the near vicinity to give them some protection. These proposals were vetoed by Canby, who was convinced that the Modocs were more interested in talking than fighting, and plans went ahead for the next meeting with Captain Jack on April 11.

On the morning of the eleventh, General Canby, Meacham, Dyar, Thomas, and Frank Riddle and his wife rode to the meeting place expecting to meet Jack and four of his leaders. When they arrived they found there were eight Indians, and, contrary to an earlier agreement, a number of them were openly carrying weapons.

Canby ignored the fact that some of the Indians were armed, and the parley got underway with the usual handshaking. Jack reiterated his demand that the soldiers leave the country and that they be allowed to live where they wanted to while Canby pointed out that only the President could order the troops removed, or decide where the Indians should live. After considerable oratory on both sides, Jack suddenly gave a signal and two Indians with their arms full of rifles appeared from the nearby rocks where they had been concealed. Before the Commissioners could move Captain Jack pulled a revolver and shot Canby in the face, while another Indian shot Thomas through the chest. Meacham ran but went down as a ricocheting rifle bullet felled him with a glancing blow across the forehead. Dyar and Riddle, who were standing when the melee started, had a better chance and, in a dodging run, managed to outdistance their pursuers. Tobey was knocked down but alarmed the Indians by calling out that the soldiers were coming. She was not hurt. After stripping the clothes and boots from Canby and Thomas, who were dead, and from the unconscious Meacham, the Indians took off for their stronghold on a run, well aware that they would shortly have a real fight on their hands.

Although the murders had taken place on April 11, it wasn't until four days later that the army was ready for its second attack on the stronghold. Its greatly augmented forces now consisted of four batteries of artillery, five infantry companies, four troops of cavalry, and seventy-two Indian scouts from the Warm Springs Reservation. The first day the approach was so cautious that most of the troops didn't even get within rifle range. The second day was a little better, and by nightfall Colonel Gillem thought he had the Modocs completely surrounded. He was unaware, however, that Major E. C. Mason, commanding the forces approaching from the east, had flatly disobeyed orders.

Instead of effecting junction with the forces coming up from the south as he had been ordered to do, he had his men dig in safely out of range and even held his artillery so far back that their shells fell short of the Modoc camp. This left a gap in the lines, and during the night the Modocs simply walked out of the trap and disappeared into the maze of cinder cones, caves, and lava beds nearby.

Four days later the Modocs had been located, and Captain Evan Thomas was ordered to take a sixty-four man patrol and find out if mortars could be taken to a small butte overlooking their camp. The detachment reached the slopes of the butte and sat down for lunch, completely unaware that twenty-four Modocs were concealed in the rocks waiting for them. When the Indians opened fire the panic was frightening. The officers tried to rally their men to dislodge the Indians above them but with little success. Twenty-three of the soldiers including Captains Thomas and Wright were killed and nearly as many severely wounded. The rest ran the four miles back to Gillem's camp or concealed themselves in the rocks until nightfall. As usual, the Modocs hadn't lost a man. This disaster led to Gillem's removal, and on May 2 Colonel Jeff C. Davis was placed in charge, the third officer to assume this responsibility.

Davis had two immediate tasks that had to be accomplished quickly. He had to find the Modocs and he had to select a field commander who could keep his men from running for cover at the first hostile shot. Captain H. C. Hasbrouck, a recent arrival, was given this assignment, and as soon as the general area of the Modoc camp was located he took the field with five days' rations for his three troops of cavalry and the Warm Springs Indian scouts. The night of May 9 they camped on a small lake, unaware that the Modocs had them under close surveillance. At dawn the next morning the Modocs charged the camp, expecting their attack would create the same panic and losses that had resulted from the previous battle. They almost succeeded. In the first rush, several soldiers were killed or wounded, and the horses stampeded. This time, however, Hasbrouck and his officers managed to rally their men, and a prompt counterattack routed the Modocs and captured most of their pack animals and supplies, including their spare ammunition.

This was a serious blow to the confident Modocs. One of their sub-leaders had been fatally wounded and his death further shattered their morale. One group of fourteen fighting men with their families promptly deserted. Within a few days ten of the women and children from this band were captured, and when some of the women were sent back to assure their men they would not be shot out of hand, these too came in to surrender.

From here on it was only a matter of time. Jack still had thirty-seven fighting men but although the army did not know it, these too had broken into small groups and scattered. With the help of the captured Modocs a number of these bands were located and prevailed upon to surrender. Finally, on June 1, Captain Jack himself, convinced that further fighting was useless, gave himself up, and the Modoc War was over.

PART IX

The Southern Plains 1874

Introduction

Comanches, Cheyennes, Kiowas, and Arapahoes left their reservations in Indian Territory (Oklahoma) in great numbers in the summer of 1874. Isatai (or Ishatai), a young Quahadi Comanche medicine man, was primarily responsible for the widespread desertion. He promised the Indians that the Great Spirit would turn aside the bullets of the white men. General Nelson A. Miles (in his book, Personal Recollections) explains why these Indians were ripe for Isatai's "medicine": the buffalo herd was being destroyed rapidly by hide hunters; the Indians' annual food allowances were usually exhausted in six or seven months; these nomadic Indian horsemen found reservation life particularly confining and galling. General Miles felt that the actions of the Indians in slipping away from the reservation to hunt, thereby supplementing the government rations, was a natural thing.

Following a religious gathering (The Sun Dance) near Fort Sill early in the summer of 1874, many of the deserters followed Isatai into the Texas Panhandle. There they joined forces with other bands who had never recognized the treaties and who had continued their nomadic life on and near the Llano Estacado (Staked Plains). The Indians were particularly bitter toward the hide hunters for their wanton destruction of the southern buffalo herd—which was food, shelter, and clothing to the tribesmen. It was only natural for their first move to be against the hide hunters.

Lieutenant General Phil Sheridan, Commander of the Division of the Missouri, acted promptly on learning of the wholesale desertions, which were followed by news of the fighting at Adobe Walls. He sent word to the Indians that if they did not return to their reservations by August 1 they would be treated as hostiles. He ordered his field commanders to prepare for a fall and winter campaign.

Late in August 1874 an unfortunate misunderstanding at the Wichita Agency led the soldiers from Fort Sill to fire on a surrendering band of Nokoni Comanches. It was ration day at the agency and just about all the Indians who had remained on the reservation were there. A general fight developed. The agency house was burned, several civilians killed, and a number of soldiers wounded. Immediately following this unnecessary fight the Indians, fearing reprisals, fled across the Red River into Texas. They joined forces with those who had deserted earlier.

The Indians having failed to return to their reservations by August 1 (indeed, additional Indians had left), General Sheridan ordered his field forces into action. This campaign was well planned. Colonel Ranald Mackenzie and the Fourth Cavalry moved north from Fort Concho (now San Angelo) in Texas. A column under Colonel Davidson moved west from Fort Sill; one under Major Price moved east from New Mexico; and General Miles' command moved south from Fort Dodge, Kansas. Each column was to act more or less independently but with the common objective of finding the hostiles, defeating them, and sending them back to their reservations.

Colonel Mackenzie's column consisted of eight troops of the Fourth Cavalry and four companies of infantry (to guard his supply camps and wagon trains). In addition, he had a few Tonkaway and Seminole scouts under the command of Lieutenant Thompson and Sergeant John B. Charlton. In all, Mackenzie had 15 commissioned officers, 450 enlisted men, and three acting Assistant Surgeons. Lieutenant H. W. Lawton, who was killed in the Philippines many years later, was the quartermaster for this column and earned the praise of all participants. He was harassed by sand, thunderstorms, wet northers, and mud that made the moving of supply wagons difficult. The Fourth Cavalry was a hard-hitting, fast-moving, veteran Indian-fighting regiment even at the beginning of this campaign.

17. THE SECOND BATTLE OF ADOBE WALLS

J. C. DYKES

Isatai, or Little Wolf, the Comanche medicine man, urged the Indians to make the destruction of Adobe Walls their first objective. He promised that the trading post would be taken and all the white men killed while they slept. There would be scalps, food, guns, ammunition, and liquor for the taking. Isatai told the tribesmen gathered at the war council in June 1874 at the mouth of Elk Creek on the North Fork of the Red River that the Great Spirit had told him how to make paint that would turn away the bullets of the whites. The Comanches, Cheyennes, and Kiowas in considerable numbers were at this war council on the invitation of the Comanches. There were also a few Arapahoes and Apaches present.

The idea of a big raid of the combined forces of Comanches, Kiowas, and Cheyennes into Texas originated with the Cheyennes, who were particularly angry over the invasion of the Texas Panhandle by the hide hunters. The camp of the Cheyennes was on the headwaters of the Washita in present-day Hemphill County, Texas and the hide hunters were moving ever closer to their hunting grounds. After the Sun Dance of the Comanches near Fort Sill was over and the chiefs of the various bands of Comanches had voted for the raid, Chief Quanah Parker called the war council. The Kiowas were led by Lone Wolf and Woman's Heart, but another band of Kiowas under Chief Kicking Bird refused the invitation and counseled peace. The Cheyenne warriors were under the leadership of Stone Calf and White Shield. Quanah Parker, half-white, whose mother Cynthia Ann Parker had been captured as a little girl on a raid into Central Texas, and Chief Big Bow led the Comanches. Isatai, the young Comanche medicine man, untried as a warrior, was the real moving force in the undertaking. At the end of the war council the Cheyennes and Kiowas agreed to join the Comanches in the raid. Many of the Indians were well armed with modern weapons purchased from Mexican traders (Comancheros) although many of them also carried bows and arrows. It was about one hundred miles from the spot of the war council to Adobe Walls and when the powwow was over the well-mounted warriors started for the trading post. They were joined by other small bands en route.

Dodge City, Kansas, was headquarters for many of the buffalo hide hunters in the early seventies. By 1873 the herd in western Kansas was so nearly killed off that the buffalo men were seeking new hunting grounds. The great southern herd on the High Plains of Texas seemed to offer the greatest possibilities for profits. A few of the more daring hunters made brief exploratory hunts into the Panhandle and came back to Dodge City with glowing reports of the grass and the size of the herd. John and Wright Mooar, brothers from Vermont, employed a large number of skinners and were one of the big hide outfits. When they announced their intention of moving into the Texas Panhandle in the spring of 1874 many of the smaller outfits decided to go along.

A. C. (Charlie) Myers, former hide hunter and successful merchant and hide shipper at Dodge City, decided he would steal a march on his fellow traders at Dodge by establishing a trading post in the Panhandle. His plan was to buy the hides at his post and send them back to Dodge City in the wagons that brought his goods down. His idea was so good that seven skinners decided to take along a stock of liquor to open a saloon near Myers' post. Tom O'Keefe loaded his smith tools into a wagon. He knew the trading post would need a blacksmith shop. When the wagon train left Dodge City in late March there were about thirty wagons, loaded with the goods of Myers, Hanrahan, and O'Keefe and with the supplies the various hide hunters were taking with them. The wagons were accompanied by about fifty heavily armed buffalo hunters and skinners on horseback. After considerable scouting for a suitable location, Myers decided on a spot in sight of and about a mile northeast of Bent's old trading post. Adobe Walls or Adobe Fort, abandoned in about 1844 by Bent, had been utilized by Kit Carson in his campaign against the Kiowas and Comanches in the fall of 1864 (Chap. 9). The new site was on the west side of a little creek and near the center of a meadow. There was a good view in all directions: events were later to prove the importance of this fact.

The southern herd had not started its annual migration northward when the caravan reached the Canadian River, so the hunters were glad to lend the post founders a hand on construction. Myers put up a picket store of small logs set in trenches (to form the walls). It was about thirty by sixty feet in size and housed a stock estimated to be worth fifty thousand dollars. Hanrahan built just south of Myers. The saloon was a soddy, or sod house, twenty-five by sixty feet. O'Keefe's smithy was a driven-picket house of about fifteen by fifteen feet between the store and the saloon. Shortly after these buildings were started Charles Rath, another Dodge City trader, arrived with a stock of goods valued at about twenty thousand dollars, and he built a sod house just south of Hanrahan's saloon. All four buildings had sod roofs on a framework of poles. Myers also built a picket corral, about two hundred by two hundred feet, which cornered on his store. By May 1, 1874, all four were open for business, and the new trading post became the center of activities for the hide hunters in the Panhandle. Despite the fact that no adobe was used in the construction of the new post, the hide hunters named it "Adobe Walls." Despite thirty years of weathering, the thick old adobe walls of Bent's post were still four or five feet high when the new post was built.

The hide hunters fanned out from the trading post but maintained contact as they delivered hides to Myers and Rath. Hanrahan's saloon was a favorite gathering place when the hide hunters were at Adobe Walls. Hunting was good and getting better as the great southern herd of buffalo moved slowly northward. Indian scouts and small hunting parties watched the building of the trading post with growing dismay. They noted the habits of the hide hunters and in late May and June constantly harassed the smaller outfits. Even the Mooar brothers, with one of the largest numbers of hunters and skinners in the Panhandle, were attacked. The Indians responsible for these swift raids on the camps of the hide hunters were most likely Cheyennes. However, some small bands of Comanches had never surrendered and continued to lead a nomadic life on the Staked Plains, and they may have been involved in these forays. It does not seem likely that these Indians were a party to Isatai's great plan to wipe Adobe Walls from the map. The raids alerted the hide hunters and while they continued to kill buffalo, they were careful about their campsites and about getting too far from other outfits.

In the meantime, Lee and Reynolds, the post traders at Fort Supply in the northwest part of Indian Territory (now Oklahoma), learned of the powwow taking place between the Comanches, Kiowas, and Cheyennes. They learned, too, from their Indian informants (probably Kiowas who had refused to join the raiders) that the most likely target of the combined tribesmen was Adobe Walls. Lee and Reynolds were close friends of Robert M. Wright, partner of Charles Rath in hide buying and trading. Lee and Reynolds decided to send Amos Chapman, a half-breed, to Adobe Walls to warn Rath and persuaded the commanding officer at Fort Supply to send along an escort of five cavalrymen. This party arrived at Adobe Walls about June 18 and informed Myers, Hanrahan, and Rath of the possible raid. According to their knowledge of Indian habits and what they could learn from their Indian informants, Lee and Reynolds estimated that the attack would take place on June 27. Some of the hide hunters, who were at the post when the soldiers arrived, feared that Chapman was a spy for either the Army or the Indians. The statement by one of the soldiers that they were looking for horse thieves didn't help. Trouble seemed so imminent that Rath hid Chapman in a Mooar hide wagon. Chapman told the Mooars the story.

The Mooars had started the move into the Panhandle. Myers and Hanrahan were, as we have seen, the first traders, and Rath had moved in before the first two were open for business. These five men were, more than any others, responsible for establishing the post. They talked the matter over and decided to keep the warning brought by Chapman a secret from the hide hunters. Of the founders only Tom O'Keefe, the blacksmith, was left ignorant of the danger. Many years later Wright Mooar said that the traders feared that the hide hunters would desert the post and return to Kansas. This would have left the post at the mercy of the raiding redskins.

Trouble for the hide hunters continued to pile up. Tom Wallace and Dave Dudley were killed on Chicken Creek while their partner, Joe Plummer, was at Adobe Walls for supplies. John (Antelope Jack) Holmes, a young Englishman, and a German known only as Blue Billy, were killed on a tributary of the Salt Fork of the Red River while hunting with Anderson Moore. The Mooars were followed almost to Adobe Walls by a raiding party. The Indian scare was on in earnest and many of the hide hunters gathered at the trading post. After a few idle days some of the hunters ventured out from the post to the north and west where buffalo were plentiful. The general consensus was that the Indians would attack only to the south and east of Adobe Walls. The divide between the Canadian and Red Rivers was a favorite hunting grounds of the Indians. The hide men agreed that it was not safe to hunt in that country.

John and Wright Mooar decided to load their wagons with hides and go back to Dodge City. Myers also loaded his big wagons with hides and started them for Kansas. The Mooars asked Myers and Rath if they intended to stay at Adobe Walls. They said they did. The Mooars didn't believe them. The Mooars were right. Myers and Rath, on horseback, caught up with the wagon train at Beaver Creek. This was a day or two before the date that Lee and Reynolds had predicted the Indians in force would attack the post. Of the five warned by Chapman, only Hanrahan remained at Adobe Walls.

Young Billy Dixon did the killing for his two skinners. His small outfit was one of those which deserted the divide country south of Adobe Walls after the Indian raids on the Plummer and Moore camps had resulted in four deaths. Jim Hanrahan employed seven skinners but was spending more and more time in his saloon. The hunters he hired were not keeping his skinners busy. He offered Dixon a partnership and they agreed to hunt northwest of the post where the danger of Indian attacks would be less. The Dixon-Hanrahan wagons were loaded on June 26 for an early morning start on the twenty-seventh. Billy Dixon bought a new Sharps forty-four rifle at Rath's store. The Shadler brothers, Ike and Shorty, freighters, arrived from Dodge City on the twenty-sixth with supplies for the traders. They unloaded and then reloaded their wagons with hides for the return trip to Dodge City. They decided to sleep on their wagons outside Myers' pole corral and to make an early start on the morning of the twenty-seventh.

Jim Hanrahan had a problem the night of the twenty-sixth. It did not seem likely to him that Lee and Reynolds could actually predict the day on which the Indians would attack. However, the desertion of the post by Myers, Rath, and the Mooar brothers prior to the twenty-seventh put him on the spot. He decided to resort to trickery rather than to risk the jibes of the hide hunters for predicting an attack that didn't materialize. The possibility of an attack at dawn occurred to Hanrahan. About two o'clock on the morning of the twenty-seventh he fired his pistol into the air. Oscar Sheppard (or Shepherd) and Mike Welch were sleeping in the saloon when they heard Jim shout, "Clear out!

The ridge pole is breaking!" A dozen or so of the men were soon milling around. After considerable commotion someone found a forked prop pole on the woodpile that would support the ridge pole. Hanrahan announced drinks on the house—some of the hunters had several.

For many years the hide hunters believed that the crack of Hanrahan's pistol was the cracking of the ridge pole in the saloon. True, they could see no crack. It did not occur to them to raise the question as to why Hanrahan was awake and fully dressed at 2 A.M. Such eminent students of Indian history as George Bird Grinnell and Rupert Norval Richardson accepted the story of the cracking of the ridge pole as a reason for the failure of the surprise planned by Isatai and the Chiefs to come off. By many of the participants, the cracking of the ridge pole was regarded as divine intervention in the fate of Adobe Walls. A pre-warned, half-doubting but worried Irish saloon-keeper was really responsible for preventing the surprise attack from being a complete success.

Hanrahan did his best to keep the men up with free liquor. However, many of them had been up late playing cards and drinking. They began to drift back to their bedrolls for a nap before dawn. Several hide outfits were due to start hunts the morning of the twenty-seventh. Hanrahan did not give up. He suggested to his new partner, Billy Dixon, that he get an early start for the hunting grounds. Dixon agreed and Billy Ogg was sent for the horses.

The Indians camped the night of the twenty-sixth some five or six miles east of Adobe Walls. Estimates of the number of warriors vary widely but there were surely several hundred. One thousand well-mounted and armed warriors is the top number mentioned but it is believed that seven hundred is more nearly correct. Not all the warriors had guns. The Indians spent the night of the twenty-sixth making medicine and readying for the attack. Each warrior put on his war paint and many painted their ponies. Long before daybreak the Indians lined up for the attack —most of them carried shields of dried, almost flint-hard, buffalo hide. On the right of the long line was Isatai the medicine man on a painted pony. He was naked except for a coat of his magic yellow paint. The Indian strategy was a pre-dawn attack. Isatai had promised that they would find the men at the trading post asleep and easy victims.

Billy Dixon rolled his bedding and tossed it on his wagon. As he reached for his new Sharps he spotted the charging Indians. He thought at first that the Indians intended to run off the horse herd and decided to get in a few shots. He shot once and found that the raiders were headed directly for the buildings. He ran to the nearest building, the saloon, and as he reached it was joined by Billy Ogg. Ogg was exhausted from his sprint across the meadow and fell to the floor as soon as he was inside the saloon. Many of the men had slept outside in the balmy June night air and they rushed to one or the other of the buildings as soon as Dixon's shot and shouts gave the alarm. O'Keefe ran from the saloon to Rath's store and aroused those sleeping inside. By this time the men could hear the thunder of the hoofs of the Indian horses and the whoops of the warriors. Ike and Shorty Shadler, asleep at their wagons, were engulfed in the first wild charge—both were killed and scalped. Their big dog suffered a like fate. All the others were under cover.

Billy Dixon, Billy Ogg, William Barclay (Bat) Masterson, Oscar Sheppard, Mike Welch, Hirma Watson, James McKinley, and "Bermuda" Carlisle were with Hanrahan in his saloon between the two stores. In the Myers store, north of the saloon, the defenders were Fred Leonard (Myers' clerk), James Campbell, Edward Trevor, Frank Brown, Harry (or Charlie) Armitage (a Dixon skinner), "Dutch Henry," Billy Tyler (hide hunter and new arrival at the trading post), Billy (Old Man) Keeler (cook at the Myers' store), Mike McCabe (an expert skinner known also for his big sprees when he hit town after a hunt), Henry (Harry) Lease (hide hunter), and "Frenchy" (a Dixon skinner). In the Rath store, south of the saloon, James Langston (Rath's clerk), George Eddy (Rath's bookkeeper), Andy Johnson (Rath's livestock and hide-yard tender), Sam Smith, Tom O'Keefe, and Mr. and Mrs. William Olds were holed up. The Olds had arrived only a few days before the attack to open an eating place in the Rath store. Twenty-six men (the Shadler brothers had been lost in the first charge) and one woman were left to fight several hundred painted, yelling warriors. The buildings in which the buffalo hunters took refuge were constructed to protect the supplies of the traders from the elements, but not for defense. There were no portholes through which to fire, and the first charge of the Indians carried them right up to the buildings.

The defenders made out with what they had. They piled sacks of flour and grain against the doors and windows and along the walls of the two stores. They found cracks to fire through and in the first half hour gave such a good account of themselves that the Indians withdrew. One Comanche and two Cheyennes—one a son of Chief Stone Calf—were killed and many others wounded. The Indians charged to the calls of a dark-skinned bugler several times before ten o'clock. Several of the defenders were former soldiers and understood the bugle calls. The trapped men were ready each time the Indians charged. By ten o'clock the Indians had learned the range of the big buffalo guns and were trying to stay out of it. They kept up their fire at the buildings but made only an occasional charge or sneak attack. The bugler was shot down while ransacking the Shadler wagons. Several redskins were killed or wounded as they rode from one group of warriors to another, believing they were out of range of the buffalo guns.

By four o'clock the fighting was over. The range of the big guns and the marksmanship of the buffalo hunters were too much for the Indians. The only white casualty, other than the Shadlers, was newcomer Billy Tyler. He and Fred Leonard had run out of Myers' store early in the fight to look after the horses in the corral. Indian fire drove them back to the store and Tyler took a bullet through the lungs as he stopped in the door to get off one more shot. Bat Masterson, learning of the wounding of Tyler, ran safely from the saloon to Myers' store to be with his friend. Tyler called for water but there was none. Old Man Keeler ran to the well in the corral, pumped a bucket of water, and got back untouched. His dog followed him as he ran to the well and died with twenty bullets in his body. Bat gave Billy a drink and bathed his face but the wounded man died shortly thereafter. When the defenders in the saloon ran short of ammunition, Billy Dixon and Jim Hanrahan dashed safely through a hail of bullets to Rath's store. The defenders wanted Dixon, a fine shot, to stay with them. Hanrahan made his way back to the saloon with a load of ammunition, untouched. All the defenders were valiant.

The Indians were mighty unhappy. The surprise attack had failed. Chief Quanah Parker's horse had been killed under him. Later Quanah had been put out of the fight for the day when he was struck from behind by a nearly spent bullet that glanced off a boulder. Stone Calf's son was dead. The Indians had only two scalps—the Shadlers'. The food captured was the small amount in the Shadler wagons. In one respect, the raid had been success-ful—they had killed or run off all the defenders' horses. They had also killed the Shadler oxen (but too close to the buildings to retrieve them for food). The defenders were afoot but that was small solace for the Indians, who had been promised an easy victory and instead had lost many warriors. The Cheyennes were particularly bitter towards Isatai, the young Comanche medicine man. Isatai had watched the action from afar, despite the taunts of the Cheyennes. From afar but not far enough—his horse was shot from under him—the horse he had so carefully covered with the magic paint that he said the Great Spirit had told him how to mix to turn away the bullets of the white men. Isatai's only excuse was that one of the Cheyennes had broken his "medicine" by killing a skunk en route to Adobe Walls. Isatai lived out his life in disgrace. Later some of the Indians translated his name into English as Coyote Droppings rather than as Little Wolf.

Late in the afternoon of the twenty-seventh other hide hunters slipped through the loose Indian lines surrounding the trading post to join the defenders. Jim and Bob Cator came in from their camp to the north and the Bellfield outfit came in with two teams. By the sixth day after the fight there were about a hundred men at Adobe Walls. The Indians continued to watch the post but made no further attacks. Henry Lease, riding a Bellfield horse, left for Dodge City to get help on the night of June 28. He man-aged to get through and two relief parties set out for Adobe Walls. One, of forty tough buffalo hunters led by Tom Nixon, started from Dodge City—the other, of soldiers, from Fort Leav-enworth. The defenders were busy—they constructed sod look-outs on the roofs of the two stores. These were reached by climbing crude ladders. On July 2 the sentinel on the Myers store saw a band of about thirty Indians to the north. He gave the alarm and William Olds, who had been watching from the roof of Rath's store, had started down the ladder—when his gun went off accidentally, blowing off the top of his head. He fell dead at the feet of his wife. A day or so before, Billy Dixon made his famous shot. Using a big Sharps Fifty he shot an Indian from his horse at a distance the hide hunters called "a mile"—it actually measured 1538 yards. This was the last time the Indians got within range of the big guns.

James Hanrahan, the last of the founders of the trading post, decided to abandon it. About the fourth or fifth of July a group of the defenders started the trek to Dodge City. Nixon's relief party escorted the rest back to Kansas. The Indians burned the abandoned buildings. The hide hunters had been driven from the Texas Panhandle, and in this respect the big raid was an Indian victory. The Indians broke up into small bands following their failure to capture Adobe Walls. They raided ranches and small settlements in Colorado, Kansas, New Mexico, and Texas and attacked several wagon trains. About eighty whites were killed in these lightning-like raids in the summer of 1874.

Did the various bands agree to rendezvous in Palo Duro Canyon following their raids? Or was it a matter of fearing to return to the reservation knowing that there would be reprisals against those involved in the summer raids, and of seeking a safe place to winter? Winter came early to the Staked Plains in 1874—a cold wet norther roared down across the Panhandle on September 24. Most of the Comanche, Kiowa, and Cheyenne bands were snug in the canyon when the norther struck.

18. THE BATTLE OF PALO DURO CANYON

J. C. DYKES

It was just as the first faint streaks of dawn came in the east on September 28, 1874, that the Fourth Cavalry arrived at the edge of that wide gash in the Llano Estacado known as Palo Duro Canyon. Below them on the floor of the canyon the troopers saw the winter lodges of the Comanches, Kiowas, Cheyennes, and Arapahoes. The search was over.

Palo Duro Canyon was one of the last strongholds of the Indians of the Southern Plains. The canyon is 120 miles long and in the deeper parts the floor is over a thousand feet lower than the rim. It is located in what are now Briscoe, Armstrong, Randall, and Swisher Counties, Texas, and was formed by water erosion—in the upper reaches by Palo Duro Creek, an intermittent stream, and in the lower by the Prairie Dog Town Fork of Red River, formed by the joining of Palo Duro and Tierra Blanco Creeks. Cedar, cottonwood, and wild china furnished fuel, and the grass was abundant on the protected floor of the canyon. Palo Duro is a Spanish name meaning "hard wood" and comes from the hard cedar brush from which the Indians made arrows. The recesses of the canyon and of nearby breaks at the edge of the Caprock were favored winter campsites of the Indians because of the protection they provided against the dreaded Plains northers and the easy access to fuel, water, and grass.

There was no trail from the rim to the canyon floor at the point where the Fourth Cavalry sighted the tepees far below them. The troops turned down the canyon rim (southeastward) and soon located an Indian game trail they could use for the descent. As the first troopers were about halfway down the trail, an Indian gave a warning whoop, discharged his rifle, and began waving his blanket. He was killed, but only after he had succeeded in giving the alarm. The Indians stampeded up the canyon, trying to round up their horses as they fled.

It seems fairly clear that the Indians did not expect the Fourth to find them so quickly or to attack so suddenly. On the night of the twenty-sixth about 10:30 P.M., while Mackenzie and the Fourth were still some miles south of the Canyon on the High Plains, the Indians had attempted to stampede the horses. Mackenzie had learned his lesson well in the campaign of 1871 and this time the horses were securely staked, with "sleeping parties" inside the herd. The attack was renewed about five o'clock on the morning of the twenty-seventh but the firing was at long range and little damage was done. After daylight Troops E and H charged the Indians, who mounted and galloped off, there being about three hundred of them. The Indians soon disappeared as completely as if the ground had opened to swallow them.

The Fourth returned to camp and after eating and checking guns and gear set out to the north about 3 P.M. After a twelve-hour march there was a halt, but within a half hour after the troopers had spread their blankets on the wet ground they were ordered to saddle up. Mackenzie's scouts had arrived with news just after the troopers bedded down. By 4 A.M. they were riding north again, and at dawn they found the Indians in the canyon. Almost certainly Indian scouts had watched the troopers bed down at 3 A.M. Evidently they then withdrew and hastened to the canyon to report. The diversionary tactics of September 26 and 27 had failed and the Fourth was getting perilously close to the Indian winter quarters. One wonders what the Indian strategy would have been on the morning of the twenty-eighth if the Fourth had not surprised them in camp.

Troop A, Captain (Brevet Lieutenant Colonel) Eugene B. Beaumont commanding, was first down the narrow trail, and as soon as the last man and horse had reached the bottom, A Troop mounted again and started up the canyon (northwest) after the fleeing Indians and their poines. Troops H and L soon joined A. The Indians left tepees, buffalo robes, blankets, food—in fact, all their possessions—behind as they fled, so complete was the surprise. Troop A was successful in capturing most of the Indian horses after a fast two-mile dash up the canyon. As the Indians recovered somewhat from the unexpected attack, they began to shoot from positions high up the sides of the canyon walls and from behind trees and boulders on the floor. Troops D, I, and K dismounted and after taking up protected positions facing the Indians kept up a long range exchange with them.

About noon Colonel Mackenzie saw some Indians on the rim of the canyon and, fearing that they would try to block the trail the Fourth had used, ordered Captain Gunther to take Troop H back down the canyon to the trail and climb to the rim, to assure an open retreat line. Troop H won the race easily, as the Indians had to cross a deep side canyon to reach the Fourth's down trail.

While Troops D, I, and K held the Indians in check, the rest of the command pulled down the lodges, chopped up the lodge poles, gathered and piled the Indians' belongings, and made numerous huge bonfires. The villages or groups of lodges were scattered along the canyon floor for a distance of more than two miles and, as the Indians saw all their possessions go up in smoke, they increased the tempo of their firing but with little effect against the cool veterans of the Fourth Cavalry.

Courtesy National Archives

PROBABLY THE LAST PHOTOGRAPH
OF LIEUTENANT COLONEL GEORGE A. CUSTER
(CHAPTER 20)

Courtesy National Archives

THE INDIAN LEADERS
Red Cloud   *Sitting Bull*
Gall   *Crow King*
(CHAPTER 20)

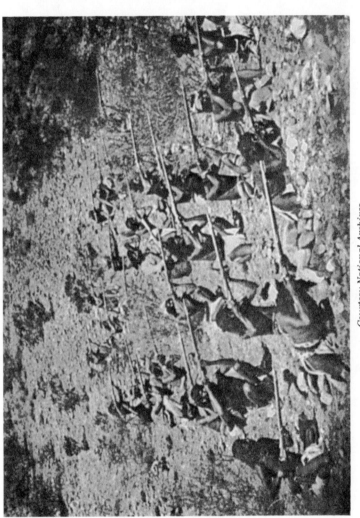

Courtesy National Archives

APACHE SCOUTS STRIPPED FOR BATTLE (CHAPTER 21)

THE RENEGADE APACHES KILL A WHITE RANCHER
(CHAPTER 21)

MILES FOLLOWED ORDERS
AND TRIED TO WIN WITH THE REGULARS
(CHAPTER 21)

D. Harper Simms Collection

Kayitah   *Martine*
THE SCOUTS WHO NEGOTIATED THE SURRENDER

This photo was made years later on the Reservation.
(CHAPTER 21)

Courtesy Oregon Historical Society
THE ARMY'S UMATILLA ALLIES
(CHAPTER 22)

Courtesy Historical Society of Montana

BANNACKS CAPTURED BY GENERAL MILES

(CHAPTER 22)

THE MILK CREEK BATTLE MONUMENT
(CHAPTER 23)

DULL KNIFE'S DEFIANCE
by Maynard Dixon

Dull Knife refusing to lead his
band back to the reservation in
Indian Territory (Oklahoma).
(CHAPTER 24)

Courtesy Nebraska State Historical Society

BURYING THE DEAD AT WOUNDED KNEE
(CHAPTER 25)

Troop A drove the horse herd down the Canyon to the escape trail and then up the narrow, twisting trail to the rim—no mean feat. As soon as the bonfires began to burn out, Colonel Mackenzie ordered the Fourth out of the Canyon. By 4 P.M. the battle of Palo Duro Canyon was over and the Fourth was back on the Staked Plains with the captured herd of horses.

Mackenzie formed the Fourth Cavalry into a "hollow square" with the captured Indian ponies inside the square. The living corral marched about twenty miles before reaching the wagon supply train at Tule Canyon at 1 A.M. The captured ponies were driven into a corral formed by the wagons and a strong guard was mounted. After a cup of coffee the Fourth turned in, having first fed their horses a full ration of corn.

On the morning of the twenty-ninth the Fourth had its first real meal in forty-eight hours. After breakfast, Colonel Mackenzie ordered a detail to kill the captured Indian horses. After the Tonkaway scouts had selected the best for their own use and to replace the cavalry horses which had been wounded or died during the campaign, the order was carried out. The number killed has been variously estimated at from a thousand to twenty-two hundred. The destruction of the horse herd was the second and fatal blow that Mackenzie dealt the Indians in this battle—the first was the burning of their lodges and other possessions on the floor of the canyon on September 28.

The battle of the Palo Duro cannot be classed as great on the basis of the number of Indians (or troopers) killed. The losses of the Fourth were negligible, while the Indians, according to interviews with participants after they returned to their reservation, lost from fifty to sixty warriors. In addition, the Indians lost fifteen warriors including the famous Kiowa chief, Woman's Heart (a participant in the assault on Adobe Walls in June), in the skirmish near Tule Canyon on the twenty-seventh. There is no doubt that the Fourth could have killed many more warriors in the battle on September 28. But this would have meant exposing the troopers to fire from the Indians in very strong positions on the slopes of the canyon walls and the storming of boulder- and tree-protected positions the Indian occupied on the canyon floor. At one point on the morning of the twenty-eighth,

Troop H lost six or eight horses as a result of Indian fire from positions high up the canyon wall. Captain Gunther ordered his men to dismount and to clear the bluffs. Colonel Mackenzie countermanded the order and told the captain that not a trooper would have lived to reach the Indians' position.

Colonel Mackenzie's strategy was sound. He surprised the Indians in their winter quarters, not a war camp. Their women and children were with them and so were all their possessions, their wealth being reckoned primarily in horses and buffalo robes. The surprise attack which caused the Indians to flee up the canyon with only their arms, followed by the quick capture of the horse herd, allowed Mackenzie to keep them at a distance while he burned their belongings. This saved the lives of a number of Cavalry troopers and made it unnecessary to hunt down and kill the warriors, who, once over their initial panic, had taken up strong positions on the steep sides and floor of the Palo Duro.

Mackenzie's job was done—he had made it mandatory that the Indians go back to the reservation. Winter was coming on—there had been a wet norther on September 24—and the Indians—without horses, buffalo robes, or food—had no choice. The dream of the wild, free life was over for the moment and almost immediately the Indians began to drift back to the reservations. By October 3, when the Fourth marched north again, not an Indian was to be found in the side ravines and arroyos or anywhere else in the Palo Duro.

Colonel Mackenzie's strategy was based on considerable experience on the frontier. He had participated in the 1871 campaign to drive Kicking Bird's band of Kiowas onto the Fort Sill reservation. Later that fall he campaigned against the Quahadi Comanches on the Staked Plains. He fought the Indians and Mexican bandits on the Rio Grande, and in 1873 he had created an international incident by his famous raid into Mexico to destroy a bandit stronghold.

In a letter to a friend many years later, Captain Robert G. Carter, who was with Colonel Mackenzie as his field adjutant in both his Staked Plains campaigns (1871 and 1874) and on the raid into Mexico, described him as follows:

He was five feet, nine inches, in height; was very thin and spare and did not weigh over 145 pounds. Later, when he was made a brigadier general he gained flesh and may have weighed 160, but never 175 pounds. Most of the time he commanded the Fourth Cavalry. He was fretful, irritable, oftentimes irascible and pretty hard to serve with. This was due largely to his failing to take care of himself and his three wounds received during the Civil War, plus a bad arrow wound in his thigh in the 1871 campaign. He kept late hours, ate but little and slept less than anybody in the regiment. But he was not a martinet and was always just to all the officers and men. He finally broke down from worry and neglect in keeping up his strength by proper food and sleep.

Mackenzie was a poor rider. He could not ride more than 25 to 30 miles without being in great pain and yet he rode 160 miles in 32 hours when we crossed the Rio Grande River in 1873, without, so far as I can recall, a single murmur or sign of exhaustion, although many of our men after going without sleep for 3 nights had hallucinations and showed signs of exhaustion and incipient insanity.

He was so careless about his clothes on a campaign that in 1871—when we followed the Northern or Quahadi Comanches out on the Staked Plains and lost them at dusk in a black, sleeting norther—the men had to pull a buffalo robe off a pack mule and wrap it about him to keep him from freezing to death.

Mackenzie hung on like a bull dog until the Indians begged him to let go. He had more brains than Custer, better judgment, and he carefully planned his attacks, providing for all emergencies, inspecting the arms and ammunition, and ordering all surplus ammunition to be carried by the men instead of placing it in the saddle pockets to be secured by the Indians by stampeding the horses.

Furthermore, all of his officers were loyal to him. There was no Reno or Benteen clique and there was always *good team-work. He had many faults, but I always thought that his wounds and his intense concentration upon his work—the work that kills—and his ambition to succeed was the cause of his breakdown and I really regarded him as our* best, most reliable *or* dependable *Indian fighter. If Grant selected him to hold down those conditions in 1876 [threatened election riots], it was because he thought he was the best man fitted for the job, just as he expressed in his memoirs, "Mackenzie is the most promising young officer in the army." He had an indomitable will, wonderful powers of endurance and unsurpassed courage.*

Mackenzie and the Fourth Cavalry in the three days, September 27–29, made the rest of the 1874 campaign just a mopping-up operation. They destroyed the Southern Plains or Horse Indians' ability to make war—particularly the ability to raid into Mexico and to fall unexpectedly on isolated ranches, frontier settlements, and wagon trains. The Kiowa and the Comanche lodges were the first in the path of the charging Fourth and their losses were particularly heavy. The Cheyenne lodges were the farthest from the point of attack and the Cheyennes saved a few horses by mounting and deserting their allies. The Indians, surprised, defeated, and now poor in worldly goods (horses and robes), went back to Indian Territory and their reservations to live on government rations. The battle of Palo Duro Canyon was a great Indian fight because of its results—it opened the way for the settlement and development of the famed Staked Plains of Texas and New Mexico. In 1876 Charles G. Goodnight, Texas and Colorado cowman, moved a herd of cattle into the Palo Duro Canyon. For many years the battleground of September 28, 1874, was a part of the great JA Ranch—a partnership venture between Colonel Goodnight and a wealthy Irish family, the Adairs. It was the first permanent ranch established in the Texas Panhandle.

PART X

The Northern Plains 1876

Introduction

The plan used on the Southern Plains in 1874 to defeat the Comanches and their allies proved so successful that General Phil Sheridan, commanding the Division of the Missouri, used it again in the campaign of 1876 against the Sioux and their allies. This was the simple tactic of convergence, *the sending of a number of columns of troops into the country where the Indians were known to be, to hunt them out and bring them to battle. The story of the Indian Wars (there were some notable exceptions, of course —see Chaps. 10, 11, and 12) was generally one of the Army spending much of its time and energy in trying to locate the hostiles. The Indians, on the other hand, spent most of their time and energy trying to evade the soldiers and to avoid any contest where the odds were not overwhelmingly in their favor.*

General Sheridan knew that the Sioux, accompanied by a considerable number of Cheyennes, were somewhere in the Powder River country. Many of the bands of these tribes had failed to report to the reservations when ordered to do so by the Commissioner of Indian Affairs in December 1875. The recalcitrant tribesmen had been joined by other restless Sioux and Cheyennes, who deserted the Great Sioux Reservation in the spring of 1876. This reservation, embracing that part of the present State of South Dakota west of the Missouri River, was created in accordance with the treaty made with Sioux and Cheyennes at Fort Laramie (Wyoming) in 1868.

The Laramie treaty also set aside as unceded Indian territory a vast tract of land vaguely limited to "that country north of the

North Platte River and east of the summits of the Big Horn Mountains." Sitting Bull, medicine man of the Hunkpapas, remained with a small band in the unceded territory. Northern Pacific Railroad surveying parties, with military escorts, invaded the unceded territory in 1872 and 1873, but the Custer expedition to the Black Hills in 1874 was a major cause of the angry disaffection of the Indians. Geologists accompanying the expedition discovered gold in the Black Hills, and a stampede started, which the Army failed to halt. The Black Hills held a special religious significance for the Sioux and were well within the boundaries of their reservation. The desecration of their holy places plus the inefficiency of the administration of Indian affairs on the reservation ended the uneasy peace that had prevailed since 1868.

In 1875 chief after chief, with their bands, quietly left the reservation to rendezvous in the unceded territory. The Indian agents, with the reservation nearly deserted and border tensions and depredations increasing, prevailed on the Commissioner to issue the order that virtually wiped out the provision of the Laramie treaty concerning the unceded territory—by barring its use by the Indians. This order to the Indians to return to the reservations only added fuel to the flame and was directly responsible for an appeal by the Commissioner of Indian Affairs to the Army to drive the Indians out of the unceded territory and back to the reservation.

Convergence on the hostiles resulted in Brigadier General Alfred H. Terry's column marching west from Fort Abraham Lincoln, Dakota Territory (located across the Missouri from the present site of Bismarck, North Dakota). His column included the Seventh Cavalry, Lieutenant Colonel (Brevet Major General) George Armstrong Custer commanding. General George Crook marched north from Fort Fetterman and Colonel John Gibbon, with about five hundred men from the Second Cavalry and Seventh Infantry, moved east from Fort Ellis in western Montana. The columns were ordered to co-operate but each was really an independent striking force, and their first responsibility was to find the Indians. What happened when they did is set forth in Chapters 19 and 20.

In the weeks following the Little Bighorn fight, reinforcements *poured into the area and Terry and Crook joined forces. With their thirty-six hundred men they were unable to find the Sioux. A part of Crook's troops did succeed in capturing American Horse's village at Slim Buttes, on the northern tip of the Black Hills, and in November Colonel Ranald S. Mackenzie and the Fourth Cavalry, veterans of the Comanche campaign of 1874 (Chap. 18), destroyed Dull Knife's village in the Big Horn Mountains. General Nelson A. Miles intercepted Sitting Bull's band in October and after a two-day running fight, induced five of the principal chiefs and over two thousand of their followers to surrender and to return to the reservation.*

When Crook and Terry left the field for the winter, Miles remained with the Fifth Infantry and part of the Twenty-second Infantry to garrison a post at the mouth of the Tongue River (near the present site of Miles City, Montana). Miles, not satisfied to spend the winter in camp, conducted an amazing winter campaign that brought the Sioux to terms. The Indians did not like to fight in the winter and it is likely that they regarded Miles' tactics of searching out their winter camps as highly unethical. Even when the temperature dropped to fifty below and deep snow covered the ground the infantry was on the move—for example, in January 1877 Miles attacked Crazy Horse's band on the Tongue when the snow was a foot deep, and during the fight it started to storm again. The Indians were defeated. Miles maintained an extensive Indian spy system and his intelligence of the moves of the hostiles was of a high order. He harried them from winter camp to winter camp, and the surprise attacks plus the judicious use of artillery (kept under canvas-covered frames with the wagon train until the enemy was engaged) made conditions so disagreeable for the Sioux that they were ready to return to their reservations. Whenever there was an opportunity Miles negotiated with them, and his diplomacy and personal integrity won the respect of several of the chiefs, who surrendered (unconditionally) and with their bands were escorted back to the Indian agencies. By the summer of 1877 the fighting was all but over.

Only Sitting Bull and a small core of die-hards refused to surrender. They fled across the border into Canada that summer of

1877 and for four years raided back into Montana in search of food and loot. Miles, from his base at Fort Keogh, kept close watch on Sitting Bull's foragers, and his patrols continually harassed them. His band dwindling and his chiefs defecting, Sitting Bull finally surrendered at Fort Buford in 1881.

19. THE BATTLE OF THE ROSEBUD

J. A. LEERMAKERS

Only students of the Indian Wars of the '60s and '70s appreciate the significance of General George Crook's fight on the Rosebud on June 17, 1876, with the Indian forces which so soundly defeated the Seventh Cavalry on the Little Bighorn eight days later. Indeed, it seems reasonable to say that the Battle of the Little Bighorn would not have been fought or would have ended quite differently had Crook's campaign been successful or had he taken what appears at this late date to have been reasonable action, by sending information about the fight to the military forces under Terry.

The Rosebud battlefield is in Montana. It is about forty miles north of Sheridan, Wyoming, and sixteen miles north of Decker,

225

Montana, from which it is reached over an all-weather gravel road. A large sign to the right of the road clearly marks the location. The Custer battlefield on the Little Bighorn is about thirty-five miles northwest, on the other side of the low Rosebud Mountains.

Crook's campaign of 1876 was part of the general plan of convergence. He had made an unsuccessful foray from Fort Fetterman against the "hostiles" in March, which culminated in the Reynolds fight on the Little Powder River. Colonel James Reynolds' troops succeeded in surprising a winter camp of Cheyennes but let victory slip from their grasp by retiring from the field.

Crook set out on the old Bozeman Trail from Fort Fetterman on May 29 with fifteen companies of cavalry and five of infantry, totaling 1002 men and 47 officers. In addition, there were a number of civilian packers and teamsters. Frank Grouard, Louis Richards, and Baptiste Pourier were guides. Five representatives of the press accompanied the expedition, including John J. Finnerty. On Clear Creek, a party of 65 miners fell in with the column. They remained with the troops and took an active part in the Rosebud fight. On June 8 Crook received dispatches that a large group of Shoshones from their Wind River reservation would soon join him. On June 9, on Tongue River, the camp was vigorously attacked from the surrounding hills by a party of Sioux and Cheyennes who were driven off after wounding two soldiers and killing a few horses. After several days, Crook moved back to the junction of the two forks of Goose Creek, near present Sheridan, Wyoming, where he went into camp.

On June 14, 176 well-armed and well-mounted Crow Indians joined the camp, accompanied by the three guides who had been sent some days earlier to enlist their help in the campaign. Captain John G. Bourke, soldier and historian, states that the Crows informed Crook of Gibbon's position on the Yellowstone, opposite the mouth of the Rosebud, and of the location of the hostile Indians on Tongue River to the north. Grouard says that he told Crook the Indians were on the Rosebud. The night of the fourteenth, 86 Shoshones, also well armed, came into camp, bringing the number of Indian allies to 262. Three Texas hunters came in with the Shoshones. The entire force thus totaled well over 1300.

Crook now made his final plans for an offensive. The wagons were to be left behind, and each officer and cavalryman was to carry four days' rations in his saddlebags, one blanket, and one hundred rounds of ammunition in belts or pouches. Infantrymen who could ride were to be mounted on mules from the pack train. If a hostile camp were located and successfully attacked, the troops would push on to join Gibbon on the Yellowstone.

June 15 was spent in making final preparations and in mounting on mules the 175 infantrymen who could ride and who elected to go along on the march. The others remained to guard the wagons and supplies left behind.

At 5 A.M. on the sixteenth, the command headed west to Tongue River, which it followed downstream to the northwest. In the early afternoon, scouts far in advance reported that they had found the trail of a very large village of the enemy, and the Indian allies became much excited. The column then turned to the left, over an elevated tableland, toward the headwaters of the Rosebud. Buffalo were found widely scattered over the country-side, and the Indians killed a number, with no regard for the warning which their gunfire might give the Sioux and Cheyennes. The march continued to the extreme source of the south fork of the Rosebud, where camp was made after a day's journey of between thirty-five and forty miles.

When Crook left Fort Fetterman the last part of May, the Sioux and Cheyennes were in camp on the Rosebud about twenty miles above the mouth of the stream, where Bradley, on scout with Gibbon's command, saw the smoke of their village. It was here that the Indians who had wintered on Powder River were joined by large numbers of Sioux and Cheyennes from the agencies. The total number of warriors in the combined bands is estimated to have been about two thousand. The Indians slowly moved up the Rosebud and were informed by a party of Cheyennes from the reservation that troops were out looking for them. About June 10 they set up camp a few miles north of the present Busby, Montana. There the Sioux had a great Sun Dance in which Sitting Bull took an important part, giving one hundred pieces of flesh (skin sliced from his arms with a sharp knife). And he had a vision of defeating the soldiers, which fired the Indians with enthusiasm for a fight. The Indians left the Sun Dance camp and moved up the Rosebud to Davis Creek, about twenty miles north of the battle area, on the fifteenth of June. The next day they went west up Davis Creek. They crossed the divide between the Little Bighorn and the Rosebud, and camped the night of June 16 at the forks of Reno Creek.

The Indians were well informed of the movements of Crook's forces. Wooden Leg and ten other Cheyennes who had been scouting for them, had found them in the vicinity of Sheridan, Wyoming, and had brought word back to the Davis Creek camp. On the evening of the sixteenth, Cheyenne scouts under Little Hawk reported that the troops were on the upper branches of the Rosebud, about twenty miles away.

There are a number of different accounts of the happenings on the night of the sixteenth in the Indian camps. It is known, however, that a large force of Sioux and Cheyennes used the cover of night to reach a point in the hills near the Rosebud about five miles from Crook's camp.

The stage was set in the early morning of June 17. The soldiers were in their camp at the head of the south fork; the Indians perhaps five miles downstream, hidden behind a high hill north of the valley of the river. There were something over a thousand soldiers, civilians, and Indian allies with Crook; a thousand Sioux and Cheyennes awaited their march down the river. The troops and their allies were well armed with breech-loading rifles; the Indians with some old and a few semi-modern rifles as well as their primitive weapons, the bow and arrow and spear. Both troops and Indians were well mounted. The Indians had an advantage in their knowledge of the terrain, but Grouard also knew the country intimately. So did Pourier and most of the other scouts, and all the Crows and Shoshones. The hostiles had just ridden twenty miles and their horses were tired; the troops were reasonably fresh. Many of Crook's troops were unseasoned in Indian warfare; the Sioux and Cheyennes were veteran warriors.

All in all, the odds were about even—except for one factor. Crook thought that the Indian camp was downstream only a few

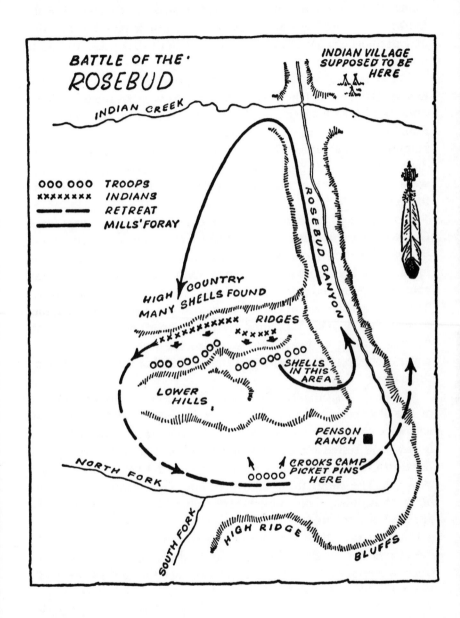

BATTLE OF THE·
ROSEBUD

INDIAN VILLAGE
SUPPOSED TO BE
HERE

INDIAN CREEK

ROSEBUD CANYON

ooo ooo   TROOPS
xxxxxxxx   INDIANS
――――   RETREAT
━━━━   MILLS' FORAY

HIGH COUNTRY
MANY SHELLS FOUND

RIDGES

SHELLS
IN THIS
AREA

LOWER
HILLS

PENSON
RANCH

NORTH FORK

CROOKS CAMP
PICKET PINS
HERE

SOUTH FORK

HIGH RIDGE

BLUFFS

miles, at the lower end of the so-called Rosebud Canyon. It was known that there had been a succession of camps on the Rosebud, and perhaps Grouard had led him to believe that there was still a camp there.

The canyon of the Rosebud deserves special mention because it was given so much prominence by eyewitnesses who subsequently wrote about the battle. Crook writes of a deep canyon; Bourke that "it formed a veritable cul-de-sac, the vertical walls hemming in the sides"; Finnerty, the reporter, describes it as a dark, winding, and narrow defile; Grouard states that the sides were a thousand feet high and that the Indians had all of this fortified.

It is difficult to understand these exaggerated descriptions. Granted that the sides of the canyon were overgrown with timber, nowhere are there vertical narrow walls. The sides are sloping and the bottom at least a quarter mile wide at all points. The country is open and the Rosebud flows through a wide flat valley. The hills, where most of the fighting occurred, rise in a succession of several low folds separated by the beds of small dry watercourses leading eastward and south to the river. There is little cover except rock outcroppings at the east end of the field, toward the canyon.

At sunrise on June 17, the troops started down the south fork of the Rosebud, and at some time between 8 and 10 A.M.—the accounts vary—they halted short of the Big Bend, unbridled the horses, and rested for about a half hour. A shot was heard from the north, and very soon a small number of Crow scouts came racing to the camp from that direction. They reported a large body of hostiles, who immediately followed over the hills and attacked the column.

Finnerty says that the Indian allies were panic-stricken and the troops deployed up the hill. Grouard claims that the troops were not prepared and that the Crows met the first attack and saved the column, fighting for twenty minutes before the troops entered the fight; after this the Crows and Shoshones kept back of the troops. On the other hand, Captain Anson Mills, battalion commander (Senior Captain), reported that he was the first to see the Indians from a high hill on the south of the river and alerted the troops. The Indian accounts report the meeting of their scouts with the Crows and the retreat of the latter to the camp.

Mills gives the disposition of the troops, by companies, during the fight, but space does not permit a detailed account here. After the initial attack, the troops charged. Mills was on the extreme right, and his description of the Indians and the fighting is vivid:

> *We met the Indians at the foot of this ridge, and charged right in and through them, driving them back to the top of the ridge. These Indians were most hideous, every one being painted in most hideous colors and designs, stark naked, except their moccasins, breech clouts and head gear, the latter consisting of feathers and horns; some of the horses being also painted, and the Indians proved then and there that they were the best cavalry soldiers on earth. In charging up towards us they exposed little of their person, hanging on with one arm around the neck and one leg over the horse, firing and lancing from underneath the horses' necks, so that there was no part of the Indian at which we could aim.*
>
> *Their shouting and personal appearance was so hideous that it terrified the horses more than our men and rendered them almost uncontrollable before we dismounted and placed them behind the rocks.*
>
> *The Indians came not in a line but in flocks or herds like the buffalo, and they piled in upon us until I think there must have been one thousand or fifteen hundred in our immediate front, but they refused to fight when they found us secured behind the rocks, and bore off to our left. I then charged the second ridge, and took it in the same manner and fortified myself with the horses protected behind the larger boulders and the men behind the smaller ones.*

The fighting now shifted to the left, where the soldiers were hotly pressed. Lieutenant Bourke rallied the Crows and Shoshones, who fiercely attacked the hostiles in hand-to-hand fighting, the troops stopping their firing for fear of hitting their Indian allies. The Sioux and Cheyennes pressed the attack in this sector so vigorously, Finnerty states, that only the courage of the officers and men saved the troops from annihilation.

During the fighting the men of the pack train and the Montana miners were in the center of the line, protected behind some rocks in advance of the troops. According to Bourke, their sharp-shooting was so effective that the Indians stayed well away from them. Finnerty also praises their coolness and deadly fire. When Mills pulled out of his position, these men held the space he had occupied.

The Indian accounts of the fighting stress the intensity of their charges and the hand-to-hand combat. The warriors showed surprising spirit. Abandoning their old practice of hovering at a distance and taking few chances, they rode in among the troops to engage in hand-to-hand encounters. According to Wooden Leg, the "Indians fought and ran away, fought and ran away." In part of the fighting, the soldiers were split in twos and threes, the Indians charging in and out among them.

Walter S. Campbell (Stanley Vestal), Indian historian, says that Sitting Bull was with the warriors all day, urging them on, but was too sore from the Sun Dance to take an active part in the fight, and that Crazy Horse was the real leader. Crazy Horse held the tribes together for a time, but the firing became so intense they split up into small groups, riding in and out among the troops. At one time the Sioux started to retreat. Crazy Horse and several other chiefs rallied them and drove the soldiers and their Indian allies back to the valley.

From all the accounts it is apparent that both Indians and troops fought hard and bravely; had the troops shown any sign of weakening, they would have been overwhelmed, as Custer was a few days later.

About noon, the fighting had shifted from Mills' front, and Crook ordered him to take eight companies of cavalry and proceed down the canyon to take the village. Crook was to follow with the rest of the command. The ride down the canyon was uneventful, although there was constant danger and fear of attack from the timbered sides. Mills reported that when he reached the vicinity of the village—which was, in reality, nowhere near—a messenger arrived with recall orders from Crook.

The battle ended at about 2:30 P.M. The Indians later said they were tired, their horses exhausted and many killed, and their ammunition used up, so they broke off the fight and returned to their camp. That night the camp moved to the valley of the Little Bighorn River.

There are three explanations of the recall of Mills' battalion: (1) the fear of ambush, (2) the need of the troops to attack the Indians from the rear, and (3) Crook's realization that he could not support Mills. Perhaps a combination of all three factors entered into Crook's decision. On Mills' return, Crook went into camp on the Rosebud, near where the first attack had occurred.

Crook reported 10 killed, including one Indian scout, and 21 wounded in the fight; 13 hostile scalps were taken. Bourke stated that the total loss was 57 killed or wounded; Finnerty, about 50 killed and wounded including the friendly Indians; and Grouard, 28 soldiers killed and 56 wounded, with one Indian scout killed and three wounded. The Indians later said their losses were 11 killed and five wounded. The troops buried their dead that night on the banks of the Rosebud, and great pains were taken to obliterate any traces of the graves.

On the morning of June 18, the command arose at dawn and set off on the return to the base camp on Goose Creek. Travois had been constructed, on which the wounded were dragged. The column moved relatively slowly because of the wounded and camped for the night on a tributary of the Tongue River, a few miles from camp. The Crows left that night, promising to return later. The next morning the command arrived back at the wagon train where, according to Mills, "General Crook and all of us made very brief reports of the fight, having little pride in our accomplishment."

Crook decided to send the wagon train to Fort Fetterman for supplies, and on the twenty-first the train left taking the wounded with it. On the same day the Shoshones left. Crook also sent for reinforcements, and while awaiting them occupied himself with hunting and fishing in the Big Horn Mountains. On or about July 12, dispatches arrived from General Terry about the fight of the Seventh Cavalry on the Little Bighorn; on July 13 supplies and reinforcements arrived from Fort Fetterman. Crook finally resumed the campaign on August 3.

The fight on the Rosebud marked a departure from the usual tactics of the Indians. For the first time a large number of tribes combined in a common cause, and although during the fight the warriors apparently acted as individuals or in small bands, they exhibited unprecedented group impetuosity, courage, and persistence. Indian warfare had up until this time consisted in taking few chances and attacking only when the odds were generously favorable. For some reason—desperation, the leadership of Crazy Horse and other Chiefs, or the incitement of Sitting Bull's vision —they fought spiritedly on land removed from the immediate defense of their village. To the military forces, this kind of Indian warfare was almost unprecedented. The Plains Indians were not supposed to take the offensive.

Crook's failure to win a decisive victory must be attributed at least as much to the Indians' courage and fighting ability as to any real or imagined shortcomings in military planning or execution. A new spirit and purpose came at the end of the Indians' freedom. Although inevitably they would have been broken, had the Indians developed these characteristics earlier, the price of their subjugation would have been higher than it was.

20. THE BATTLE OF THE LITTLE BIGHORN

ROBERT M. UTLEY

On July 6, 1876, a telegram was handed to the editor of the New York *Herald*: "Bismarck, D.T., July 5, 1876:—General Custer attacked the Indians June 25, and he, with every officer and man in five companies were killed. Reno with seven companies fought in intrenched position three days. The Bismarck Tribune's special correspondent was with the expedition and was killed." The next morning, newspapers all over the country proclaimed in lurid headlines the death of Custer and his command. The news stunned the East and alarmed the West. On that morning everyone from the man in the street to the man in the White House heatedly discussed the fate of Custer. As a topic of conversation, the fate of Custer was to lose little appeal in the next eighty-five years.

The Custer disaster came as the tragic climax of eight years of growing bitterness between red man and white. In 1868 the principal bands of Sioux and Cheyenne had gathered at Fort Laramie, Wyoming, to make peace with the United States. They had signed the Treaty of 1868, which brought to a close, on terms highly favorable to the Indians, the costly Red Cloud War.

The Laramie Treaty, it will be remembered, provided for creation of the Great Sioux Reservation in that part of the present State of South Dakota lying west of the Missouri River. Here those Indians who wished could settle near fixed agencies administered by the Indian Bureau. The treaty also set aside as unceded Indian territory a vast tract of land limited vaguely to "that country north of the North Platte River and east of the summits of the Big Horn Mountains." Most of the Sioux chose to live on the reservation. But a small band of irreconcilables, under the nominal leadership of the Hunkpapa medicine man Sitting Bull, remained in the unceded territory.

The westward advance of the frontier soon destroyed this *modus vivendi*. In 1872 and 1873 surveying parties staked out a line for the Northern Pacific Railroad in the Yellowstone Valley of Montana. In 1874 an exploring expedition under General Custer discovered gold in the Black Hills, sacred hunting grounds of the Sioux. Gold-seekers rushed to the region, and public opinion forced the Government to open negotiations for its purchase. The Sioux were angry, and the corruption and inefficiency that had long characterized the Indian Bureau did not improve their temper.

Tension mounted. Finally, in December 1875, the Commissioner of Indian Affairs ordered all Sioux living in the unceded country to gather within the Great Sioux Reservation by January 31, 1876, or be classed as hostiles subject to military action. When few complied, the Secretary of the Interior asked the Secretary of War to send troops after the hostiles.

Brigadier General George Crook and eight hundred men marched north from Fort Fetterman, Wyoming, on March 1,

1876. On March 17 part of this force, under Colonel J. J. Reynolds, surprised a winter camp of Cheyennes on the Little Powder River. Reynolds let victory slip from his grasp, and Crook, disheartened, returned to Fort Fetterman.

From the office of the Military Division of the Missouri in Chicago, Lieutenant General P. H. Sheridan then devised a more comprehensive campaign, with three columns to converge on the Indian country. Early in April 1876 Colonel John Gibbon and about five hundred men of the Second Cavalry and Seventh Infantry marched east from Fort Ellis, in western Montana. General Crook, his command reorganized, left Fort Fetterman on May 29 and marched north toward the head of Rosebud Creek.

The third and strongest column, over nine hundred men commanded by Brigadier General Alfred H. Terry, marched west from Fort Abraham Lincoln, Dakota Territory, on May 17. Backbone of Terry's command was the Seventh Cavalry, led by the dashing Lieutenant Colonel (Brevet Major General) George Armstrong Custer.* All twelve troops had been drawn together for the campaign, but the regiment still numbered only about six hundred men, many of them recruits. The exploits of the Seventh had become legend throughout the nation in the decade since the Civil War, and its commander had unlimited confidence that it could defeat any gathering of Indians on the plains. A Gatling Gun detachment from the Twentieth Infantry, and two companies of the Sixth Infantry and one of the Seventeenth to guard the wagon train, made up the balance of Terry's force.

General Terry had taken command at the last minute. Custer was to have headed the Fort Lincoln column. But in testifying before a Congressional committee he had criticized members of President Grant's personal and official family. He had been publicly rebuked and deprived of his command. Only at the last moment had the President, at the behest of Generals Sheridan and Terry, reluctantly permitted him to go along in command of his regiment but subordinate to Terry. Custer smarted under the

---

* Custer's actual rank was lieutenant colonel. He had been breveted major general during the Civil War and was thus entitled to be addressed as "General Custer."

humiliation, but whether or not it influenced his military judgment has long been a topic of controversy.

The crossing of the Little Missouri brought a flurry of excitement. Custer led a scouting party down the river to investigate rumors of Indians, but found no fresh signs. The troops pushed on through the badlands of Dakota and Montana and emerged in the valley of the Powder River a short distance above its confluence with the Yellowstone. Both Terry and Gibbon were to draw their supplies from river steamers plying the Yellowstone, and at the mouth of Glendive Creek Terry established a supply depot. A battalion of the Sixth Infantry came up the river from Fort Buford to man it. A week later the base was moved to the mouth of the Powder.

On the Powder Terry divided the Seventh Cavalry. The right wing, under Custer, marched along the south bank of the Yellowstone to the mouth of Rosebud Creek. Major Marcus A. Reno and the left wing struck south to scout the headwaters of the Powder and the Tongue. They rode clear into the valley of the Rosebud, where they found a fresh Indian trail that led across the Wolf Mountains and into the valley of a small stream that the Indians called the Greasy Grass, but which maps labeled the Little Bighorn. On this very day, June 17, General Crook was only forty miles to the south, also in the Rosebud Valley. A large force of Sioux under Crazy Horse blocked his advance and, after a sharp engagement, compelled him to fall back and establish camp on Goose Creek. Ignorant of Crook's reverse, Reno turned north and, on June 21, joined the rest of the Seventh at the mouth of the Rosebud.

That evening an air of excitement and expectancy pervaded the camp. The men argued over the evidence and speculated on what moves would be made. They agreed that all signs pointed to action. The band and wagon train had been left at the Powder River. During the morning Colonel Gibbon's Montana column had broken camp across the river and marched upstream to the west. The steamer *Far West*, commanded by Captain Grant Marsh, lay moored to the bank. Aboard, Terry conferred with Custer, Gibbon, and Major James Brisbin, who commanded Gibbon's cavalry.

The council of war concluded, Custer strode down the gang-plank of the *Far West* and ordered his trumpeter to sound "officers' call." The officers of the Seventh quickly assembled at the tent flying the red and blue pennant with white crossed sabers that marked regimental headquarters. Briskly, Custer outlined the plan for trapping the Sioux. Since the trail discovered by Major Reno led towards the Little Bighorn, the Indians were probably camped on that stream. The Seventh would march up the Rosebud, cross the Wolf Mountains, and move on to the Little Bighorn from the south. Terry would go with Gibbon, ascend the Bighorn, and enter the Little Bighorn Valley from the north. The Sioux would then be crushed between the two forces. The cavalry would travel light, carrying only essentials and relying on a mule train for rations and ammunition. Custer abolished the wing organization and made troop commanders responsible directly to him.

By noon the next day the regiment was prepared for the march. Terry, Gibbon, and Brisbin had remained behind to see the Seventh off, and joined Custer for a final review. Major Reno led the twelve troops past the four officers to the accompaniment of massed trumpets. Custer scarcely concealed his pride in them. But the mule train, an innovation in the Seventh, was already giving trouble. Packs slipped or stubborn animals shook free of their cargo. Terry's mild criticism brought a flush to Custer's face. The officers shook hands; Terry handed Custer a written copy of his instructions, and Custer, waving a last good-by, spurred to the head of his regiment. Dour old Gibbon, suffering from intestinal colic, flung a parting admonition. "Now Custer, don't be greedy. Wait for us." "No," came the answer, "I won't."

The following day, June 23, the regiment struck the hostile trail and passed through three abandoned campsites. Treading hooves pulverized the sandy soil, raising clouds of dust and covering horse and rider alike with fine yellow particles. The twenty-fourth was a repetition of the twenty-third. The troopers picked their way through what seemed to be one deserted camp after another. They were actually riding through the continuous camp of the same village. They also overlooked the significance of another portent. Numerous wickiups—temporary brush shelters housing a single warrior whose family had remained at the agency—cluttered the floor of the valley.

That night, twenty-eight miles from reveille, the regiment bivouacked in the shade of a steep bluff. The Crow Indian scouts, on loan from Gibbon, came in and reported that the trail ahead turned west and led over the Wolf Mountains into the Little Bighorn watershed. Custer pondered a moment, then, his decision made, had the exhausted officers roused and summoned to his bivouac. In short, nervous barks he outlined his plan. A night march would carry them across the mountains. While the troops concealed themselves and rested during the twenty-fifth, the scouts could reconnoiter and Terry and Gibbon would have time to reach the Little Bighorn. The Seventh would then attack the enemy on June 26.

Orders passed quickly. The troopers wearily remounted and the regiment pulled itself up the slope. The night grew black. Confusion spread through the ranks as they groped blindly through the maze of creek beds and ravines. Soon even Custer saw the futility of continuing the march. At 2 A.M., ten miles from the earlier camp, the cavalry halted to await daylight.

Meanwhile, Lieutenant Charles A. Varnum, Chief of Scouts, had taken his Crows and Arikaras ahead and found a mountaintop from which to scan the country west of the mountains. The scouts called it the Crow's Nest. Dawn revealed a furrowed plain falling away from the divide and stretching west to the snow-capped Big Horns on the horizon. A thread of green traced the meandering course of a small creek flowing from the divide toward the Little Bighorn, fifteen miles distant.

With the first light the scouts grew excited. They made vigorous signs and tried to point out for Varnum the cause of their excitement. Charlie Reynolds, civilian scout and veteran plainsman, saw it too. "Look for worms," he said. But the Lieutenant's untrained eye could not detect on the benchland west of the Little Bighorn the tiny dark smudge that, to the scouts, represented a large herd of ponies.

In the valley cut by the tree-lined Greasy Grass, the hostile camp shook itself awake. It was a village larger than the plains had ever known. From the Missouri River agencies the standard of Sitting Bull had drawn thousands of discontented Indians. A horde of Sioux—Hunkpapas under Gall and Crow King, Inkpaduta's band of Yanktonnais and Santees, Minneconjous under Lame Deer and Hump, Crazy Horse with the Oglalas—as well as Northern Cheyennes under Two Moon, had assembled in an immense native city. The population numbered close to fifteen thousand, with over three thousand fighting warriors. They were confident of their strength, having defeated Crook only a week earlier. Many owned rifles, some the new Winchester repeater. The hostiles had been in the Little Bighorn valley only a few days. The ponies were thriving on the pasturage of the Greasy Grass. Hunters, scouting miles in every direction, brought fresh meat daily. Toward this powerful alliance rode Custer's six hundred cavalrymen, ignorant of the odds—a day ahead of Gibbon's infantry and cavalry and Lieutenant Low's Gatling Guns.

Back at the Crow's Nest Lieutenant Varnum had sent for Custer. But the sun had risen and an obscuring mist hung over the hills below. With his glasses Custer searched the prairie, but could see no pony herd. The scouts were mistaken, he said, and returned to the regiment.

Although he had not seen the pony herd, Custer knew that the village had to be nearby. He understood also that his presence would soon be known to the Sioux leaders, for Indians had been seen watching the activity on the Crow's Nest, and Sergeant Curtis, retracing the route of the night march to search for lost supplies, had found a group of warriors opening a box of hard bread dropped from a pack mule. In Indian warfare surprise was essential. If the Sioux learned of the approach of soldiers, they would probably flee in all directions. Although Gibbon was not yet in position (actually he was lost in the maze of badlands along the Bighorn), Custer quickly reached his decision. The first trumpet call in three days echoed in the hills, and the Seventh Cavalry jolted expectantly up the slope to the crest of the divide.

Shortly after noon the command topped the divide and halted. Custer and his adjutant, Lieutenant W. W. Cooke, moved to one side. As they talked, Cooke made notations in his memorandum book. Captain Frederick W. Benteen and H Troop, in the lead, surveyed the wrinkled landscape. They were at the head of a small stream (later to take the name of Reno Creek) that merged in the distance with the faint trace of green which marked the Little Bighorn. Custer and the adjutant concluded their discussion and Cooke rapidly broke the regiment into battalions.

The first three troops in line—H under Captain Benteen, D under Captain Thomas B. Weir, and K under Lieutenant Edward S. Godfrey—made up the first battalion. Benteen, senior captain of the regiment, commanded. He signaled left oblique and the three troops wheeled towards a line of bluffs two miles distant with orders to "pitch into anything you might find." No sooner had the battalion disappeared among the hills than Chief Trumpeter Voss galloped after it with further instructions to continue to the second line of bluffs if nothing were found at the first.

The next three troops in line were M, A, and G, under Captain Thomas French, Captain Myles Moylan, and Lieutenant Donald McIntosh, respectively. These Cooke assigned to Major Reno. Custer himself took direct command of Troops C, E, F, I, and L, led by Captain Thomas W. Custer (the commander's brother), Lieutenant Algernon E. Smith, Captain George W. Yates, Captain Myles W. Keogh, and Lieutenant James Calhoun (Custer's brother-in-law). Lieutenant Edward G. Mathey was placed in charge of the mule train, and Captain Thomas McDougall's B Troop, detailed to guard the packs, brought up the rear. Reno's 112 men started down the left bank of what later became Reno Creek, while Custer's 231 troopers took the right bank. The two columns rode parallel, one on each side of the stream, making for the Little Bighorn.

Fifteen minutes later Custer motioned Sergeant Major W. W. Sharrow forward and sent him to Benteen with further instructions: if no sign of Indians were found, continue the march towards the Little Bighorn and send word of any new developments. Two hours and ten miles later Custer and Reno encountered a lone tepee standing in the valley on the right bank of the creek. The two columns halted. Peering inside, the Arikara scouts saw the body of a Sioux warrior (killed in the battle with Crook on June 17) and jubilantly set fire to the lodge. But Custer was more intent upon a heavy cloud of dust rising from behind the rampart of bluffs that hid the Little Bighorn from view. It could mean only one thing, the Sioux village. To Custer, it also meant fleeing Sioux.

Fred Gerard, civilian scout, had mounted a nearby knoll. Suddenly he pointed towards the river and shouted, "There are your Indians, General, running like devils!" Custer saw some forty warriors bolting for the stream. He ordered the Arikaras to pursue, but they refused. He then turned to Cooke and barked some orders. Cooke wheeled his mount to Reno. "General Custer directs that you take as fast a gait as you deem prudent and charge afterward," he relayed, "and you will be supported by the whole outfit."

Reno's battalion moved out at a trot, Custer following. The Indian scouts fell in with Reno. The command descended the slope to the river, a low hill on the right intervening to mask Custer's battalion. As the formation hit the stream, the thirsty horses stopped to drink and plunged the column into confusion.

Captain Keogh and Lieutenant Cooke, who had accompanied Reno to the river, turned their horses and started back to Custer. They were soon overtaken by Fred Gerard, who told them that the Sioux were not fleeing, as Custer thought, but were riding forth to meet Reno. Gerard returned to Reno, while Cooke and Keogh hastened to give Custer this information. They found that he had left Reno's trail and turned right, heading north towards the ominous dust cloud.

Meanwhile, Benteen had found the "valley hunting" excursion exhausting to men and horses as the terrain grew steadily rougher. Lieutenant Francis Gibson, out in front observing from each succeeding ridge, detected nothing. Finally the battalion turned right and intersected the trail of Custer and Reno. Halting at a morass near the forks of Reno Creek, the cavalrymen watered their horses. As they resumed the march the pack train, McDougall's B Troop riding herd, arrived. The thirsty mules plunged into the morass and promptly became mired.

Sergeant Daniel Kanipe of C Troop galloped up to McDougall. He had been detailed by Custer, he explained, to bring the packs up with all possible haste. He had given the message to Benteen, who had ordered it carried back to McDougall. The packers doubled their efforts to re-form the mule train.

Ahead, Benteen reached the burning tepee, where he met another messenger from Custer, Trumpeter Giovanni Martini. He had been pursued by Sioux, and his horse was bleeding from a bullet wound. Martini saluted and handed Benteen a crumpled scrap of paper torn from Cooke's memorandum book: "Benteen: Come on. Big village. Be Quick. Bring Packs. W. W. Cooke, Adjt. P. S. Bring Pacs."

At the ford of the Little Bighorn, Reno's horses had finished drinking and the major re-formed the three troops on the left bank of the river. It was 2:30 P.M. by Lieutenant George D. Wallace's watch when the column took up the trot toward the dust cloud rising from behind a strip of timber two miles down the Little Bighorn Valley.

Reno rose in his stirrups and signalled the battalion into battle line, Troop A on the left, M on the right, and G in the rear as reserve. Varnum's Arikara scouts formed on the left of A Troop. The cavalry raced down the valley towards the timber.

The Arikara scouts panicked and the left flank began to disintegrate. Reno motioned McIntosh to oblique his reserve troop into the left of the line. The storm of dust grew in intensity, and large numbers of mounted warriors began to appear. Glancing to the rear, Reno saw no sign of the support promised by Custer. Flinging his arm into the air, he shouted, "Prepare to fight on foot!" Before even striking the enemy, the charge ground to a milling halt.

The troopers detailed to hold the horses grabbed the reins of the horses and galloped to the rear. A thin skirmish line stretched across the valley, the right flank anchored on a bend of the river, the left flank reaching for the low hills that rose to the tableland on the west. Carbines cracked at the whooping warriors. The recruits fired rapidly and wildly, but the Indians did not better. Officers paced the line attempting to control and direct the fire.

Fearing that his horses would stampede, Reno pulled Troop G from the line and formed it as a horse guard. The line stretched taut in an effort to close the gap. But the Sioux were now filtering around the exposed left flank and threatening to mass in the rear. Reno saw the threat. He scanned the terrain and picked out a natural parapet, formed by the changing course of the river, within the fringe of cottonwood trees on the right flank. Quickly he ordered the line shifted into the timber and re-formed in the new position.

This movement brought little improvement. Matted underbrush made control of the battalion almost impossible. Warriors worked their way into the timber and infiltrated the disjointed line. Others gathered on the east bank of the river to fire into Reno's rear. Arrows and bullets of every caliber laced the cottonwood grove but produced few casualties.

The battalion had fought about ten minute on the skirmish line and half an hour in the timber when Reno, astride his horse in a clearing, decided to seek still another position. He shouted the command to mount, but only those nearby heard and obeyed. The word spread, however, as some followed the example of others and climbed into their saddles. At this crucial moment a stray bullet struck the Arikara scout Bloody Knife in the head. Blood and brains spattered Reno in the face and his self-control snapped: "Dismount!" he cried. Then, regaining his composure: "Mount and get to the bluffs!"

Confusion spread, but most of the men managed to assemble on the plain next to the timber. With Reno at their head, they began to cut a path through the swarms of tribesmen blocking the way to the river. Red and blue mixed, fighting hand to hand. Charlie Reynolds caught a bullet in the chest and died. Lieutenant McIntosh was cut off and engulfed by a horde of Indians. Retreat turned to rout, every man for himself, no rear guard to check the pursuit. Varnum rushed to the head of the command and shouted, "For God's sake, men, don't run; don't let them whip us." Reno retorted, "Sir, I am in command here."

The troops reached the river a mile below the original ford, where the banks were four to six feet high. Some jumped their mounts into the water, while others slid down the bank to the stream. Sioux crowded the waterside, firing at the helpless soldiers. Lieutenant B. H. Hodgson, struck by a bullet, splashed into the water. Clutching the stirrup of a passing horseman, he reached the opposite bank. Here he sat firing his revolver at the Indians across the river until hit again and killed.

On the east side of the river steep cliffs and hogbacks, scored by deep ravines, rose two to three hundred feet above the valley. As the troopers emerged from the river they raced across the narrow strip of bottom land into the shelter of a hogback, then made their tortuous way to the top of the bluffs. Halfway up the spine of a hogback Dr. J. M. DeWolf and his orderly were killed. As the first men gained the summit they could see below the last few bunches of troopers pulling themselves from the river and starting up the escarpment.

Reno's battalion was completely off balance and easy prey for a concerted Sioux attack. But the Indians failed to press their advantage. Their fire slackened and they began to leave in increasing numbers to ride downstream. Squaws went among the dead and dying troopers scattered along the line of retreat to mutilate and plunder the bodies. Twenty-nine men were dead and seventeen, including Lieutenant C. C. DeRudio, missing.

A dust cloud rising from the slope to the east announced the approach of Captain Benteen's three troops, advancing at a gallop. As they mounted the hill, Reno ran out to meet them. "For God's sake Benteen," he shouted, "halt your command and help me. I've lost half my men." At a motion from Benteen the battalion dismounted and spread a skirmish line forward to enclose the remnant of Reno's command.

It was four o'clock and no one knew what had happened to Custer. A faint crackle of carbine fire wafted across the hills. Then two distant volleys echoed from downstream. A high hill to the north cut off vision, but Varnum dredged a fleeting memory from events of the past hour. As Reno's men had gone into action in the valley, he had caught a glimpse of the Gray Horse Troop (Troop E) on the bluffs across the river. Custer must have decided to support Reno by charging the lower end of the Indian village. Or perhaps the rising dust cloud had intensified his fear that the Indians were escaping, and he had led his battalion in pursuit.

Reno appeared to have no intention of responding to the obvious distress signal, even though Cooke's hastily scrawled note brought by Trumpeter Martini fairly pleaded for swift action. Captain Weir fidgeted with impatience and finally, without authority, led his troop north along the rim of the bluffs. Seeing

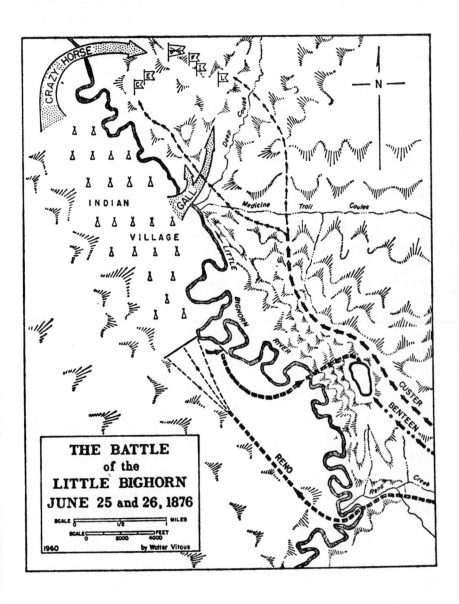

THE BATTLE
of the
LITTLE BIGHORN
JUNE 25 and 26, 1876

D Troop move out, Reno ordered H, M, and K Troops to its support. On the summit of the high hill (later named Weir Point) Weir halted to await these reinforcements. From here he surveyed the distant hills downstream. They were swathed in smoke and dust. Here and there an indistinct horseman could be seen racing to and fro amid the billowing clouds. Weir's further advance was suddenly blocked by hordes of savages pouring up the ravines that drained the hill. Every sage clump soon concealed its painted warrior, and a heavy fire compelled the four troops to dismount and return the fire.

The smoke and dust observed by Weir and his men concealed the closing scene of Custer's annihilation. The details of the "last stand" have for eighty-five years remained a mystery that invites speculation and controversy because no one can ever be sure of them. Custer's progress may be followed with reasonable accuracy to the point where Trumpeter Martini, the last surviving member of the regiment to see him alive, left with the message for Benteen. Thereafter, the placement of the bodies and the confused and contradictory testimony of Indian participants furnish the only clues. Based on this evidence, here is what might have happened.

Shortly after Reno had been ordered to cross the river in pursuit of the forty Indians discovered by Fred Gerard, Custer veered from his trail and headed directly for the dust cloud rising from the Little Bighorn valley. The way led up a long shallow ravine towards the precipice falling away to the river. Captain Keogh and Lieutenant Cooke returned from Reno with news that the Indians were not running away. Sergeant Major Sharrow came back bearing the message directing Benteen to continue his march towards the Little Bighorn. Clearly, battle was imminent. Custer therefore sent Sergeant Kanipe back to McDougall and the pack train to hasten the ammunition to the front.

At the head of the ravine the troops found themselves just below the crest overlooking the valley. Custer, who had ranged nervously in every direction, rode rapidly to the top of a high hill (Weir Point) and scanned the valley, with its sea of tepees stretching for three miles along the bank of the river. Turning in his saddle and sweeping off his hat, he yelled, "Hurrah, boys, we've caught them napping." He galloped down the hill and the five troops took up the trot down a brushy draw leading into a large coulee (since named Medicine Tail Coulee) that emptied into the river.

Turning to Trumpeter Martini, who had been detailed from H Troop as orderly trumpeter for the day, Custer said, "Orderly, I want you to take a message to Captain Benteen. Ride as fast as you can and tell him to hurry. Tell him it's a big village and I want him to be quick, and to bring the ammunition packs." As Martini checked his horse, Adjutant Cooke said, "Wait, Orderly, I'll give you a message." He scribbled a few lines in his memorandum book, tore out a page, and handed it to Martini. "Now Orderly, ride as fast as you can to Captain Benteen. Take the same trail we came down. If you have time, and there is no danger, come back. But otherwise stay with your company." Saluting, Martini wheeled his horse and galloped back up the trail.

The battalion turned left into Medicine Tail Coulee and almost immediately collided with a large force of Sioux under Gall pouring across the river to meet the new threat. His advance blocked, Custer veered to the right and fought a rear-guard action north to a high ridge one half mile long and parallel to the river. Freed by Reno's retreat from the upper end of the village, more warriors swelled Gall's ranks and he pressed the battle ridge from the south. Crazy Horse led another force down the valley, crossed the river, and moved against the ridge from the north.

Caught in broken terrain unsuited to mounted action and hopelessly outnumbered, the cavalry fought on the defensive and largely on foot. The Indians, too, dismounted. At the southern point of the battle ridge Calhoun and L Troop deployed to stem Gall's advance. F and I troops, caught in the flank by Two Moon's Cheyennes, scattered along both sides of the ridge. C and E Troops, carried by the tide of battle into a deep ravine between the ridge and the river, were destroyed by Indians under Lame White Man.

At the northern point of the ridge the survivors of the five troops, about fifty men, gathered around Custer for the last stand. On the west slope they shot their horses and arranged them in a tight circle as barricades. In the center the headquarters guidon hung limp in an atmosphere heavy with dust and powder smoke. Next to it stood Custer, a broad-brimmed felt hat shading his face. He had shed his coat and wore a blue shirt and fringed buckskin trousers jammed into troop boots. Two stubby English Webley Bulldogs blazed in his hands.

Crazy Horse had crushed Yates and Keogh and linked with Gall, who had overwhelmed Calhoun. The Sioux and Cheyennes arched volleys of arrows overhead to shower the defense perimeter on Custer Hill. They worked their dismounted circle closer and closer for the death blow. Custer went down, a bullet in his head, another in his chest. The entire battle had lasted hardly an hour.

Organized resistance ended. For the few scattered troopers who were still alive hope may have revived if a gust of wind ever parted the smoke enough to permit a view to the south. A faint trace of blue capped Weir Point—Captain Weir and his blue-clad men advancing to the sound of firing. But the Indians had seen it too, and they rode south in large numbers. Weir stopped and dismounted to defend the hill.

After heavy fighting the four troops on Weir Point gave ground. Lieutenant Godfrey deployed part of Troop K and covered the movement. Rejoining the rest of the command, Weir's men saw that the pack train had at last arrived and that Reno and Benteen were organizing a defense perimeter.

The terrain proved excellent for defense. With one exception, a ridge to the north, the position dominated the surrounding hills. A saucer-shaped depression in the center formed a shelter for Dr. H. R. Porter's hospital and the pack mules and cavalry horses. On the west the bluffs fell away precipitously to the river. On the east and south the ground sloped gently for several miles to Reno Creek.

Almost immediately the Sioux hit this position. The seven troops fought desperately on all sides, while the Indians, emboldened by their triumph over Custer, sought to overrun the hill and destroy the rest of the regiment. Darkness came quickly, however, and the warriors withdrew.

Throughout the night the valley was a riot of savage celebration. Lit by huge fires, the village vibrated with the throb of drums and the chant of the war dance. From the bluffs the cavalrymen watched the firelit activity below as they scooped out shallow rifle pits with their mess gear. Some thought they heard bugle calls, and convinced themselves that Custer was at last coming to their aid.

As the first light of day brushed the hilltops, a single rifle cracked. It was the signal. The Indians had worked into positions entirely surrounding the hill, and they brought every part of Reno's lines under heavy fire. The defenders returned the fire, and thus opened the second day of fighting.

The soldiers were disposed in an irregular circle around the hospital. Reno had five troops drawn up in a semicircle on the north rim of the swale where the hospital was located. Troop A was deployed behind barricades of dead horses and mules along the more exposed eastern side of the depression. Benteen, with Troop H and the pack train detail, held an elongated hump jutting south from the hospital area. This was the key to the entire position.

Sensing that to breach Benteen's lines would mean victory, the Indians increased the pressure on his defenses. But he held firm. In full view of the enemy he stalked his line directing the fire and inspiring the men with an example of courage. Finally, instructing Lieutenant Gibson to hold at all costs, Benteen went to Reno and asked for reinforcements. He returned with Captain French and Troop M, and strung the new men along the east rim of the ridge. The Indians were already massing for a charge. Anticipating them, Benteen roused his men to their feet for a counterattack. Firing carbines and pistols and yelling at the top of their voices, the soldiers poured down the slope. The Indians broke and fled towards the river, dragging their dead and wounded with them. Benteen's men climbed back up the hill and dropped into their rifle pits.

After a short debate, the Indians again prepared to storm the position. Benteen hurried over to Reno and demanded that a general counterattack be launched. Reno agreed and told Benteen to give the word. At Benteen's signal the seven troops charged in four directions and again the Indians scattered. Eighty-five yards from the assault line Reno called the men back to their holes.

These charges made the Sioux and Cheyennes more cautious. Thereafter they contented themselves with keeping up a desultory fire, and by late afternoon only an occasional bullet kicked up the dirt on Reno Hill. A few at a time the warriors disappeared. Fearing a ruse, the soldiers remained in their rifle pits. In the hospital Dr. Porter tended the wounded. They cried for water, but the little that had been obtained from the river by volunteers facing Sioux rifles was not enough to go around.

The enemy fire died out entirely. As Reno's men watched in bewilderment the Indians set fire to the dry grass in the valley. A wall of smoke blotted out all activity in the village. At about seven in the evening an immense mass of humanity emerged from behind the smoke screen and climbed to the benchland across the valley. Seven tribes of Sioux and Cheyennes and a gigantic pony herd formed a procession of aboriginal might. As it crawled away towards the Bighorn Mountains, the Civil War veterans compared the array to Sheridan's cavalry on the march in the Shenandoah Valley.

That night, as the soldiers buried their dead, Lieutenant De-Rudio, Sergeant O'Neill, and the scouts Fred Gerard and Billy Jackson found their way into the lines. They had been left in the timber during the retreat the day before, and had spent a harrowing thirty-six hours dodging savages. Reno counted his casualties. Both in the valley fight and on the hill, he had lost forty-seven killed and fifty-two wounded. The command moved closer to the river, both to get nearer to water and to escape the stench of decaying horseflesh.

Next morning, June 27, the cavalrymen observed the approach of another column. Some were convinced that Custer had at last arrived. Others thought it was Terry. Still others argued that the Indians were returning. The column resolved itself into the blue of army uniforms. It was not Custer, for no Gray Horse Troop could be seen. Someone said that it must be Crook, and three cheers went up for Crook. Lieutenants Hare and Wallace galloped across the river. As they neared the approaching troops they recognized the fluttering guidons of the Second Cavalry followed by the ranks of Gibbon's Seventh Infantry. Reining in beside General Terry, Hare and Wallace saluted and burst out with the same question, "Where is Custer?"

On Reno Hill Lieutenant James H. Bradley, who commanded Gibbon's Indian scouts, rode into the lines. Dismounting beside Godfrey, he explained that he had just counted 197 bodies dotting the hills five miles down the river.

Custer's battalion had been wiped out. Of 231 soldiers in five troops not one man had escaped. Their stripped and mutilated remains were found scattered over the sage-covered hills. A ring of dead horses on the northern point of the battle ridge marked the last stand of Custer. His body, stripped but otherwise untouched, lay in the center of the circle, his wounds scarcely visible, a peaceful look on his face. Later, the burial detail found but one sign of life, Captain Keogh's horse, Comanche. Terribly wounded, he was led to the mouth of the Little Bighorn. With Reno's wounded he took his place on the deck of the *Far West* for the trip to Fort Lincoln. Comanche lived another fifteen years, venerated as the only survivor of the Battle of the Little Bighorn.

The Sioux had won their greatest victory in the long conflict with the white man. But it proved an empty victory. The nation was shocked by the Custer disaster, and the Army high command flooded the Sioux country with troops. For the Sioux and the Cheyenne, the future held only hunger, defeat, surrender, and for some, death.

PART XI

Apaches vs. Apaches
1871–86

Introduction

Before 1871 civilian and military leaders in the Southwest had but one policy regarding Apaches—extermination! Army orders in 1868 were to "capture and root out the Apaches by every means, and to hunt them as you would wild animals." Cash prizes were offered for Apache scalps.

This was the picture when General George Crook, already an experienced and respected Indian campaigner, was placed in command of the Army's Department of Arizona. Instead of attempting extermination, however, Crook launched a policy of pacification of Apaches, the expression of a point of view not highly popular in the Territory.

In line with this policy, Crook's first step was to enlist a considerable number of Apaches as scouts. This not only subtracted from the total number of Indians he would have to fight; it also provided him with troops who knew the tricks and the hideouts of their hostile tribesmen.

General Crook came to have special admiration for his Apache scouts, calling them the best scouts he ever had. More particularly he came to admire the Chiricahua scouts, for he depended more and more upon them as the campaign finally came to focus primarily on the Chiricahua band. The Chiricahuas were known to be the best warriors of all the Apaches, and Crook knew that it would take Chiricahuas themselves to match the cunning and fathom the strategy of this wild tribe.

His faith was well-founded and his strategy sound. In two years most of the hostile Apaches were subdued and at peace, busily learning to till the soil and raise livestock.

But this peaceful era was short-lived. Crook was transferred to another area in 1875. Almost immediately, trouble between whites and Apaches reappeared. Unscrupulous Indian agents conspired with land grabbers to push the Apaches around. The Indians, provoked by this treachery and incited by a few die-hard leaders, began to retaliate in the only way they knew. Many bands, including the Chiricahuas, left their reservations and waged war over a wide territory in Arizona, New Mexico, and Mexico proper.

The Chiricahuas, after the death of their wise chief, Cochise, fell under the influence of Geronimo. Crafty and contentious, Geronimo was not a hereditary chief but prevailed because Taza and Naiche, sons of Cochise, lacked their father's strength of leadership.

In 1882, with the situation steadily worsening, Crook was reassigned to Arizona and moved swiftly and firmly to straighten things out. As before, he brought a few bands at a time back to the reservations. He set up an Indian police force and drove squatters off Indian lands. He re-established Indian farming operations and found markets for Indian produce.

Most of the five hundred-odd Chiricahuas were still on the loose. In 1885, however, Crook surrounded them at their stronghold in the Sierra Madres of Mexico and obtained their pledge to return and live peaceably on a reservation.

Most of the Chiricahuas kept their pledge to General Crook and for them this was truly the end of the warpath. They were settled on Turkey Creek, seventeen miles southwest of Fort Apache, under the command of Lieutenant Britton Davis. Davis' wise counsel and leadership gained him the lasting friendship and co-operation of all but a few chronic malcontents, like Geronimo, whose sullen hatred of the whites was building up to the final and fiercest chapter of the Apache wars in the Southwest.

21. THE APACHE SCOUTS WHO WON A WAR

D. HARPER SIMMS

A baseball game was under way at Fort Apache the afternoon of May 17, 1885. Umpiring the contest between two post nines was Lieutenant Britton Davis, young but seasoned veteran of Apache campaigns under General George Crook, Commander of the Department of Arizona, U. S. Army.

Davis was at Fort Apache that Sunday afternoon waiting for a reply to a telegram he had sent two days earlier. The telegram had reported to Captain F. E. Pierce, Davis' superior at San Carlos, the details of serious trouble being stirred up by certain rebellious leaders of the Chiricahua Apaches at Turkey Creek.

Davis had asked Captain Pierce to relay to General Crook at Fort Whipple his request for authority to deal decisively with the troublemakers and eliminate, if he could, that principal source of unrest among his otherwise peaceful charges. But the telegram would never be answered because Captain Pierce had dismissed the report as unworthy of the General's attention. Nor did he bother to make any response to the waiting junior officer.

This was not the first time, nor the last, that an unheeded warning has led to tragic consequences in American military history. But Britton Davis still didn't know the cause for delay when, at about four o'clock, the ball game was interrupted by the arrival of two fast-riding Apache scouts.

The riders were Chatto, first sergeant of Davis' Company B of Chiricahua scouts, and Mickey Free, his half-breed Apache interpreter.

Their news was bad. As Davis had feared they might, the *tizwin*-drinking malcontents—Geronimo, Chihuahua, Mangus, and Naiche—had succeeded in fomenting an uprising, and had broken away from the reservation taking with them about one fourth of the band.

Thus began an arduous sixteen-month campaign that would pit five thousand regular troops and several hundred scouts against a handful of renegade Apaches. It would finally bring an end to the Indian wars in the Southwest, but in doing so would produce one of the greatest miscarriages of justice ever to blot the mottled record of white man's treatment of the Indian in America.

It would set off an incredible display of petty bickerings and controversy in the military ranks. And it would unfold an unparalleled story of a major military campaign won by Indian scouts who served the Army against hostiles of their own tribe and families.

The hostile band, somewhat reluctantly accepting Geronimo's petulant leadership, headed straight for the Mexican border. Lieutenant Davis and his scouts followed for a few hours, but when they saw how much of a lead the renegades had gained, they turned back to get orders from General Crook and to prepare for a long campaign in Mexico.

And long it was. In addition to Chatto and the Apache scouts under Davis and another group of scouts under Lieutenant Charles B. Gatewood, the immediate pursuit was also mounted by Captain Allen Smith with two troops of the Fourth Cavalry. Crook ordered Davis to enlist another hundred scouts. The remaining Chiricahuas volunteered almost to a man, according to Jason Betzinez, one of the few men still living who were in the band at that time. Betzinez recently told of this experience and said he was rejected as a scout because of his kinship to one of the hostile leaders.

General Crook set all other available troops in motion and before many days, several separate forces were in grueling pursuit. Temperatures up to 128° punished the soldiers but the Apache scouts seemed inured to the heat. Not only did they know every water hole, but in addition were able to travel great distances without water. Tough as our frontier soldiers must have been, the Apaches were infinitely more durable in that climate and terrain. Soldiers became footsore, their boots cut to shreds on the sharp rocks in a matter of days. The Apaches, however, could actually travel barefoot in that rough land if necessary. This toughness of foot was just one of the attributes which made the Indians so valuable to Crook.

Tactics of the campaign called for the scouts to deploy widely on each side of an advancing column of soldiers. The Apaches thus covered the roughest country, saving the white soldiers from the more rigorous aspects of the march as well as performing a job for which they were better equipped than the whites. Keen eyesight, skill at tracking, and built-in knowledge of the haunts and habits of the adversary made the Chiricahua scouts obviously indispensable to successful action, especially when moving against other Chiricahuas.

Even with the help of the scouts, however, this chase of Geronimo was long and costly. Time after time, the pursuing forces managed to intercept the fast-moving hostiles only to lose them in the rough terrain after a brief skirmish.

But Crook held his troops relentlessly on the trail and the pressure began to tell on the renegades, who lost horses and ran short of food and ammunition. Finally in January 1886, some

sixty miles below Nacori near the Aros River, the renegades sig-
nified their willingness to talk terms with a force under Captain
Emmett Crawford.

At this critical moment, however, Mexican troops, presumably
mistaking the Indian scouts for hostiles, attacked Captain Crawford's force, fatally wounding Crawford himself in the melee.

Soon afterward, the hostile Chiricahuas again sent word that
they wished to parley and agreed to meet Crook at Cañon de los
Embudos, near the border, two months later, if the general would
come without regular soldiers.

On March 25, 1886, Geronimo and his lieutenants met General
Crook at the appointed place. This historic conference was photo-
graphed by a man named Fly, from Tombstone. The renegades
had, by this time, refitted, and were in top physical condition,
well fed and armed. They were alert, suspicious, and ready for
instant action. Crook knew that he and his handful of aides were
in a critical situation, one which called for all the skill and
diplomacy this great soldier had amassed in his years of dealing
with Indians.

But after three long conferences, replete with the oratory so
dear to Indians, Crook accepted Geronimo's surrender, stipulat-
ing that the hostiles would be sent to prison for two years and
then permitted to return to their reservation. The forces grouped
to return to Arizona, Crook going on ahead to make arrangements.

The Apaches, conducted by Lieutenant Marion P. Maus and
his scouts, were permitted to keep their arms and to travel
separately. This was done, Crook explained later, because the
newly surrendered Apaches were so skittish and fearful—either
of attack by Mexican troops or treachery on the part of the
whites. The general felt he must acquiesce in this request to
demonstrate his good faith and to hold the confidence he had
managed to gain in the parley.

Without troops, of course, Crook was in poor position to enforce any demands. So it is hard to say whether events would
have been different even if he had wanted to disarm the Apaches.

At any rate, during the second night out, a disreputable white
rancher smuggled a quantity of liquor into the renegade camp.

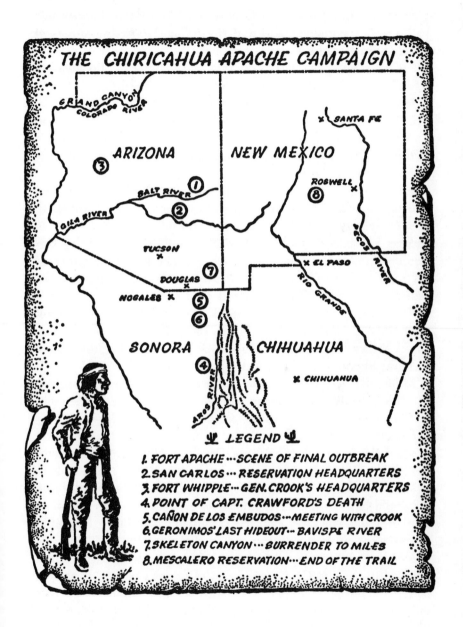

THE CHIRICAHUA APACHE CAMPAIGN

ARIZONA

NEW MEXICO

GRAND CANYON
COLORADO RIVER

③

SANTA FE ×

ROSWELL ×
⑧

SALT RIVER ①
②
GILA RIVER

TUCSON ×

DOUGLAS ×
⑦

NOGALES ×
⑤
⑥

× EL PASO

PECOS RIVER

RIO GRANDE

SONORA

CHIHUAHUA

④

× CHIHUAHUA

AROS RIVER

⚜ LEGEND ⚜

1. FORT APACHE ··· SCENE OF FINAL OUTBREAK
2. SAN CARLOS ··· RESERVATION HEADQUARTERS
3. FORT WHIPPLE ·· GEN. CROOK'S HEADQUARTERS
4. POINT OF CAPT. CRAWFORD'S DEATH
5. CAÑON DE LOS EMBUDOS ··· MEETING WITH CROOK
6. GERONIMOS' LAST HIDEOUT ·· BAVISPE RIVER
7. SKELETON CANYON ··· BURRENDER TO MILES
8. MESCALERO RESERVATION ··· END OF THE TRAIL

Geronimo and Naiche got wildly drunk. For reasons known only to him, the bootlegger also told the Indians terrifying stories of what lay in store for them as prisoners. This, plus fear of punishment for their spree, led Geronimo and Naiche to slip away in the night, with thirty-four men, women, and children.

Maus reported this to Crook and brought the main body of prisoners on to Fort Bowie. A group of scouts started once again on Geronimo's trail. But the citizenry, always looking for a chance to crucify Crook, seized upon Geronimo's escape to heap calumny on the general's head.

Even Crook's own military superiors censured him. President Cleveland and General Phil Sheridan, Commanding General of the Army, not only castigated him for allowing Geronimo to escape, but said he had acted without authority in offering surrender terms to the renegade leader. Furthermore, they criticized his tactics, casting doubt on the trustworthiness of the Apache scouts upon whom Crook had relied so fully.

This was more than Crook could take, and he asked to be relieved of his command. On April 2, 1886, Brigadier General Nelson A. Miles was appointed to succeed Crook, with orders from General Sheridan to finish the job posthaste.

Miles was assigned two thousand additional troops, bringing the forces under his command to five thousand men. Their objective: *to bring in thirty-six men, women, and children.*

General Sheridan ordered Miles to make use of regular troops, another thinly veiled criticism of Crook's tactics. But Miles' light cavalry units, substituted for the scout companies, got nowhere against the elusive hostiles. Before long the new commander saw he would have to use Chiricahua scouts. That, plus his introduction of the heliograph (mirrors reflecting sun rays) for rapid communication, hastened the end of the campaign.

Aware that Geronimo had never been captured outright, Miles decided to try a method reminiscent of Crook's tactics. It was, in fact, a suggestion from one of Crook's old Chiricahua scouts that influenced the general to attempt another approach to the hostiles.

Consulting his Apaches, he chose two trusted Chiricahuas, Martine and Kayitah, both of whom had relatives in the hostile camp, and sent them into Mexico with Lieutenant Gatewood to attempt direct peace talks with Geronimo. Approaching the Bavispe River country of Sonora, the small group found signs that the renegade camp was near. Martine and Kayitah moved ahead alone, carrying a white flour sack tied to a branch as a truce flag.

Jasper Kanseah, who, along with Martine and Kayitah, lived to old age at Mescalero, New Mexico, recently retold his version of that event.

Kanseah was on watch when the approaching scouts were first sighted. Geronimo ordered his men to open fire, but his order was countermanded by someone who recognized Martine and Kayitah. The renegade leader was finally persuaded to allow the scouts to enter the camp.

At first the scouts' efforts appeared fruitless, for Geronimo seemed adamant. But he was tired of fighting and, after a long palaver, finally agreed to meet Gatewood. Kayitah stayed in the hostile camp as a token of good faith, while Martine hurried back to Gatewood with the news.

At his meeting with Gatewood, Geronimo was persuaded to come to a meeting with General Miles at Skeleton Canyon, on the Arizona side of the border. He kept the appointment and on September 6, 1886, after a two-day harangue during which Geronimo made a vain effort to stipulate terms, the renegade chief agreed to an unconditional surrender.

This marked, at long last, the end of the Indian hostilities in the Southwest. It marked the end of a long and bitter war with Apaches that was, in truth, won by Apaches.

Accounts of the expeditions and battles in which these Apache scouts served General Crook and General Miles so nobly make this conclusion clear, even to a present-day reader. Captain John G. Bourke, participant in most of the campaign and faithful recorder of much of Crook's career, left no question about it in his book, *On the Border With Crook*. He wrote:

> *Not a single Chiricahua had been killed, captured, or wounded throughout the entire campaign—with two exceptions—unless by Chiricahua Apache scouts who, like*

Chatto, had kept the pledges given to General Crook in the Sierra Madre in 1883.

Crook himself declared: "It is not too much to say that the surrender of Naiche, Chihuahua, Geronimo, and their bands could not have been effected except for the assistance of Chatto and his Chiricahua scouts."

And how were they rewarded for this?

The scouts were, in fact, forgotten in the long and bitter arguments over, and investigations of, the terms of Geronimo's surrender. What was promised the Chiricahuas and what was not depends on which account you read. Credit for the surrender was the subject of jealous bickering among Army officers for many years. Charges of collusion between the military and land-grabbing political leaders in Arizona were never clarified, but whatever the motives, the result was all bad for *all* the Chiricahuas.

For along with the hostiles taken in the final campaign, the scouts and the peaceful remainder of the tribe at Fort Apache were assembled and shipped off to prison in Florida. Chatto, faithful first sergeant of Britton Davis' gallant Company B, wearing a medal fresh from the President of the United States, was imprisoned with the rest.

No one was spared. Incredible as it may seem, even Kayitah and Martine, the scouts who had risked their lives to induce Geronimo to surrender, went to prison along with the chief renegade himself. Martine had never in his life fought against white troops. Kayitah had once been on the warpath, but had long since deserted the hostiles and volunteered as a scout.

The tribe was held for eight years, in military prisons in Florida, and later in Alabama. Many of the Chiricahuas, unaccustomed to the damp climate and confinement, died there. In 1894 they were moved to the Fort Sill military reservation in Oklahoma Territory. Not until 1913 were friends of these Apaches successful in obtaining an Act of Congress that freed the Chiricahuas after a quarter of a century of prison and exile. Some stayed on in Oklahoma, where tracts of farm land were allotted to them. Most of the tribe chose to join a closely related band, the Mescaleros, on a mountain reservation in southern New Mexico that more nearly resembled their homeland. None were permitted to return to Arizona.

The Chiricahua scouts are all gone now. The measure of their service in bringing peace in Arizona is little known and seldom noted. But those who search out the story of the Apache scouts find it one of the most intriguing and amazing chapters in the chronicles of the Old West.

PART XII

Trouble in the Mountains
1877–79

Introduction

At first the rising tide of white settlement advanced slowly into the valleys and the high country on the western slope of the Rockies. However, the westward movement was accelerated when gold was found on the Nez Perces' land and both silver and lead on that of the Utes. The demand of the mining interests, reinforced by those of an ever increasing number of home-seekers, led to continued pressure on the Indians to release part of the lands assigned to them under the various treaties with the Great White Father.

The actions of the Indian agents, some thoroughly dishonest, some foolish, and some completely stupid, also helped increase Indian hostility. In addition, Congress failed to appropriate adequate funds for rations for the tribes now deprived of many of their hunting grounds. As a result the Indians were often hungry. They were angry and spoiling for retribution. This was the general picture in the high country in the late 1870s.

The direct cause of the Nez Perces' outbreak in 1877 was the abrogation of their treaty by the government. They were offered a new treaty under which they would cede a considerable part of their best land to the government. This was nothing new to the Nez Perces—they had been asked several times in the past to part with land and had done so peacefully. The government expected that they would give in again, for this tribe had a long and honorable record of peace and friendship with the white man. The chiefs of all the bands except one did sign the new treaty. The Southern Nez Perces refused to give up their tribal *homes and burial grounds in the Wallowa Valley in the north-eastern corner of Oregon. Chief Joseph would probably have succeeded in getting the southern band to sign had not his hand been forced by a small war party of young braves. These warriors went on a raid and killed a score or more of white men, women, and children. Joseph knew that the raid ended the slim chance there had been for peace and took the lead in preparing to leave their homeland. His fighting retreat was a masterpiece of military strategy but hardly qualifies as a decisive Indian battle.*

The mistake of a clerk and the government's bullheaded refusal to correct it was an immediate cause of the Bannack War of 1878. The Camas Prairie was the primary source of the camas root, one of the principal foods of the Bannacks. However, in describing the Bannack Reservation a clerk included a non-existent Kansas (instead of Camas) Prairie in the boundaries of the tribal lands. The government refused to correct the mistake and permitted white settlers to move on to the Camas Prairie. Hogs ate many of the roots and cattle covered the prairie. This was too much for the Bannacks who had only the year before served the Army well during the Nez Perce retreat. However, this was one of the few times, perhaps the only time, that the Bannacks had allied themselves with the white man. Their record differed from that of their hereditary foes, the Nez Perces, as they had almost continuously resisted the encroachment of the white man. Only the chance to even some old scores with their ancient enemies had led the Bannacks to join in corralling the Nez Perces in 1877.

The name Bannack, later changed by common usage to "Bannock," is derived from their own Indian name Banakwut. They belonged to the Shoshonean branch of the Uto-Aztecan linguistic stock, being a branch of the Northern Paiute. From historic times, the tribe ranged in western Wyoming, into Idaho south of the Salmon River, and along the Snake River from southern Montana into eastern Oregon. They murdered John Reed's Astor party on Boise River in 1814. Alexander Ross, Hudson Bay Company fur trader, made contact with them in 1824. He called them "robbers" and said they lived by "plunder," with "their hand against every man, and every man's hand against them." For their depredations against white settlers and overland immigrants, General Connor virtually decimated the tribe's warriors on Bear River in 1867. The Fort Hall Reservation was established for them in 1869, but they continued their nomadic life, partly from habit and partly to supplement the starvation rations they received on the reservation.

Strangely enough, it was the over-zealousness of well-meaning Indian Agent N. C. Meeker, working earnestly in their behalf, that brought on the Ute troubles of 1879. Mr. Meeker, the former agricultural editor of the New York Tribune, founded a colony on the Cache la Poudre River in 1869, which he named Greeley, in honor of his close friend and partner, Horace Greeley.

"Father Meeker," as the younger newspapermen in the territory called him, became very interested in the Indians. In 1877 he succeeded in becoming agent at the White River Ute Agency. He moved it to a better farming area known as Powell's Bottom, some distance from the former location on the White River. Here he began intensive programs of teaching the Utes farming methods, while his attractive daughter, Josephine Meeker, assisted in running his newly established school.

The Utes strongly resisted sending their children to school. However, the idea of farming was their chief irritant. Since farms went with fences, and vice versa, the Indians were continually having difficulties with their ponies stumbling over the fences and receiving assorted injuries therefrom.

Meeker did not have the patience that it would have taken to make farmers out of the Utes. He made a bad mistake—he tried to enforce his authority and compel the Utes to do his bidding. The Utes resisted stubbornly and finally violently.

22. THE BANNACK INDIAN WAR OF 1878

FREDERICK A. MARK

From a dozen camp fires scattered among the Bannack lodges at the head of a small aspen-fringed mountain valley, the smoke curled lazily into the clear, crisp sky one spring morning in 1878. The face of Buffalo Horn, chief of the Bannacks, was solemn as he stepped from his tepee and gazed east onto Camas Prairie below him. With field glasses he had retained from his scouting duty with General Howard in the Nez Perce campaign the year before, he scanned the prairie before him for traces of the white man's cattle trespassing on the sacred camas ground of his tribe. While he stood there, lean and tall, his intelligent face hardened as he observed the breakfast smoke of cattlemen's camps.

Buffalo Horn was determined not to give up Camas Prairie, which his tribe had used since historic times and had reserved with the Portneuf lands in the treaty with the United States Government at Fort Bridger in 1867, even though some ignorant clerk had erroneously substituted the name Kansas for Camas. Buffalo Horn had visited Fort Boise a few days before, and on the basis of his good reputation and excellent military service as a scout under several military commanders against the Nez Perce and Sioux, he had been authorized an issue of ammunition by the Territorial Governor.

His plan of battle was clear in his mind. He would not make the mistakes of Nez Perce Joseph and Sitting Bull. He had little respect for the tactics of the Army's commanders.

Buffalo Horn's mind was made up. The injustices of the white man would be tolerated no longer. His son and another Indian mounted their ponies and rode out upon the prairie. Soon they came to the cattle camp of three white men who were herding part of the twenty-five hundred head of cattle. By the time the young braves arrived at the cattle camp the sun shone with brilliance on the snowy heights of Soldier Mountain behind them and on the ragged Sawtooth Mountains to the north. On the pretext of trading a buffalo robe, they parleyed with the white men, then suddenly shot Lou Kensler and George Nesby. The two wounded men made their escape on horses; the other man, William Silvey, escaped into the brush and later found a horse to hasten his departure.

The wounded men met two freighters, who relayed the news of the attack to a rancher, who delivered the message to Fort Boise. The attack was not unexpected, since Captain R. F. Bernard at that post had already received orders from General Howard at Vancouver, and was on his way to Camas Prairie to quell anticipated trouble from the Indians. It was already known the Malheur and Umatilla Indians were in concert with the Bannacks and that war was imminent.

In the meantime, Buffalo Horn was having trouble in his own camp. Chief Tendoy, one of his band, was against war and, taking some of his warriors, women, and children, had left for his reservation on Lemhi River. Buffalo Horn felt that he had ample reason to go to war, since his band was on short rations, and the agent was being investigated for shipping Indian supplies to Eastern relatives.

Indians to the westward were making evident preparations for war. Eagle Eye of the Weiser tribe, took rations at his supply point, the Malheur Agency, and headed east. The next day, the Malheur Paiutes under Chief Egan departed from the reservation with forty-six Bannacks. Their trail led southeast. Conditions on the Malheur reservation were even worse than those on the reservations in Idaho Territory. The Indians accused the new agent, Rinehart, of harsh and inhuman treatment and starvation rations. While there was much to be desired from the politically appointed agents, the principal fault was that of Congress, with its years of failure to promptly ratify treaties made with the Indians, and its meager appropriations for support of the reservation.

Chief Egan had a reputation for being a pleasant, industrious, and courteous Indian. He was respected by the military authorities. He consented to lead the hostiles as Chief only after threats against him by the Paiutes.

On June 2 Captain Bernard arrived on Camas Prairie, and his cavalry forced Buffalo Horn and his hostiles into the lava beds near the head of Clover Creek. Buffalo Horn soon broke away and descended from the hills to the Overland Road on Snake River, near King Hill, where he plundered freight wagons and improved his supply of ammunition and arms. Passing down the river about five miles, the hostiles crossed at Glenn's Ferry, then cut the ferry adrift.

Major Patrick Collins, now in command of Bernard's column, followed the hostiles to the mouth of the Bruneau, finding en route the bodies of John Bascom and two other men killed by the Indians. Meanwhile, the Territorial Governor and Generals Crook and Howard were preparing military orders to place enough volunteers and troops in the field to cut off the hostiles before they reached their allies in Oregon. In this they failed.

The hostiles passed up Bruneau River, killing settlers found in their way. Bruneau John, an Indian friendly to the settlers, had preceded the hostiles to the valley and warned the ranchers. Large numbers of settlers fortified themselves in a four-room dugout on Robinson's ranch. Fletcher Haws and Jack Sweeney were not so fortunate; they were caught on the range and killed.

Major Collins returned to Fort Boise, and Captain Bernard again took command. He followed the hostiles, now numbering three hundred or more, over the divide to the headwaters of Owyhee River. On June 8 Colonel Robbin's scouts, proceeding ahead of Bernard, located the hostiles' camp on Battle Creek. At the same time, Captain Harper with some twenty volunteers approached from Silver City and engaged the Indians. In a running battle, a part of Harper's volunteers bolted, and the group barely escaped annihilation. The volunteers fled after four were shot from their horses and killed. But in the engagement Buffalo Horn was killed. Credited as being a gallant fighter, he was shot at close range, screamed, and fell from his horse.

General Howard arrived at Fort Walla Walla from Vancouver June 9; and after conferring with Colonel Wheaton, the commanding officer, departed hastily for Boise. By June 18 Howard had almost nine hundred troops in the field, most of which arrived overland from adjoining states and territories. The troops consisted of a column of foot troops under Major Joseph Stewart, Fourth Artillery; a column of three cavalry companies under Captain Bernard, First Cavalry; a company under Captain Thomas McGregor proceeding from Camp Harney to join with Bernard; a column under Colonel C. Grover, First Cavalry, consisting of cavalry and infantry units; a column of five companies of the Twelfth Infantry under Captain Harry Egbert; and two companies of the Fourth Artillery under Captain John Egan. By June 16 these columns had orders to move toward the enemy in the area around Stein's Mountain, Oregon. In the meantime, Captain John Bendire moved his troops from Fort Hall on Lincoln Creek to guard the Agency at Ross Fork.

The hostile force had now effected a union with Egan's Malheurs, many of the Northern Paiutes, Eagle Eye's Weisers, some Shoshones, and probably some Umatillas. Reports were rampant of ranch raiding and killing of settlers in the Stein's Mountain area, an extremely rough, barren, and inaccessible region even to this day.

Replenishing his supplies at Silver City, Bernard, the colorful

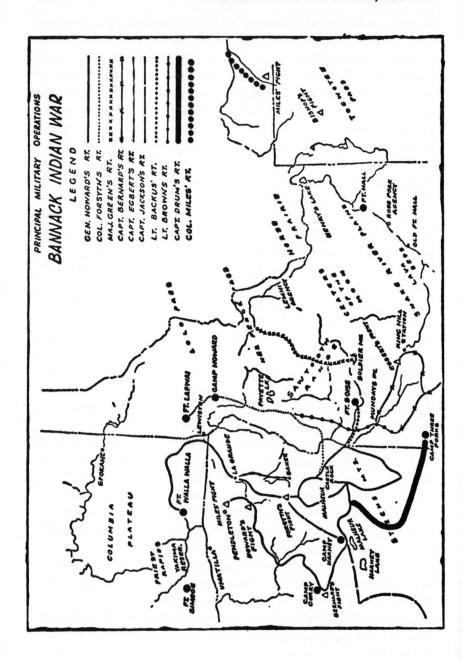

cavalry captain, was again in the saddle pressing hard to the west over broken wasteland toward Stein's Mountain in Oregon. General Howard had left his advance headquarters on Winnimucca Road and was following Bernard, his progress greatly slowed down with supply wagons. Bernard's cavalry companies and nine howitzers moved fast. On June 21 he drew rations at Camp Harney and proceeded forty-five miles west near a point on Silver Creek, where scouts had located the hostiles. The Indians had now consolidated their force into eight hundred or more warriors, with their women and children moving before them.

At Silver Creek Bernard made contact with the hostiles. Approaching their camp unobserved June 23 at eight o'clock in the morning, he formed his column about four hundred yards from the Indian camp and advised his troops that any found retreating would be shot and that they might just as well be killed by the Indians as by their friends. With these words, and others more encouraging, he attacked. The troops were outnumbered at least three to one, but the Indians immediately withdrew into the crags behind them, which were inaccessible to the mounted cavalrymen. Bernard re-formed his lines twice and charged, but he could not dislodge the hostiles. Three cavalrymen were killed and three wounded. Bernard now requested reinforcements. General Howard, with his troops, arrived on June 25.

In the interim the Indians withdrew northward and crossed the divide to the John Day River. Small parties were raiding ranches throughout the John Day country, killing all who came in their path, and driving large herds of cattle and horses before them. The people of Canyon City were terrified. Bernard pressed forward at a fast pace while Howard was lumbering far behind with his wagons and infantry.

The hostiles reached Fox Valley July 2. Bernard's scouts were observing them while he waited for Howard's reinforcements. The Indians had now chosen the high, craggy divide between the John Day and Grand Rivers as their line of advance, and Howard was forced to transfer his supplies to pack horses. Obviously, the hostiles intended to effect union with the Umatillas and Northern Columbia tribes before attempting a stand against

Howard's columns. On July 5 Howard and McGregor formed a junction at Pilot Rock with Colonel Wheaton's troops arriving from Fort Walla Walla under the command of Captain C. B. Throckmorton, and a cavalry company from Fort Lapwai, Idaho territory, commanded by Captain W. H. Winters. Scouts located the hostiles on the north slope of the Blue Mountains near the divide between Butter and Birch Creeks. Howard was fearful the Indians, then crossing the Columbia River, contemplated an assault on the Umatilla Agency and Pendleton. Settlers had deserted the whole countryside around Pendleton.

General Howard, accompanying Bernard's cavalry, rushed two columns forward at sunrise July 8. The advance on the hostiles was made over extremely rough terrain and heavy timber. The Indians were attacked from several points, and in their hasty retreat they left tons of camp supplies and some abandoned their horses, in order to gain ground more inaccessible to the troops. The Indians were blasted from their positions and retreated to higher ground. They made a second stand on a higher ridge and fell back again before the withering fire of the troops. Howard now continued his frontal attack with rushes from both flanks. The Indians hastily retired several miles into the mountains, and the troops stopped the assault because of the sheer exhaustion of men and animals. The hostiles' women and children, proceeding ahead of the braves, were moving eastward toward the Grande Ronde valley. Five enlisted men were wounded, and one died of his injuries. Now nearly two thousand Indian malcontents were in the vicinity.

Advance bands of Egan's hostiles were reported crossing the Columbia River below Umatilla on July 8. The Bannacks and Paiutes offered the Umatillas two thousand horses in return for assistance, advising they would need no help once they crossed the Columbia. The Umatillas refused and the hostiles fired on them, killing several.

In the vicinity of Willow Springs, a group of fifty white volunteers were attacked and five were killed. After posting troops to guard all trails leading to the Snake and Salmon Rivers, to prevent further northward movement of the hostiles, Howard departed for Lewiston and the mouth of the Grande Ronde. Captain Bernard started overland to prevent movement of the Indians over the Lolo and Nez Perce trails into Montana territory.

But new and unexpected fighting was still to take place. On July 10 the hostiles descended from the mountains and destroyed the Cayuse station on the stage road between Le Grande and Pendleton. Getting word of this new attack, the Indian Agent at Umatilla sent word to the troops near Alta, some eighteen miles away, urging them to defend the Agency. About four o'clock the same afternoon, George Coggan was killed, and Alfred Bunker was wounded, then burned alive, by the hostiles. Traveling all night the soldiers arrived at the agency at daylight. While the troops were eating a well-earned breakfast, hostiles appeared at the edge of the clearing and, surprised to see troops there, hesitated. The commanding officer immediately deployed his men and opened fire on the hostiles. He wondered if the Umatillas might join the hostiles; some did, but they raised a white flag before nightfall and surrendered.

Bitter fighting continued into the next day through the thickly wooded mountains. During the night the Umatillas offered aid to the commanding officer, a Captain Miles, but in the meantime the command passed into the hands of Colonel Wheaton, and the Umatillas on their own initiative took up pursuit of the hostiles. Contacting Chief Egan, they advised him they had come to join his band. While engaged in conversation with Egan and a few of his warriors, the Umatillas suddenly opened fire, killing Egan and several braves near him. Chief Egan's head was later brought to the agency for identification. The morale of the hostiles was now broken; both war chiefs were dead. Breaking up into small bands, they dispersed to the east and south, and across the Columbia River.

With this turn in events, Captain Bernard was ordered back to Umatilla. Colonel Forsyth, freshly arrived from Chicago, pursued a band of hostiles south to the headwaters of the John Day River; and in exchanging fire with the band's rear guard, five soldiers received wounds and one volunteer was killed.

River boats, heavily armed, patrolled the Columbia above and below Umatilla landing. A few Indians were captured and large amounts of supplies were left on the banks by the hostiles when they were fired on. The hostile Chief Moses, in the Yakima country, had trouble restraining his braves from actively engaging in the war. Numerous depredations were carried out by his tribesmen. At least one rancher and his wife were killed, and the warehouses at Priest's Rapids on the Columbia were burned. Yakima City organized a strong volunteer group and built strong blockhouses for defense.

But the great crescent-shaped movement of the Indians bursting out of Idaho Territory and across Oregon had spent its force. After traveling hundreds of miles, the hostiles now broke up into very small groups and headed eastward in a great fan-shaped pattern. Reports of Indian movements came from Burnt River, the Wallowas, Powder River, and the Grande Ronde, indicating to General Howard that the hostiles were headed toward Central Idaho, Stein's Mountain, the Snake, and Owyhee Rivers.

Along the Salmon River small groups of hostiles were reported threatening settlers and firing on Chinese miners. By mid-August Major Sanford and Captain Egbert had followed them back into Southern Idaho Territory. At the mouth of Bennett Creek, a tributary of Snake River, Captain Dove attacked a hundred hostiles. Reinforced by Captain Egbert's column, the attack was resumed under cover of darkness and the Indians were driven into the lava beds. Major Green moved east to the wild headwaters of the Lost and Salmon Rivers. Indians had attacked a group of freighters near Lemhi Pass. Green captured several squaws and a few horses. The commands of Egbert, Bernard, Sanford, and Drum were kept busy in late August and September rounding up small bands of Indians in the southern part of Idaho Territory.

At Payette Lakes, near the center of the Territory, small bands of hostiles killed five citizens. In the extreme northeast corner of the Territory, a small band of Bannacks fired on Dr. F. V. Hayden's geological survey party and captured all their horses. A few days later, Captain Egan recaptured fifty-six horses from a group of hostiles.

In early September Colonel Nelson A. Miles, at Fort Ellis, Montana Territory, received orders to intercept a group of hostiles approaching either Boulder or Clark's Fork Pass. With seventy-five cavalry and Crow scouts, Miles immediately departed for Clark's Fork Pass, some 115 miles away. Arriving at the pass scouts were placed at high points and the next day observed a band of hostiles approaching about twelve miles away. They went into camp at noon six miles from Miles' concealed camp. Approaching the Indians at daybreak, Miles formed a skirmish line and attacked. Eleven of the warriors were killed and most of the remainder captured. Captain Bennett and one Crow scout were killed, and one soldier wounded.

Other hostiles drifted into Wyoming Territory. Near Wind River Lieutenant Bishop, Fifth Cavalry, captured some who escaped Miles. Fifty miles northwest of Togwotee Pass on Dry Creek, a tributary of Snake River, Bishop attacked a band of Bannacks on September 12. One Indian was killed; five women, a few children, and eleven horses were captured.

The Indian war was over. Much to the displeasure of post commanders, Indian prisoners were held at several military posts from Fort Omaha to Fort Hall. On February 10, 1879, Captain W. H. Winters delivered some six hundred Indian prisoners to Fort Simcoe, Washington. Some were permitted to return to their old reservations during the next two years; others never got back.

Although the war involved the military posts from the Platte to the Columbia, including regular troops and volunteers from a half dozen states, the casualties, white and red, were relatively small. Only nine soldiers were killed and 24 wounded. There were 24 citizens killed and 34 wounded, including those attached and not attached to troops. There were 78 Indians reported killed and 66 wounded; however it is quite likely at least double that number were casualties. Compared to the Nez Perce War of 1876–77, in which 123 citizens and soldiers and 171 Indians lost their lives, it is evident the military commanders in the present struggle must have been sympathetic to the Bannack and Paiute cause. Their principal efforts were toward preventing the Indians from consolidating a large force in one place, and their operations were chiefly directed to "herding" the Indians rather than killing them.

Following his inspection of the Fort Hall Reservation, just prior to the war in April, 1878, General Crook stated:

The apportionment of rations for the supply of this agency was ridiculously inadequate; the Indians complained that three days out of seven they had nothing to eat, and the agent told me the allowance had never been adequate.

Crook added at a later date:

. . . that it was no surprise . . . that some of the Indians soon afterward broke out into hostility, and the great wonder is that so many remained on the Reservation. With the Bannacks and Shoshones, our Indian policy has resolved itself into a question of war-path or starvation, and being merely human, many of them will always choose the former alternative, where death shall at least be glorious.

23. BESIEGED ON MILK CREEK

JACK P. RIDDLE

The Ute Indians had generally been a peaceful tribe so far as whites were concerned, until September 29, 1879, when they ambushed Major T. T. Thornburg's troops on Milk Creek, murdered Indian Agent Nathan C. Meeker, and killed eleven other white men. In addition, they abducted and violated Meeker's wife and daughter, and Mrs. Shadrick Price of the White River Agency near the present Meeker, Colorado. The trouble was brewed through Meeker's general lack of understanding of Indians and his inability to adjust his own life and that of eleven employees at the agency headquarters to frontier conditions. His actions cost the lives of Major Thornburg, nine U. S. soldiers, and thirty-seven Indians at Milk Creek.

Meeker was a kindly man with admirable intentions of helping the Northern Utes become progressive, self-sustaining citizens. But his former life as a poet and correspondent for Horace Greeley's New York *Tribune* fitted him poorly for the position of Indian Agent. With Horace Greeley, he started the colonizing project at the present Greeley, Colorado. While the colony thrived, Meeker lost money, and in the spring of 1878 willingly accepted the position of Indian Agent at the White River Agency. His predecessor at the agency, the Reverend E. H. Hanforth, had initiated irrigation agriculture, a program viewed as despicable and insulting by these traditionally nomadic hunters, who considered hoe work a job for squaws and ignorant white men.

Meeker also attempted to promote an aggressive farming program. His first reform action was to transfer the White River Agency fifteen miles to Powell's Valley, about four miles down the White River from the present location of the town of Meeker, Colorado. The deep, fertile Powell's Valley soils were admirably adapted to the production of the irrigated crops that Meeker hoped would enrich the tribal coffers. The valley also produced strong tall grass, some of the best horse pasture on the reservation. The fencing in and ploughing of their best horse range riled some of the Utes, who finally yielded half-heartedly to the persuasions and pressures brought to bear on them by Meeker and his white assistants. The Indians grudgingly agreed to spend three thousand dollars of the agency's funds to build an irrigation ditch. They worked reluctantly and erratically at ditch and fence construction, at grubbing sagebrush and plowing, and at planting and harvesting crops. Workers played hookey regularly to rest in the shade and to hunt. About this attitude Meeker said: "A great deal of talking and entreaty were required all the time; once in about a week all would stop work without apparent cause, though evidently in bad humor, but after a few days would be at work again."

The Utes were accustomed to summering in the high mountain valleys at the head of White River and other western slope streams. Hunting, fishing, playing games, and resting, they enjoyed there a form of gracious living that Meeker's tight reservation policy denied.

Ute tempers flared when Meeker prevented their taking these long trips to mountains and elsewhere by ruling that rations would be provided weekly and given only to the heads of families.

Dissension also increased because of the government's disgraceful delay in delivering clothing, provisions, and annuity goods to the Indians. Northern Ute annuity and other goods were stored at Rawlins, Wyoming, until freighted to the White River Agency. Indians often suffered for months for lack of food and clothing that lay in Rawlins' storehouses, because either muddled or crooked government operatives and contractors failed to deliver them to the agency.

On March 17, 1879, Meeker wrote the commandant of Fort Steele, Wyoming, that some of his Indians were buying up large amounts of ammunition at several (renegade) stores on the Snake and Bear Rivers and taking this and their annuity goods north to their allies.

From March to August of that same year the tension continued to mount between the White River Utes and Agent Meeker. A small group of Utes paid a call on Governor Pitkin of Colorado seeking action to curtail Meeker's fence-building and plowing, as well as his continual pecking at their extracurricular activities.

In a letter dated August 11, to E. A. Hoyt, Commissioner of Indian Affairs, Washington, D.C., Meeker said:

> *These Ute Indians are not to be trusted, and I have hitherto informed you that instead of forming them into a police I have been obliged to keep up a police of white men to watch them, for the greater part of them are almost constantly off the reservation, trading, running and stealing horses, and intimately associated with the ruffians, renegades and cattle thieves of the frontier, and now I am pretty well convinced that certain cattlemen intend to operate with the Indians next winter to run off little bunches of our cattle at a time, to the railroad. I have a strong belief that a raid is to be made on our herd through the connivances of the Indians. And what I want*

is sufficient military force to be sent hither to awe these savages, so that they will stay at home.

On September 10, 1879, Agent Meeker told his troubles to Governor Pitkin in Denver:

We have plowed 80 acres and the Indians object to any more being done and to any more fencing. We shall stop plowing. One of the plowmen was shot at last week. On Monday I was assaulted in my own house, while my wife was present, by a leading chief named Johnson, and forced out of doors, and considerably injured as I was in a crippled condition, having previously met with an accident— a wagon falling over me. The employees came to my rescue. I had built this Johnson a house, given him a wagon and harness and fed him at my table many, many times. The trouble is, he has 150 horses and wants the land for pasturage, although the Agency was moved that this same land might be used, and the Agency buildings are on it. I have had two days' council with the chiefs and head men of the tribe who concluded, after a sort of a way, that I might plow, but they will do nothing to permit me to, and they laugh at my being forced out of my house.

Thus began the problem that was to be solved in a painful and expensive way. Messages began crossing the desks of the various adjutants and generals from Fort Steele to Chicago and Washington. There was an exchange of messages between the Department of Interior and the Secretary of War. Such people as Crook, Sherman, John Pope, and others became involved. All of which led to a telegram which read as follows:

Headquarters Department of the Platte
Assistant Adjutant Generals Office
Fort Omaha, Nebraska, September 16, 1879
To: Commanding Officer
Fort Fred Steele, Wyoming
Under orders from the General of the Army, you will at once move with sufficient number of troops to arrest such

Indian chiefs belonging to White River Agency as are insubordinate, and you will enforce obedience to the requirements of Agent Meeker. You will afford him such protection as the emergency of the case requires and hold the ringleaders as prisoners until an investigation can be had. You are authorized to suspend orders for movement of "E" Company, Third Cavalry, and to use this Company if necessary. Report receipt of this by telegraph and if you require additional troops.

By Command of General Crook:
(Signed) R. Williams
Assistant Adjutant General

Major T. T. Thornburg and his command left Fort Steele, Wyoming, as ordered and marched south over the blue shale flats toward the White River Agency. He had 33 supply wagons and 140 men, including two companies of cavalry and two companies of infantry. The army moved south to the present site of Craig, Colorado, then crossed the big sagebrush flats and struck the Yampa River where it joins Elkhead Creek a little over sixty miles north of Meeker's headquarters. Here Thornburg had a surprise meeting with the Ute sub-chief, Captain Jack (not to be confused with the Modoc chief of that name) and nine other braves. This was the first knowledge the Utes had that the army was heading for the agency, because Meeker had purposely kept the plans a secret for fear of a bloody uprising. Though outwardly calm, the Utes were thoroughly angry about the advancing army. Intentionally showing no ill will, Captain Jack left camp and notified the Utes that the army was coming to force them into submission. The next day Thornburg advanced his command up the Yampa and crossed near the present location of the Carey Ranch. He moved over the divide into Williams Fork and camped there September 27. Here Captain Jack and his party again parleyed with Thornburg. The Utes asked the major to take five soldiers as escort and ride with them to palaver with Meeker at the agency. Joe Rankin, Chief of Scouts, feared an Indian ruse to isolate Thornburg from his troops so they could kill him. The major accepted Rankin's advice and told Captain Jack that he would move his

troops to a point near the agency, where he would gladly negotiate with the agent and the Utes. Jack tried then to get Thornburg to make permanent camp at least fifty miles from the agency
as a gesture of good will toward the Indians. The major refused
his request, and Jack and his party left in a huff.

Thornburg's command started its march on the morning of the
twenty-ninth at 6:30 A.M., reaching Milk Creek at about 10:00
A.M. After watering the cavalry horses at the stream, two companies, E of the Third Cavalry, and F of the Fifth Cavalry, under
the immediate command of Major Thornburg, turned off the
road, taking a trail that bore away to the left, while Company
D, Fifth Cavalry, remained with the train which followed at a
distance of perhaps a mile. At this time no sign of Indians had
been observed, except a freshly started fire in the bottomland
grass, an occurrence with which they had grown so familiar that
no apprehension was excited by it. Guide Rankin and a small
party of soldiers were in the advance and, upon passing over
some high ground midway between the road which they had left
and the trail, discovered over three hundred Indians lying in
ambush along the high ridges which completely covered and
commanded the road. With a quick and soldierly perception of
the situation, the commanding lieutenant turned back and made
signals for the command to retrace it steps. Just as the leading
company, F of the Fifth Cavalry, was descending a ridge into
the valley beyond, it was ordered to the side of the hill on its left
flank. Company E, Third Cavalry, was halted on the high grounds
it occupied, and both companies at once dismounted and deployed as skirmishers.

The soldiers' line, at this time, roughly resembled the letter V,
the point being toward the Indians, with the side of it formed by
Company F, Fifth Cavalry, projecting considerably beyond the
point of junction, and being deflected to the left so as to prevent
the enemy from turning their flank. At this time attempts were
made by Major Thornburg, in person, to communicate with the
Indians. But efforts in this direction was met by a shot. At once a
hot fire was opened upon the soldiers and the fight began all
along the line.

The Indians displayed admirable skill in the selection of the ground upon which to give battle. And it was soon apparent that the Army's position was untenable in the face of an enemy superbly armed and greatly superior in force.

With sound judgment and a quick and thorough perception of the situation, Major Thornburg determined to form a junction with Company D, Fifth Cavalry, which was protecting the wagon train, and with that end in view directed the companies engaged to fall back slowly. The command retired as directed in perfect order, the horses being kept well protected between the skirmish lines of the two companies. Thus, the savages were prevented from breaking through Army lines. Failing in their efforts in front, the Indians endeavored to cut the command off from the train which had parked on the right bank of Milk Creek. To accomplish this purpose, the warriors passed around the army's left flank beyond carbine range and concentrated in great force upon a knoll to the left of, and completely commanding, the soldiers' retreat. Major Thornburg, discovering this new danger, directed Captain John S. Payne to charge the knoll with twenty men. They swept the Indians off the hill. Then, without attempting to hold the hill, he fell back upon the train and the way was opened for the retirement of the horses. Captain Payne, on returning to the wagon train, took immediate steps for its defense.

Major Thornburg doubtlessly started for the train shortly after giving Captain Payne his orders. Thornburg was shot and instantly killed just after crossing the river, within five hundred yards of the wagons.

In the meantime, Company E, Third Cavalry, with a detachment from Companies E and F, Fifth Cavalry, began to withdraw. The latter covered the retreat.

Upon reaching the train, Captain Payne found it circled on the right bank of Milk Creek, about two hundred yards from the water.

The animals were crowded within the corral formed by the wagons, and Payne at once directed some twenty or more of the wounded horses to be led out and shot at the mouth of the corral, so that their bodies might provide a continuous line of defense and afford cover for Army sharpshooters. As soon as these arrangements were completed the men were ordered to unload the wagons and to use bedding and filled grain and flour sacks for breastworks. One cannot speak too highly of the men's conduct at this time. Though exposed to galling fire, by which some men and many horses were struck down, they worked with alacrity and courage, and in a short time their corral was in as good a state of defense as the means at hand would permit.

A deep round rifle pit was scooped out within the enclosure to serve as a hospital for the wounded.

As two officers and men had not returned to camp, Payne sent a sergeant with twelve men to try to find them. Shortly, Payne was relieved to see the missing troops enter the entrenchments. Although wounded in action, Payne provided superb leadership to his troops.

A new and critical danger then threatened. The Indians, taking advantage of a high wind blowing directly towards the besieged camp, fired the tall grass and sagebrush along the creek. At the moment this peril was realized, Payne observed that John Gordon's supply train, filled with annuity goods, was parked within seventy-five yards of his position, and so situated as to command his approach to water. Seeing this, he feared the enemy might reach Gordon's train under cover of the smoke from the burning grassland. He directed that the grass on that side be fired, and in a few moments was gratified to see Gordon's train in flames. The fire from down the valley approached with great rapidity and struck the exposed point of the corral, igniting bundles, grain and flour sacks, wagon sheets, and all in its path, and for a few moments threatened destruction. At this time the Indians made their most ferocious attack, but the Army men kept their heads and sprayed the Utes with such a lethal fire that they retreated with heavy losses. Several Army lives were lost and many wounds received, but the fire was extinguished and the greatest danger passed. From this time, about 2:45 P.M., until nightfall, the Utes kept up a furious fire, killing fully three fourths of the animals and wounding several so badly they were ordered killed by Captain Payne.

At dusk a large body of Indians charged down behind Gordon's still burning train, delivering volley after volley of vicious fire. They were repulsed easily, and fled after suffering the loss of several warriors.

At night the Army's dead animals were hauled off; a full supply of water for twenty-four hours was procured; the wounded were cared for; and more entrenchments were dug. By daylight the corral was in good condition for defense. Couriers were sent out with dispatches at midnight without being detected by the Utes. A general feeling of confidence inspired the men. Ammunition and rations were distributed, and Payne felt that his command was ready to make a heroic stand the next time the Indians gave battle.

During the next day the Utes kept up an almost incessant fire, killing all the Army animals except fourteen mules. Nothing important happened during the night of the thirtieth. But after that time the enemy gave the soldiers no rest. On the night of October 1 their water party was fired upon at short range, and one man of Company F, Fifth Cavalry, was shot through the face. The water party guard returned this fire with effect, killing one Indian.

On the morning of October 3, Captain Francis S. Dodge with Company D, Ninth Cavalry, arrived on the scene. They had made a forced march from Middle Park (Colorado), southeast of the scene of action, to aid the encircled troops. While en route on the first of October, they found a penciled note attached to some sagebrush by the road which read: "Hurry up—the troops have been defeated at the Agency!" and signed "E.C.C.," one of the couriers dispatched earlier by Payne. Oddly enough the Utes allowed Dodge and his command to enter the area without a single shot being fired at them. The Indians apparently believed Dodge to be the vanguard of a much larger force.

Captain Dodge's small reinforcement cheered the beleaguered troopers, but the help was not enough to enable the soldiers to move out of their trap. Rations were low and the men lived mainly on corn; water was difficult to obtain, and they almost suffocated from the stench of putrifying animal carcasses.

At 5:30 A.M., October 6, 1879, the besieged army was rescued by troops under General Wesley Merritt, of Fort Russell, Wyoming Territory. Merritt had been alerted about the Milk Creek ambush by the chief scout, Joe Rankin, one of the couriers making a midnight escape the first night of the siege. Joe had made a heroic ride of over 160 miles through sagebrush hills and blue shale flats to Rawlins, Wyoming. Four hours after Rankin's telegram reached him, General Merritt was moving westward on a troop train toward Rawlins with 200 cavalry troops and 150 infantrymen. Merritt left Rawlins at 10:30 A.M., October 2, with infantrymen loaded in light wagons for a hasty trip. The rescuers made record time and reached the ashes of George Gordon's wagons at dawn, October 6.

Payne's troops lay obscure in the dawn; no sound of them could be heard. Merritt feared they might be dead but had his trumpeter sound the Officer's Call, the night signal for the Fifth Infantry. Soon the bugler in the besieged camp answered and there was a happy scramble as rejoicing men thrilled to their rescue from their devilish confinement.

Captain Dodge and Payne marched their remaining troops back to Rawlins. General Merritt advanced to the agency to discover that sub-chief Johnson and other renegades had murdered Meeker and his staff.

After the soldiers had buried the dead, Merritt established his new Army cantonment at the present site of Meeker, Colorado. Government agents rescued the kidnaped agency women and returned them to the Army. A bill was passed requiring the Utes to pay certain sums from their government annuities to Meeker massacre survivors and the families of those who were murdered. Specifically it required the Utes to pay:

> During the period of twenty years, if they shall live so long, the following sums respectively: To Mrs. Arivella D. Meeker, five hundred dollars; to Miss Josephine Meeker, five hundred dollars; to Mrs. Sophrina Price, five hundred dollars; to Mrs. Maggie Gordon, five hundred dollars; to George Dresser, two hundred dollars; to

Mrs. Sarah M. Post, five hundred dollars; to Mrs. Eaton, mother of George Eaton, two hundred dollars; to the parents of Arthur L. Thompson, two hundred dollars; to the father of Fred Shepard, two hundred dollars; to the parents of Wilmer Eskridge, two hundred dollars.

PART XIII
The Cheyennes Go Home
1878

Introduction

The Cheyennes belonged to the Algonquin family of Indians. They came out of Minnesota and lived for a time along the Sheyenne River in North Dakota. The bulk of the tribe later moved south to the Missouri River, where the Indians continued a sedentary existence until they adopted the horse. Thereupon, they became some of the greatest huntsmen and cavalrymen of all time. They occupied the Central Great Plains, lived off buffalo, and dwelt in skin tepees. They maintained a peaceful alliance with the Arapahoes, with whom they intermarried, and remained friendly with sedentary tribes along the Missouri. They warred with the Northern Dakotas, Sioux, Kiowas, Comanches, Crows, Shoshones, and Utes. The Mosaic Law of "eye for an eye and tooth for a tooth" prevailed among them and ingenious forms of killing and torture were invented and used.

George Bird Grinnell and William Bent claim that the Cheyennes were peaceful toward the whites until the United States reneged on its treaties and invaded and appropriated Indian lands. However, Grinnell wrote the classic saga, The Fighting Cheyennes, *which is primarily the chronology of Cheyenne fighting history. Early records do not bear out his statement that the Cheyennes were originally peaceful toward whites.*

Walter S. Campbell (Stanley Vestal) says they were the most warlike tribe of the warlike Plains Indians. General Frederick W. Benteen (as he eventually became) remarked that the Cheyenne and Sioux warriors who annihilated General George A. Custer's Seventh Cavalry were "good shots, good riders and the best fighters the sun ever shone on."

It was into this hotbed of potential turbulence that the white man maneuvered his western migration. Easterners greedily viewed the Great Plains and fringing mountains as a potential El Dorado with mineral-rich hills and lavish grasslands waiting only for cattle to replace the vanishing buffalo. The fact that these were Indian lands held by the sanction of treaty with the U. S. Government failed to hold back the advancing tide of whites that soon infiltrated the area. White men killed off the buffalo, the Indian's food, then began filling the ranges with cattle.

The Indians fought a defensive battle to hold their grazing lands. By 1870 they had levied a heavy toll on the settlers in varied types of depredations. They murdered vengefully to protect their homelands. The whites in turn fought passionately for their newly acquired homes and property.

The U. S. Government was thus forced to establish garrisons to patrol the Indian country to protect white pioneers. The U. S. Army suffered severe setbacks to start with. General George Crook was stalemated at the Battle of the Rosebud, and soon afterward General Custer and his Seventh Cavalry were annihilated by the Cheyenne and Sioux coalition in 1876 at the Battle of the Little Bighorn. From then on the tide of battle changed to white victories. The army under General Nelson A. Miles moved like a ravenous octopus, strangling the scattered Indian clans.

A few weeks after the Custer battle, the U. S. Cavalry surprised Dull Knife's village on Crazy Woman Creek near the Bighorns. The Cheyennes retreated but were not captured. Major Luther North and his Pawnee scouts, who were sent to burn the lodges and camp gear, found many articles which had belonged to members of the Seventh Cavalry.

Dull Knife's band wintered with Sioux Chief Crazy Horse's village in 1876–77. The next spring, Dull Knife surrendered his band to United States troops and most of his group were transferred to the Indian Territory to live with the Southern Cheyennes at the Darlington agency, at Fort Reno.

24. MASSACRE OF THE
DULL KNIFE BAND

B. W. ALLRED

The surrender of the Cheyennes to the U. S. Army and their removal to Indian Territory was a boon to the hordes of whites who began taking possession of the plains. The white settler's viewpoint of Dull Knife was generally in agreement with that expressed by Dennis Collins, an early historian who was familiar with central plains conditions. It was not a cliché of fiction that dead Indians are good Indians, for many whites firmly believed the Indians had to be killed in order to insure settlement. Their own scalps were at stake.

Said Collins,

> *Dull Knife was at Fort Reno only a short time until he began fomenting trouble. He claimed the water and grass*

were no good, and the agent was stealing his chuckaway
[rations] *and his family and friends were famishing. Dull
Knife could with less provocation stir up more strife with
less raw material to start with than any Indian I ever knew
or heard of; he complained bitterly all winter, but on
ration day he was there with the rest.*

The Indians swapped off their merchantable possessions to
border hawkers for arms and ammunition. When his ponies had
fattened on green grass the next spring, Dull Knife told the Indian agent that he was taking his band to their northern buffalo
hunting grounds. The agent gave orders for him to stay at the
agency and dispatched a troop to guard him and his band.

But Dull Knife sneaked away from sleeping guards and fled.
He skirmished with the pursuing soldiers and moved his people
northward. Collins claims these renegade Cheyennes pillaged
ranches for food and killed many whites.

The band was finally captured by soldiers and penned up at
Fort Robinson, Nebraska. There they killed their guards and ran
for the sandhills. The soldiers engaged them again and killed
many Indians.

Dull Knife claimed that he had surrendered under the guaran-
tee that he could return north again if he became dissatisfied
with the Darlington agency at Fort Reno, to which he and his
people were taken. His band was irked at the confinement and
the overriding vexations imposed by the army and Indian agency.
The living in "unhealthful" Oklahoma and the loss of the buffalo
induced a serious and infectious spiritual sickness.

The northern Cheyennes grew homesick for their dry high
home in the Dakotas, Montana, and Wyoming. They were buffalo
eaters and nearly starved on the skinny cattle issued by the government inspector. The Indian agent claims he received rations
for only nine months of the year, hence the Indians suffered from
malnutrition much of the time. They were readily susceptible to
the malarial diseases which prevailed among the Southern Cheyennes.

Some time later, Little Wolf, one of the tribal chiefs, told of their tribulations to a Congressional committee in the following words:

> *A great many have been sick, some have died. I have been sick a great deal of the time since I have been down here—homesick and heartsick and sick in every way. I have been thinking of my native country and the good home I had up there where I was never hungry, but when I wanted anything to eat I could go out and hunt buffalo. It makes me feel sick when I think about that, and I cannot help thinking about that.*

Dissatisfied Cheyennes begged Dull Knife and Little Wolf to lead them home. The Indian agent was under orders to hold them on the reservation and placed a guard to prevent their threatened escape.

One day, three of Little Wolf's braves escaped and the agent brought in Little Wolf to account for this misbehavior. When the chief and two of his men, Wild Hog and Crow, reported, the agent asked for ten Cheyennes to be held as hostages until the soldiers could run down the three absent braves and return them. Little Wolf knew the Army had little chance of retrieving the runaways and he feared his ten hostages would never be freed. Hence he refused the agent's demands. Threats were exchanged, and Little Wolf boldly told the agent he was going north and that if the Army tried to overtake him there would be a bloody fight.

He had his men returned to their camp twenty miles above the agency on the Canadian river, where he and Dull Knife prepared for flight and fighting. Both were courageous leaders, Dull Knife the strategist around the council fire, Little Wolf the fierce, brave warrior and victor of many coups.

Old campaigners claim that the Dull Knife escape was one of the most heroic marches of wartime history. The little band consisted of three hundred Indians, of which sixty or seventy were able warriors, the rest being women, children, and old men. Thirteen thousand U. S. troops converged from all directions to exterminate this courageous little band as it fought northward over leagues of the vast plains of Oklahoma and Kansas. Troops engaged the Indians a hundred miles north of Fort Reno, but the runaways struck doggedly northward and Dull Knife's eyes flickered nervously over his back trail as he prodded his band onward. They fought and marched and avoided conflict with whites as much as possible. There were four heavy engagements between Cheyennes and soldiers and only six Indians were killed, but several were wounded.

After crossing the Platte River west of Ogallala, the Cheyenne forces split. Little Wolf's band drew north and wintered in the buffalo-rich Nebraska sandhills. Dull Knife headed northwest toward Fort Robinson and Pine Ridge. Safely across the Platte, he admonished his people to leave the whites alone and live at peace in their own homeland.

The head drainages of the Niobrara and White rivers were swarming with U. S. cavalry and Dull Knife's band had an accidental meeting with soldiers on October 23, 1878. The soldiers lined up for an engagement, but nothing happened as Dull Knife raised the white flag and took his sub-chiefs to talk to the commanding officer, a Captain Johnson of the Third Cavalry. Dull Knife told him, "We have come back home to go to our old agency; you can return at once. We shall go to the agency as soon as we can get there." The meeting ended peaceably; the parties split and camped some distance apart on a small branch on the Niobrara.

Next day the Indians followed the cavalry trail and camped at night near the Army. As soon as the Cheyennes made camp, soldiers rounded up their horses and herded them to one side. This annoyed the Indians temporarily, until Army men doled out rations including sugar and coffee. Other troops arrived during the night, and by morning the Indians saw the snouts of artillery fieldpieces pointed dead center on their camp.

After breakfast, the Army officers demanded that the Indians surrender their guns and ammunition, which they did. But they kept a few rifles and pistols, hidden in women's clothing and camp trappings. Only the men were searched. They were allowed to keep knives and bows.

Then followed a hectic ten-day powwow about where the Indians were to surrender. The Cheyennes argued angrily for the

Red Cloud Agency in South Dakota (later the name was changed to Pine Ridge Agency), the soldiers insisted on Fort Robinson. Tempers reached the boiling point and a fight was threatening. Both sides dug in.

One officer told Dull Knife the Army men merely wanted them to go to Fort Robinson to surrender, after which they would be rationed and sent to the Red Cloud Agency. This statement was repeated several times during the ten-day period but Dull Knife suspected the devious ingenuity of soldiers. "Soldier has forked tongue," said the old chief. "Him who speaks much is much mistaken."

Army pressure continued, and as reinforcements increased the hapless Cheyennes were forced to accede to Army demands. So Dull Knife ordered his weary band to pack up their cluttered, dirty tepees and wade through the snow to Fort Robinson for formal surrender.

Near sundown the frozen exhausted Cheyennes dragged into Fort Robinson where they were fed and billeted in a long building set aside as Indian quarters. That night they were counted and their names listed. Indian leaders were Dull Knife, Wild Hog, Bull Hump, Tangle Hair, and Strong Left Hand.

Next morning hope was shattered when the Indians were told they would be held at Fort Robinson for three months until the Army decided whether to send them south to the Darlington Agency or to let them remain in the north with the Sioux at the Red Cloud Agency. The frustrated Cheyennes figured they were the victims of a devilish plot to swindle them out of their birthrights.

They were told they would continue to be allowed the moderate freedom of the post and nearby foothills, provided they returned to the fort each night. The commanding officer told them, "If one of you deserts, you will not be treated like this any longer. You will all be held responsible for him."

At this, Dull Knife told his people to do as commanded and said, "We are back on our own ground and have stopped fighting. We have found the place we started to come to."

For two months tranquillity reigned. The Indians were warm and well fed. They wandered freely, hunting rabbits and gathering red-willow bark along the streams, but at night each was back for the supper count. Socials were held in the barracks; soldiers danced with the girls and gave them money to buy ornaments. The Cheyennes thought the Great White Father was a mighty good chief after all.

But one day Bull Hump jumped camp and ran off to find his wife at the Red Cloud Agency. All liberty was suspended and the Indians were penned up in the quarters under guard. Three days later Bull Hump was returned.

The U. S. Army leaders then tried to induce the Cheyennes to return to Fort Reno, and to this request they bitterly objected. Dull Knife told Captain Henry Walton Wessells, Jr. (Third Cavalry), that the captain could kill him at the camp, but he would *not* go south. Wessells was insensitive, however, to the Indians' fretful pleas to remain in their homeland. Wessells' next act was to cut all rations and try to starve them into submission, but Dull Knife was a crusty old gamecock who stubbornly starved. The officers tried to induce the women and children to leave the jail, letting the men stay, but the Indians would not let this happen.

Indian tempers boiled over at this eccentric form of Army injustice and declared war on the Army. They remained sullenly in their barracks plotting an escape from their jail. Food, fuel, and water were withheld and they lived for a time on leftover food scraps, licked frost from windows, and survived the cold by bundling together in their blankets and camping gear.

James Rowland of Pine Ridge served as interpreter during this hectic incarceration. As starvation continued, the Indians told him not to enter their jail nor let others come in or they would be killed. They suffered stoically through their piteous predicament. Many were half delirious from hunger, thirst, and fear. Some claimed they were without food and water eight days; others said there was no water for three days, no food for five days.

On January 9, 1879, the gritty little band decided to break out and fight for life in the open air rather than rot in jail. They assembled the rifles and pistols that they had concealed in pieces in the squaws' clothing when forced to give up their arms and made ready to break loose at sunset. They dressed in their finest buckskins and moccasins and kissed each other good-by. Blankets, saddles, and camp gear were piled on the floor next to the windows so they could easily step from the room to the ground. Blankets were tied to their backs for use on the outside.

The soldiers were expecting the Indians to try to escape, so the commanding officer placed a chain of overlapping sentries around the building.

The Indians' coup was brilliantly planned to checkmate the well-calculated defenses of the soldiers. Little Shield and several other men were posted by the windows ready to shoot the guards. He fired the first shot, whereupon the Indians all jumped to the snow-covered ground and dashed for the creek in the moonlight. The fleeing Indians stopped at the creek to slake their thirst before ploughing westward through the snow along the frozen creek toward the hills and freedom.

Shots awakened the sleeping post personnel, who jumped to doors and windows to find out what had happened. Some of the escaping Indians observed these jittery sightseers in their white nightclothes and wondered if they were to be assailed by spirits as well as by Army guards.

Indians and soldiers ran helter-skelter. Bullets whizzed in all directions. Indian men, women, and children fell wounded or dead, their blood clotting in the snow. Army forces were soon assembled and began tracing the fleeing Indians. Many dead were scattered over the snow, and the enfeebled women and children were easy to follow. Five exhausted women with babies stopped to rest in some pines. Later their bodies were found where they had been shot by soldiers. One of the women was Dull Knife's daughter.

By daylight next day, the soldiers had brought sixty-five captives back to the post. Many of these were wounded. A six-mule-team wagon was dispatched to bring in fifty dead Indians, their frozen bodies decked like cordwood.

On this same day, Captain Wessells asked the captives if they would return south. A badly wounded girl spat back at the captain, "No, we will not go back, we will die rather. You have killed most of us, why do you not go ahead and now finish the work?"

One band of runaways took shelter in a buffalo wallow, and all but three were shot in a crossfire set up by pursuing soldiers.

A small party, including Dull Knife and his wife, his son's wife and child, and a young warrior, Red Bird, turned off from the main course followed by the Cheyennes and holed up in a big cave, nearly starving on a spartan diet of roots, moccasins, and sinew. Eighteen days later they showed up at interpreter Rowland's home at the Pine Ridge agency, where they were cared for.

Of the 150 nervy Cheyennes incarcerated at Fort Robinson, 64 were killed after escaping, 58 were allowed to stay at Pine Ridge, about 20 went to the southern Cheyennes, and the fate of the remaining eight or ten was never learned. Those who survived finally worked their way up to Fort Keogh and later were taken to the Tongue River Reservation where most of them eventually died of illness or old age.

Dull Knife died in 1883 in his high dry homeland. He lies buried on a grassy butte overlooking the valley of the Rosebud river in southern Montana.

Thus ends the tragic story of Morningstar—which is the poetic Cheyenne name for Dull Knife. The latter is the translation of his Sioux name. He provided a fighting leadership and was never intimidated. His greatest adversary was the inability of the white man to understand the Indian way of life and his ignorance of the Indian's real capacity for peace and co-operation.

PART XIV

The Ghost Dance
1891

Introduction

Few stories of American frontier history have enjoyed a greater popularity than the tale of how the Sioux under Sitting Bull and Crazy Horse beat back the attack of the Seventh Cavalry at the Little Bighorn and left that proud regiment to nurse its wounds and taste the bitter cup of defeat. Often spoken of as the "Custer Massacre," it was not a massacre, but a stand-up, give-and-take battle, in which the Seventh was defeated by its own poor leadership and the overwhelming odds.

Nevertheless, it seemed that the Indian wars were over, that never again would the Seventh face the Sioux in battle. The war which General Nelson A. Miles had waged against that tribe and its allies through the bitter winter of 1876–77 had ended with the complete surrender of most of the northern Plains Indians. The Sioux, the Cheyennes, and the Arapahoes were now broken peoples, settled upon reservations, trying to farm and to follow the white man's road.

Stubborn Sitting Bull had not surrendered. "God made me an Indian, but not a reservation Indian," he said, and retreated north into Canada with his followers. But Sitting Bull found, like many a man before and since, that he must change his mind. At last the chief began negotiations with the American authorities, and in 1881 the Canadian officials, with a sigh of relief, bade farewell to their turbulent red refugee. Sitting Bill became a reservation Indian, settling at Standing Rock, probably not many miles from where he was born.

But Sitting Bull's boast that he was not a reservation Indian was only too true. He hated and distrusted the white man all his life. He was a wily and astute politician, and the unrest and discontent incident to turning a group of fighting nomads into peaceful farmers, coupled with the inevitable misunderstandings on both sides, provided a fertile field for his troublemaking talents. Complicating the picture was the graft and corruption often present among the white men, sometimes in astonishingly high places. Agents were often inefficient, even when honest.

The Indians were promised that there would be no reduction of rations, but Congress failed to appropriate enough money to feed them; so, hard on the heels of the promise, came a ration-cut of from one third to one half. The Sioux were hungry. The warriors who once whipped Custer and drove Crook back were now living in a state of semi-starvation.

Epidemics of influenza, measles, and whooping cough swept through their ranks. Lowered resistance due to malnutrition made the mortality rate abnormally high. Many Indians lost all hope. They had nothing more to lose but their lives, and to many life seemed no longer to be of value. They were ready to grasp at any straw of hope. The hope came in the form of a new religion, the Ghost Dance.

In the late 1880s in Nevada a Paiute named Wovoka, known to the whites as Jack Wilson, was recovering from a long illness. As he pondered the strange and vivid fever dreams which had come to him, he became convinced that they represented direct, divine revelations. The doctrine which he began preaching was a strange medley of tribal beliefs and Christian concepts caught from the missionaries.

He taught that he had seen God, a majestic figure clad in flowing white robes and with long yellow hair. God showed him the nail-wounds in His hands and feet. God said that He had appeared upon earth before, to the white people who had rejected His teachings and killed Him. Now He was about to appear again, this time to the Indians. They must prepare for His coming, work, live good lives, not fight or quarrel among themselves or with other peoples. They must discard all the things they had obtained from the white men as far as this was possible but, strangely enough, they were to send their children to school.

When God came again the dead would rise and the white men would be no more. Once more the buffalo would cover the land, coming out from the caves where they had hidden from the white man.

Wovoka claimed he was given, by God, sacred songs and prayers and the sacred dance, which he was to teach the Indians. Certain paints, paint patterns, and garments were prescribed.

Delegations came to Wovoka from many tribes, who participated in the new dance, were converted, and returned to preach the new cult and set hopeless hearts beating wildly with the hope that soon the good old days would come again. Cheyenne, Arapaho, Kiowa, Comanche, Sioux—these were but a few of the tribes that caught the contagion of the new dance, the dream, the hope. Soon the Indian West was in a boiling ferment of excitement.

"Soon now, soon," tribesmen whispered to each other. War-scarred warriors in tattered denims and flour-sack shirts pondered gravely each unusual phenomenon of nature. Perhaps it was a sign sent by the "above-ones." Young men were sent out to scout for the first sign of the returning buffalo.

The Sioux first had word of the Messiah in the summer of 1889, through visitors from other reservations, and from the letters of those who were away in the schools. In the fall of that year a council was held on the matter by Red Cloud, Young-Man-Afraid, Little Wound, and other chiefs. Their attitude was summed up by one who said, "If this thing is good, we should have it. If it is not, it will fall to the ground of itself."

A delegation was sent to call upon Wovoka and investigate the new religion. The delegates were gone all winter and returned converted in the spring of 1890. Their report created an intense excitement among the Sioux, who had awaited them eagerly.

A council was called to discuss the report, but the Indian agent arrested Good Thunder and two of the other delegates. They refused to talk and in two days were released. Soon afterward, Kicking Bear, another delegate, returned from a visit to the Arapahoes and reported that they were dancing and that in the trance they saw and talked with their dead relatives.

The excitement mounted through the summer of 1890, as the

crops withered and died in the hot wind. It was a portent, a plain sign from the above-ones that this wind, which withered the crops and made useless all the toil and drudgery of the white man's road, should blow from the direction whence came this new hope. It was as if the God-of-the-South-Direction had said, "Behold, I bring to you a promise and a hope, and as a token I take away this new thing, this evil thing, which has come upon you."

25. TRAGEDY AT WOUNDED KNEE

GEORGE METCALF

As the Ghost Dance became front page news, the settlers began demanding military protection, and the Governor of South Dakota petitioned the War Department to send troops. The agent at Pine Ridge was frantically demanding soldiers to quell a threatened outbreak. All possible influence was brought to bear, and although one Senator moved to send a hundred thousand rations, Congress sent troops to overawe the hungry Sioux. A body of Nebraska Militia under General Colby arrived at Pine Ridge. Fifty Cheyennes and as many Crow scouts were employed; a battery of Hotchkiss guns was sent. Then the Seventh Cavalry, now under the command of Colonel James W. Forsyth, arrived, and once more the Sioux and the Seventh faced each other.

The presence of the troops made the Indians resentful and suspicious, but there were no hostile demonstrations. From the viewpoint of the Ghost Dancers it would have been folly to have provoked trouble. Why should they fight the soldiers? God would destroy them in the spring when He came again.

The troops loafed in camp, frankly bored and spoiling for a fight. Officers admitted that they did not know why they were there—there seemed to be no need of them. Newspaper correspondents sent out highly colored stories, but teachers and missionaries continued to move freely among the Sioux without molestation.

In mid-November orders were given that the Indians were to collect at their various agencies, and the largest part of the tribe began to do so. The more conservative element, the bulk of the Ghost Dancers, as well as many who were simply frightened by the presence of the troops, mistrusting the motives of the government, retreated into the Bad Lands. These immediately became known as "hostiles" although they had as yet committed no acts of hostility. Then, in December, it was learned that Sitting Bull was planning to place himself at the head of these dissatisfied groups.

Agent James McLaughlin dispatched a force of Sioux policemen on the night of December 14 to arrest the old chief and bring him to Fort Yates. They surrounded his house and he was awakened at dawn and told that he was under arrest. After a short talk he agreed to go in to see the agent. His Sioux followers begged him not to go, and his son taunted him with cowardice for going so readily. Stung by this the chief seated himself, saying, "I will not go." One of his followers then fired, hitting the leader of the police who instantly shot Sitting Bull, while another policeman struck him with a tomahawk. A short, sharp skirmish took place which ended in the flight of the chief's followers.

The news of Sitting Bull's death ran like wildfire among the

Sioux. From man to man and group to group, by word of mouth, smoke signals, and mirror flashes the news ran. Rumors and wild tales of all kinds were carried by the moccasin telegraph throughout the reservations.

The Sioux were panic-stricken. They feared and distrusted the Army and the police as much as the whites feared and distrusted the Sioux. The panic of the refugees from Sitting Bull's camp was infectious, and more groups joined the hostiles, hiding far back in the rough, broken country of the Pine Ridge, or in the almost inaccessible fastnesses of the Bad Lands.

It now became the task of the Army to comb this immense area in order to round up and bring these suspicious groups back into semi-confinement, and to do so if possible without bloodshed. It was a nervous, wearing job and in general was ably performed. Troops moved through the broken country, often by night marches, in search of the scattered groups of hostiles.

The most important leader still at large outside the Bad Lands was Big Foot, well known as a man of peace. His camp was near the forks of Sheyenne River, and Colonel E. V. Sumner, with a troop of the Eighth Cavalry had been detailed to watch him.

Big Foot and his headmen visited the camp of the troops, assured the officers of their friendship, and convinced them of their peaceful intentions.

But after the death of Sitting Bull, thirty of the dead chief's followers came to Big Foot's camp. When Colonel Sumner received word that these fugitives from the reservation had joined Big Foot, he ordered the entire band brought in to the Pine Ridge agency.

Big Foot went to Colonel Sumner and told him frankly that while he himself would go wherever he was ordered, he feared that there would be trouble if an attempt was made to force the women and children, who were cold and hungry, to leave the village.

Sumner, however, foresaw trouble and decided to force the Indians to come in, meanwhile sending a white man who had a friendly acquaintance with Big Foot to tell the Indians that they must obey the orders of the military and proceed to the agency. This man, with a view to frightening the Indians into a still more submissive mood, made a number of statements about the hostile intentions and savage nature of the troops which, together with the tales told by the refugees from Standing Rock, frightened the band into flight. That evening they left their village and, instead of turning toward the agency, headed south. Big Foot and his band, cold, hungry, and frightened, had "jumped the reservation" and headed for the Bad Lands.

The chief wanted to join the hostiles under Kicking Bear and Short Bull, but before making contact with that band he was intercepted by Major S. M. Whitside and four troops of the Seventh Cavalry, on December 28.

When they saw the soldiers, the Indians halted and raised a white flag. Big Foot, seriously ill with pneumonia, left the pony-drag upon which he was being carried and stumbled forward. His attempt to parley was cut short.

"Surrender or fight," said the officer, "which will it be?"

The old chief made a sudden, hopeless gesture; his hands sketched the "All done" sign. Head and shoulders bent he stood there for a moment while the wind whipped the tatters of his ragged clothing.

"We surrender," he said.

Upon receiving word that Big Foot had been arrested, General John R. Brooke sent Colonel Forsyth that night, with four additional troops of the Seventh, a Hotchkiss battery, and a company of scouts, to reinforce Major Whitside. Forsyth, as senior officer, took command of the entire force, now numbering 470 men.

Camp that night was made on the west side of Wounded Knee Creek, at some little distance from the stream. The tepees were pitched in a semicircle just within the mouth of a wide, shallow gulch which runs into a narrow, waist-deep gully. Immediately north was a low knoll upon which the artillery was placed, muzzles trained upon the camp. The stage was set and the curtain about to rise upon the final act of the tragedy of the American Indian.

Next morning it was decided to disarm the Indians before moving them on to the agency at Pine Ridge, twenty miles distant.

When called from their tepees the Indian men collected about Big Foot's tent and seated themselves quietly upon the ground. They were then told to go to their tepees, collect their weapons, and stack them in front of the tent of the chief.

The first twenty returned with only two guns. After a consultation among the officers, troops were moved to within ten yards of the group, and squads were detailed to search the camp.

The search was thorough, quick, and rough. Troopers shouldered their way into the tepees, ripped beds apart, tossed through bundles of clothing, tore open bags. Women protested shrilly and volubly as they were deprived of the knives which they wore at their belts and used in household tasks. Their men stood within the square, sullen and uncomprehending, muttering to one another as the cries of the women came to them. Protesting women tried to block the entry of troopers into their homes, and were flung aside. Here and there a tent went down as a struggling group of soldiers and women careened against it. The muttering among the men grew louder. Nervous tension mounted. Husbands and brothers, not knowing what might happen next, clutched knives beneath the blankets.

The squads came back with about forty guns, mostly old muzzle-loaders, which they piled in front of Big Foot's tent.

A young man took a rifle from beneath his blanket and walked toward the pile to lay it down. Two soldiers seized the gun and attempted to wrest it from him. A scuffle began for possession of the weapon.

Yellow Bird, a medicine man, was threading his way through the groups, preaching resistance. "When I throw a handful of dust into the air, the *wasichu's* [the white men's] eyes will be made blind," he said. "When I throw up a handful of dust . . . kill."

Suddenly he bent, straightened, flung up his arm. A puff of dust blossomed from his fingers like the smoke of a rifle-shot. Perhaps it was coincidence . . . many Indians afterward claimed it was an accident . . . but a rifle shot came from where the trio struggled for the gun. A soldier crumpled and fell forward on his face.

The nervous tension broke in an explosion of violent action.

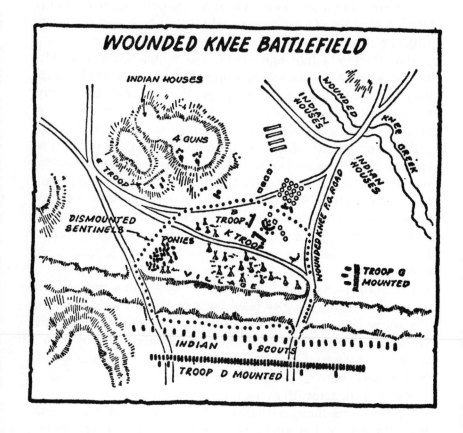

The crowd of Indians became an insane mob, screaming battle cries. A few of the murderous, stone-headed war hammers of the Sioux came out from beneath the blankets and began to swing. Knife blades flashed in the morning sun. Father Kraft, a priest—whom the Sioux knew well, liked, and respected—sprang among the frantic warriors trying to bring them to reason. He went down with a knife-wound through the lungs . . . and lived. Captain George B. Wallace fell, wounded in the leg, and died under the knives. Some Indians tried to rearm themselves with the guns piled before the tent, while others threw themselves like wildcats straight at the troopers' throats, with no weapons but their bare hands.

This was what the Seventh had been waiting for; this chance was too good to miss. A volley crashed into the Sioux at point-blank range from all four sides of the square, and half the men grouped about Big Foot's tent went down. Yellow Bird fell. Big Foot died there.

The steady roar of the Springfields was punctuated by the crash of the Hotchkiss guns from the knoll. These went into action at the first shot from below, slamming two-pound high-explosive shells into the camp among the women and children. One woman survivor received fourteen wounds from a single shellburst. Some tepees went down and others caught fire, burning fiercely over the wounded and helpless inmates.

Bullets still ploughed into the ranks of the men. Soldiers fell too, some under the Sioux knives, more from the fire of their own comrades across the square.

Hopelessly outnumbered, the few remaining warriors broke from the square and ran, scattering, hiding, looking for shelter and safety. Some broke toward the tents and their families, running desperately until overtaken in mid-stride by the heavy bullets that flung them sprawling. Others died under the thunder-bolts of the artillery.

It took two minutes to turn the camp into a burning shambles, with the surviving Indians scattered in utter rout.

The soldiers surged forward, blood-mad. They fired at every Indian who moved—man, woman, or child, well or wounded. They shot the very dogs of the camp, the horses. . . . "My father ran and then fell down and blood came out of his mouth, and then a soldier put his gun up to my white pony's nose and shot him," said a Sioux child two years afterward.

Many of the women and children fled for protection to the shallow gully which leads back toward the hills. Here they hid, crouching low. Scouts, urged on by soldiers, called to them. "Come out. We do not make war on women and children." Two small boys climbed out, and fell under a hail of bullets. Neither age nor sex meant anything to the troopers of the Seventh that day.

There is testimony that immediately after the action an officer of the Seventh said, "with much gluttonous satisfaction in his voice, 'Now we have avenged Custer's death.'"

Troops scattered in pursuit of the fleeing Indians, following them up nearby ravines, riding along the gully, and firing into the groups who were using its banks to shelter their retreat. The "wagon-guns" were turned to sweep this gully and to shell other fleeing groups.

Lieutenant (afterward Brigadier General) E. S. Godfrey, writing in 1931, said that *some time after all firing had ceased* he was ordered to pursue a group of women who were escaping down a ravine full of small pines and scattered clumps of bushes. Seeing a movement among the bushes he ordered his detachment to fire, killing a woman and three children, and badly wounding a boy of fourteen. A young soldier finished the boy at once.

This was not the only wounded Indian who was shot. One warrior fell with a wound in his leg and as he lay helpless, was shot again through the body. As an example of the terrible casualties suffered by the band it may be mentioned that this man who recovered lost his father, his mother, two brothers, a sister, his wife and a child at Wounded Knee.

The firing had been heard for miles around and now mounted Indians were gathering upon the hill crests to the west—"friendlies" from the agency. They sprang up like magic, increasing in number every minute, but they were no longer "friendlies." They had seen their kinsmen butchered, and now they were only Sioux . . . mounted and armed warriors.

The threatening attitude of these Indians, who now outnumbered his Army force, plus the approach of a blizzard, forced Forsyth hastily to gather his dead and wounded as well as his thirty-three severely wounded prisoners—all but six of whom were women and children—and fall back into the agency town of Pine Ridge. The blizzard struck long before he reached the town; and while it increased the suffering of the wounded, the storm prevented any attack being made by the rapidly gathering tribesmen.

It was not possible to return to the scene until January 1, 1891, three days after the affair, when a party accompanied by a number of civilians, war correspondents, and others, went out to bury the dead. Scattered about in the snow which now covered the scene were the frozen bodies of Big Foot and most of the warriors of his band and, among them and scattered up the ravine for a distance of two or three miles, the bodies of women and children. A few wounded had been left upon the field, some of whom still lived despite their exposure to the rigors of a Dakota blizzard. A few children were rescued from beside the bodies of mothers who, before they died, had removed their blankets and shawls and wrapped the infants in them. One baby, a girl was adopted by General Colby, and other whites adopted orphans from the band.

Dr. Charles Eastman, who accompanied the burial party, mentions the fact that some of the young women and girls had pulled their shawls over their heads and buried their faces in their hands, as if they could not face their death when the soldiers came to kill them.

Many observers mention the body of a woman which lay at the foot of the pole on which the white flag waved. All speak of the huddled groups of women and children lying dead in the gully, and of the shell-torn bodies of others, killed as they fled up the ravine after all resistance had ceased.

The bodies were collected with buckboards and wagons, and pictures taken at the time show these piled high with frozen corpses, the bodies being stacked on them like cordwood. A long trench was dug on top of the low knoll and in this common grave the victims of the massacre were piled. When it was full the earth was heaped on top and the burial was complete.

Many of the bodies went naked into the grave, the bloody clothing having been stripped from them as souvenirs. One of the burial party afterward said, "It was a thing to melt the heart of a man, to see those little children, with their bodies shot to pieces, thrown naked into the pit."

The casualties of that day will never be precisely known. In the mass grave were buried the bodies of 84 men and boys, 44 women, and 16 young children—144 in all. A number of the dead had been carried away by the Indians, and some of the prisoners died after being brought in. General Miles estimated that probably 300 Indians were killed outright or died of wounds and exposure.

Thirty-one whites were killed and 33 wounded, some of whom later died. Many of these undoubtedly fell under the fire of their own excited comrades as they shot into the mass of men within the square. Old Indians, as well as many whites who were present or knew the Big Foot band, declare to this day that most of the white casualties were caused in this manner, insisting that the Indians in the square were without guns.

General Miles speaks of the incident as a "general melee and massacre," and says again, "a massacre occurred." Miles went on to record further that "the action of the commanding officer . . . was most reprehensible," and that "I have regarded the whole affair as most unjustifiable and worthy of the severest condemnation." General Miles particularly mentioned the killing of women and children at a distance of two or three miles from the camp in bringing court-martial charges against Forsyth. Secretary of War Proctor exonerated Forsyth, the evidence not being made public.

Today one follows a good road across the reservation from Pine Ridge to Wounded Knee. The scene has changed little in the past sixty-five years . . . a few buildings, a road. One walks across the grassy little flat where the Indian camp stood. The tree-lined banks of Wounded Knee Creek are not far away to the east. Immediately to the west, a shallow, smoothly sloping gulch or "draw" leads west to the hill crest. Not far from the campsite stands the post office and trading post of Wounded Knee. A few small frame houses are scattered about within a radius of a mile, but properly speaking there is no town. The narrow, shallow ravine, up which the women and children fled, winds unchanged between the trading post and the low knoll to the northeast.

A small, white-painted frame church now stands on the knoll where the Hotchkiss battery stood on that tragic December morning, and one can stand on its doorstep and with map and notes locate the positions of each party.

Behind the church is a little cemetery, and in the center, dominating it, is a long narrow area enclosed by a low cement curb: the mass grave. Suddenly the whole episode becomes real, something very close and very vivid. A people's dream is buried here with its dead.

The grave has been marked with a simple stone shaft. It bears a short inscription telling its purpose, and three sides carry the names of some of the dead who lie beneath it. The fourth side carries but one name: "Charging Cloud, the Peacemaker, died here innocent."

As you walk back toward the road and your parked car many thoughts go through your mind; Custer, the Little Bighorn, Reno's men and their battle at the ford and the gallant defense of the hilltop. In very shame you try not to think of Wounded Knee.

All honor to the Seventh Cavalry, a brave and gallant regiment.

But, truly, they were greater in their day of defeat, than in victory.

BIBLIOGRAPHY

CHAPTER 1

J. Cecil Alter. *James Bridger*. Salt Lake City, Utah, 1925.

John G. Bourke. *On the Border with Crook*. New York, 1891.

Cyrus T. Brady. *Indian Fights and Fighters*. New York, 1904.

Edward S. Ellis. *The Indian Wars of the United States*. Grand Rapids, Michigan, 1892.

Theodore Roosevelt. *The Winning of the West*. 4 vols.; New York, 1900.

Paul I. Wellman. *Death on the Prairie*. New York, 1934.

———. *Death in the Desert*. New York, 1935.

CHAPTER 2

Jennie Broughton Brown. *Fort Hall of the Oregon Trail*. Caldwell, Idaho, 1932.

Hiram M. Chittenden. *A History of the American Fur Trade of the Far West*. 2 vols.; Stanford, California, 1954.

Bernard De Voto. *Across the Wide Missouri*. Boston, 1947.

Howard R. Driggs. *Westward America*. New York, 1942.

W. A. Ferris. *Life in the Rocky Mountains*. Denver, 1940.

L. R. Hafen and W. Ghent. *Broken Hand*. Denver, 1931.

Burton Harris. *John Colter, His Years in the Rockies*. New York, 1952.

Washington Irving. *The Adventures of Captain Bonneville, U.S.A., in the Rocky Mountains and the Far West,* in the *Complete Works of Washington Irving*. New York, n.d.

Zenas Leonard (edited by John C. Ewers). *Adventures of Zenas Leonard, Fur Trader*. Norman, Oklahoma, 1959.

Merrill J. Mattes. *"Jackson Hole, Crossroads of the American Fur Trade, 1830–1840," Pacific Northwest Quarterly*, Vol. XXXIX, No. 1, 1948.

Dale Morgan. *Jedediah Smith*. Indianapolis, 1953.

George Nidever (edited by William H. Ellison). *The Life and Adventures of George N. Dever*. Berkeley, California, 1937.

Alexander Ross. *The Fur Hunters of the Far West*, Vol. I, edited by M. M. Quaife. Chicago, 1924.

William L. Sublette. Letter in *Missouri Republican*, October 16, 1832.

John B. Wyeth. *Oregon: A Short History of a Long Journey*, Vol. XXI in R. G. Thwaites' *Early Western Travels*. Cleveland, 1904–7.

Nathaniel J. Wyeth (edited by F. G. Young). *The Correspondence and Journals of Captain Nathaniel J. Wyeth*, 1831–1836. Eugene, Oregon, 1899.

CHAPTER 3

O. Clark Fisher. *It Occurred in Kimble*. Houston, 1937.

James Kimmins Greer. *Colonel Jack Hays*. New York, 1952.

J. Marvin Hunter. *Pioneer History of Bandera County*. Bandera, Texas, 1922.

A. J. Sowell. *Early Settlers and Indian Fighters of Southwest Texas*. Austin, 1900.

Walter Prescott Webb. *The Texas Rangers*. Boston and New York, 1935.

———— (editor-in-chief). *The Handbook of Texas*. 2 vols.; Austin, 1952.

CHAPTER 4

George W. Fuller. *A History of the Pacific Northwest*. Caldwell, Idaho, 1945.

Francis B. Heitman. *Historical Register and Dictionary of the United States Army*, Vol I. Washington, D.C., 1903.

Benjamin F. Manring. *The Conquest of the Coeur d'Alênes, Spokanes and Palouses*. Spokane, 1912.

Report of the Secretary of War dated December 6, 1858, House Executive Documents, No. 2, 35th Congress, 2d Session, 1858–59. Washington, D.C., 1859.

Edgar I. Stewart. *Washington-Northwest Frontier*, Vol. II. New York, 1957.

Washington, Washington Writers' Project of the W.P.A. Portland, Oregon, 1941.

CHAPTER 5

William Norbet Bischoff. *The Jesuits in Old Oregon*. Caldwell, Idaho, 1945.

George Fuller. *A History of the Pacific Northwest*. New York, 1941.

Francis B. Heitman. *Historical Register and Dictionary of the United States Army*, Vol I. Washington, D.C., 1903

Benjamin F. Manring. *The Conquest of the Coeur D'Alênes, Spokanes and Palouses*. Spokane, 1912.

John Mullah. Topographical Memoirs of Colonel Wright's Campaign, Senate Executive Documents, No. 32, Vol. X, 35th Congress, 2d Session. Washington, D.C., 1858–59.

Report of the Secretary of War dated December 6, 1858, House Executive Documents, No. 2, 35th Congress, 2d Session, 1858–59. Washington, D.C., 1859.

Edgar I. Stewart. *Washington-Northwest Frontier*, Vol. II. New York, 1957.

Thomas Teakle. *Pacific Northwest Transcripts*, Vol. XLII, Wright Campaign, typed manuscript.

U. S. Geological Survey. *Map of Medical Lake Quadrangle*. Washington-Spokane County, 1954.

CHAPTER 6

Hubert Howe Bancroft. *History of Nevado, Colorado and Wyoming*, Vol. XXV of the *Complete Works of Hubert Howe Bancroft*. San Francisco, 1890.

Buckland Manuscript in Hubert Howe Bancroft Library. Berkeley, n.d.

Sam P. Davis (editor). *The History of Nevada*, Vol. I. Reno and Los Angeles, 1913.

Daniel Montgomery Drumheller. *"Uncle Dan" Drumheller Tells Thrills of Western Trails in 1854*. Spokane, 1925.

Sarah "Winnemucca" Hopkins. *Life Among the Paiutes: Their Wrongs and Claims*. New York, 1883.

Edith Jane Lamb. *Formation of the State of Nevada*. Unpublished thesis, University of California, 1917.

William Doyle Malloy. *Carson Valley, 1857–1860*. Unpublished thesis quoting "Tennessee's" letter #72, University of California, December 1931.

The Thompson J. West Company. *History of Nevada*. 1881.

CHAPTER 7

Edward S. Ellis. *The Indian Wars of the United States*. Grand Rapids, Michigan, 1892.

Minnesota, Minnesota Writers' Project of the W.P.A. New York, 1938.

C. M. Oehler. *The Great Sioux Uprising*. New York, 1959.

Doane Robinson. *History of the Dakota or Sioux Indians*. Minneapolis, 1956.

Louis H. Roddis. *The Indian Wars of Minnesota*. Cedar Rapids, Iowa, 1956.

CHAPTER 8

Walter S. Campbell (Stanley Vestal, pseud.). *Kit Carson*. Boston, 1928.

Dane Coolidge. *The Navajo Indians*. Boston, 1930.

William A. Keleher. *Turmoil in New Mexico*. Santa Fe, 1952.

New Mexico, New Mexico Writers' Project of the W.P.A. New York, 1940.

Ralph Emerson Twitchell. *The Leading Facts of New Mexican History*, Vol. II. Cedar Rapids, Iowa, 1912.
Ruth M. Underhill. *The Navajos*. Norman, Oklahoma, 1956.

CHAPTER 9
George Bird Grinnell. *The Fighting Cheyennes*. New York, 1915.
House Executive Document, No. 1, 39th Congress, 1st Session. Washington, D.C., 1865.
George H. Pettis. *Kit Carson's Fight with the Comanche and Kiowa Indians*. Santa Fe, 1908.
Rupert Norval Richardson. *The Comanche Barrier to South Plains Settlement*. Glendale, California, 1933.

CHAPTERS 10, 11, and 12
Fort Phil Kearny Post Returns, Orders, and Other Official Records. National Archives.
Fort C. F. Smith Post Returns, Orders, and Other Official Records. National Archives.
Carrington Map of Fort Phil Kearny Reservation and Hartz Map of Fort C. F. Smith Reservation. National Archives.
House Document No. 1324, Vol. II, Part I, 40th Congress, 2d Session.
Senate Executive Document No. 97, 40th Congress, 2d Session.
Cyrus Townsend Brady. *Indian Fights and Fighters*. New York, 1904.
Earl A. Brininstool. *Fighting Indian Warriors*. Harrisburg, 1952.
Francis C. Carrington. *My Army Life and the Fort Phil Kearny Massacre*. Philadelphia, 1910.
Margaret I. Carrington. *Absaraka, Land of the Crows*. Philadelphia, 1868.
Robert B. David. *Finn Burnett, Frontiersman*. Glendale, California, 1937.
Richard I. Dodge. *Our Wild Indians*. Hartford, Connecticut, 1882.
George Bird Grinnell. *The Fighting Cheyennes*. New York, 1915.
Grace Raymond Hebard and Earl A. Brininstool. *The Bozeman Trail*. 2 vols.; Cleveland, 1922.
F. B. Heitman. *Historical Register and Dictionary of the United States Army, from Its Organization, September 29, 1789, to March 2, 1903*. Washington, D.C., 1903.

CHAPTER 13
Cyrus T. Brady. *Indian Fights and Fighters*. New York, 1904.
Earl A. Brininstool. *Fighting Red Cloud's Warriors*. Columbus, Ohio, 1926.
George A. Forsyth. *Thrilling Days in Army Life*. New York, 1900.
Winfield Freeman. "The Battle of the Arickaree," *Kansas Historical Collections*, VI, 346–67.

George B. Grinnell. *The Fighting Cheyennes*. New York, 1915.
John Hurst. "The Beecher Island Fight," *Kansas Historical Collections*, XV, 530–38. (Hurst was with Forsyth on the Arickaree.)
Merrill J. Mattes. *The Beecher Island Battlefield Diary of Sigmund Shlesinger*," reprinted from the *Colorado Magazine*, July 1952.
Carl C. Rister. *Border Command: General Phil Sheridan in the West*. Norman, Oklahoma, 1944.
Sigmund Shlesinger. "The Beecher Island Fight," *Kansas Historical Collections*, XV, 538–47. (Shlesinger fought at Beecher Island.)
Chauncey B. Whitney. "Diary of Chauncey B. Whitney," *Kansas Historical Collections*, XII, 296–99. (Scout Whitney's battlefield diary.)

CHAPTER 14

Charles J. Brill. *Conquest of the Southern Plains*. Oklahoma City, 1938.
Cavalry Journal, Vol. XXXVII, No. 153, October 1928.
George A. Custer. *My Life on the Plains*. New York, 1874.
George A. Forsyth. *Thrilling Days in Army Life*. New York, 1900.
George B. Grinnell. *The Fighting Cheyennes*. New York, 1915.
J. E. Milner and E. R. Forrest. *California Joe*. Caldwell, Idaho, 1935.
M. F. Schmitt and D. Brown. *Fighting Indians of the West*. New York, 1948.
Edgar I. Stewart. *Custer's Luck*. Norman, Oklahoma, 1955.

CHAPTER 15

George E. Hyde. *The Pawnee Indians*. Denver, 1951.
George B. Grinnell. *Two Great Scouts and Their Pawnee Battalion*. Cleveland, 1928.
Annual Reports of the Commissioner of Indian Affairs.
Nebraska History Magazine, Vol. XVI, July–September 1935.
Letters Received, Pawnee Agency, 1873, Records of the Bureau of Indian Affairs. National Archives.

CHAPTER 16

Henry J. Brown. "The Biggest Little War in American History," *Oregon Historical Quarterly*, March 1942.
Alfred B. Meacham. *The Tragedy of the Lava Beds*, Washington, D.C., 1883.
Keith A. Murray. *The Modocs and Their War*. Norman, Oklahoma, 1959.
T. B. Odeneal. *The Modoc War*. Portland, Oregon, 1873.
Doris Palmer Payne. *Captain Jack, Modoc Renegade*. Portland, Oregon, 1938.
Jeff C. Riddle. *The Indian History of the Modoc War*. San Francisco, 1914.

CHAPTER 17

Olive K. Dixon, *Life of Billy Dixon*, Dallas, 1927.

Wayne Gard. *The Great Buffalo Hunt*. New York, 1915.

George B. Grinnell. *The Fighting Cheyennes*. New York, 1915.

John L. McCarty. *Adobe Walls Bride*. San Antonio, 1955.

J. Wright Mooar, as told to James W. Hunt. "Buffalo Days," *Holland's Magazine* (Dallas), Vol. LII, 1933.

Rupert Norval Richardson. *The Comanche Barrier to South Plains Settlement*. Glendale, California, 1933.

Walter Prescott Webb (editor-in-chief). *The Handbook of Texas*. 2 vols.; Austin, 1952.

CHAPTER 18

Harley True Burton. *A History of the JA Ranch*. Austin, 1928.

Captain Robert G. Carter. *The Old Sergeant's Story*. New York, 1926.

————. *On the Border with Mackenzie*. Washington, D.C., 1935.

————, papers of (correspondence and manuscripts), in possession of the writer.

J. Evetts Haley. *Charles Goodnight, Cowman*. Boston, 1936.

General Nelson A. Miles. *Personal Recollections and Observations*. New York, 1896.

The Palo Duro (a compilation). Amarillo, Texas, 1934.

Walter Prescott Webb (editor in chief). *The Handbook of Texas*. 2 vols.; 1952.

CHAPTER 19

John G. Bourke. *On the Border with Crook*. New York, 1891.

Walter S. Campbell (Stanley Vestal, pseud.). *Sitting Bull*. Boston and New York, 1932.

General George Crook. *His Autobiography*, as edited by Martin F. Schmitt. Norman, Oklahoma, 1946.

Joe De Barthe. *Life and Adventures of Frank Grouard*. St. Joseph, Missouri, 1894.

John F. Finnerty. *War Path and Bivouac, or the Conquest of the Sioux*. New York, 1890.

George B. Grinnell. *The Fighting Cheyennes*. New York, 1915.

George E. Hyde. *Red Cloud's Folks*. Norman, Oklahoma, 1938.

Thomas B. Marquis. *A Warrior Who Fought Custer*. Minneapolis, 1931.

Anson Mills. *My Story*. Washington, D.C., privately printed, 1918.

Mari Sandoz. *Crazy Horse*. New York, 1945.

J. W. Vaughn. *With Crook at the Rosebud*. Harrisburg, 1956.

CHAPTER 20

Elizabeth B. Custer. *Boots and Saddles, or Life in Dakota with General Custer.* New York, 1885.

Edward S. Godfrey. "Custer's Last Battle," *Century Magazine,* Vol. XLIII, January 1892.

W. A. Graham. *The Story of the Little Big Horn.* 2d ed.; Harrisburg, 1945.

————. *The Custer Myth: A Source Book of Custeriana.* Harrisburg, 1953.

————. "Come on! Be Quick! Bring Packs! Custer's Battle Plan, the Story of His Last Message, as Told by the Man Who Carried it," *Cavalry Journal,* Vol. XXXII, July 1923.

George B. Grinnell. *The Fighting Cheyennes.* New York, 1915.

Joseph M. Hanson. *The Conquest of the Missouri.* 2d ed.; New York, 1946.

George E. Hyde. *Red Cloud's Folks.* Norman, Oklahoma, 1937.

Robert Frazier Hunt. *I Fought with Custer.* New York, 1947.

Charles Kuhlman. *Legend into History.* Harrisburg, 1951.

Edward S. Luce. *Keogh, Comanche and Custer.* St. Louis, 1939.

Thomas B. Marquis. *A Warrior Who Fought Custer.* Minneapolis, 1931.

Edgar I. Stewart. *Custer's Luck.* Norman, Oklahoma, 1955.

Frederick F. Van De Water. *Glory Hunter: A Life of General Custer.* Indianapolis, 1934.

Frederick Whittaker. *A Complete Life of General George A. Custer.* New York, 1876.

CHAPTER 21

Jason Betzinez. *I Fought with Geronimo.* Harrisburg, 1959.

John G. Bourke. *An Apache Campaign in the Sierra Madre.* New York, 1958.

————. *On the Border with Crook.* New York, 1891.

Ross Calvin. *River of the Sun.* Albuquerque, 1946.

Mrs. Tom Charles. *Tales of the Tularosa.* Alamogordo, New Mexico, 1954.

John C. Cremony. *Life Among the Apaches.* San Francisco, 1868.

Britton Davis. *The Truth about Geronimo.* New Haven, 1929.

Major General O. O. Howard. *My Life and Experiences among the Hostile Indians.* Hartford, 1907.

Jasper Kanseah. "The Last of Geronimo's Warriors," *New Mexico Magazine,* June 1955.

Frank C. Lockwood. *The Apache Indians.* New York, 1938.

Elizabeth M. Page. *In Camp and Tepee.* New York, 1915.

CHAPTER 22

Robert Ballow. *Early Klicktat Valley Days*. Goldendale, Washington, 1938.

George F. Brimlow. *The Bannock Indian War of 1878*. Caldwell, Idaho, 1938.

Jennie Broughton Brown. *Fort Hall on the Oregon Trail*. Caldwell, Idaho, 1932.

Sarah "Winnimucca" Hopkins. *Life among the Paiutes: Their Wrongs and Claims*. Boston, 1883.

Adelaide Hawes. *The Valley of Tall Grass*. Caldwell, Idaho, 1950.

W. J. McConnell. *Early History of Idaho*. Caldwell, Idaho, 1913.

Osborne Russell. *Journal of a Trapper*. Boise, Idaho, 1921.

John R. Swanton. *The Indian Tribes of North America*. Washington, D.C., 1953.

Transcripts:

Thomas Teakle. *Bannock Indian War, 1878*, Vols. LV, LVI, LVII.

Fort Hall Indian Reservation (local compilation).

Martha B. Babb. Signed statement of experiences during the Bannock War of 1878. Spokane, Washington, December 1946.

Reports:

Report of Commissioner of Indian Affairs. Washington, D.C., 1878.

CHAPTER 23

Colorado, Colorado Writers' Project of the W.P.A. New York, 1941.

LeRoy and Ann Hafen. *Colorado*. Denver, 1949.

Official Reports and Documents of the Ute Uprising in the National Archives.

Wesley Merritt. "Three Indian Campaigns," *Harper's New Monthly Magazine*, 1889.

M. F. Schmitt and D. Brown. *Fighting Indians of the West*. New York, 1948.

Wilson Rockwell. *The Utes, Forgotten People*. Denver, 1957.

CHAPTER 24

Walter S. Campbell (Stanley Vestal, pseud.). *Warpath and Council Fire*. New York, 1948.

Dennis Collins. *The Indians' Last Fight, or the Dull Knife Raid*. Girard, Kansas, 1915.

George B. Grinnell. *The Fighting Cheyennes*. New York, 1915.

Mari Sandoz. *Cheyenne Autumn*. New York, 1953.

M. F. Schmitt and D. Brown. *Fighting Indians of the West*. New York, 1948.

CHAPTER 25

Elaine Goodale Eastman. "Ghost Dance War and Wounded Knee Massacre of 1890–91," *Nebraska History,* Vol. XXVI, No. 1, 1945.

George E. Hyde. *A Sioux Chronicle.* Norman, Oklahoma, 1957.

Julia B. McGillycuddy. *McGillycuddy, Agent.* Stanford University, 1941.

James H. McGregor. *The Wounded Knee Massacre.* Minneapolis, 1940.

General Nelson A. Miles. *Personal Recollections and Observations.* New York, 1896.

————. *Serving the Republic.* New York, 1911.

James Mooney. *The Ghost Dance Religion and the Sioux Outbreak of 1890,* 14th Annual Report of the Bureau of American Ethnology, Part II. Washington, D.C., 1896.

Appendix

The Potomac Corral, The Westerners

"For our own amusement and amazement"—this statement appears in our bylaws as one of the primary purposes for organizing this 10th Corral of The Westerners in 1954. Most of the organizers were corresponding members of one or more of the older corrals of Westerners. Most of them were born west of "The River" (the Mississippi) but now live in exile in the metropolitan area of Washington, D.C. Leland Case, the scholarly editor of *Together* magazine, conceived the idea of The Westerners while visiting the National Museum of Sweden. Case helped organize the first Corral in Chicago in 1944; the Tucson Corral in 1953; and, while on temporary assignment in Washington in December 1954, gave needed impetus to the formation of the Potomac Corral. There are corrals in Sweden, France, Germany, and England in addition to the thirteen in the United States.

As in the case of all other corrals, the major qualification for membership is an abiding interest in some phase of Western history or lore—military, political, agricultural, religious, social, or economic. We have learned that a Westerner is a state of mind rather than an accident of birth. Some of the most dedicated Westerners in our Corral were born in Massachusetts, North Carolina, and Pennsylvania. The roster of the Potomac Corral includes members of Congress, government officials, doctors, lawyers, professional writers, artists, book dealers, army officers (active and retired), historians, and businessmen. The members of the Corral have an impressive number of books to their credit—not all of them by the professional writers. There are two kinds of members, resident and corresponding. The resident members are those who live in or near Washington, D.C., and make up the bulk of the attendance at the monthly dinner meetings of the Corral. The corresponding members are those who live some distance from Washington and who can only occasionally attend the meetings. Both the resident and corresponding members regularly receive *Corral Dust*, our official publication.

In addition to our periodical, *Corral Dust*, the Corral plans a series of Great Western books, of which this is the first. *Great Western Rivers*, the second book in our planned series, is now in preparation for publication in 1961.

Fourteen chapters of *Great Western Indian Fights* were written by eleven resident members and the other eleven chapters by ten corresponding members. The maps were prepared by resident member William (Bill) Loechel, talented young Maryland artist, from sketches made by the various authors. The drawing on the title page and those at the head of each chapter are also his. Another Westerner, Miss Onienell Holliday of Texas and Washington, D.C., worked nights, weekends, and holidays in preparing the manuscript for publication.

The members of the Potomac Corral are proud to be the first unit of The Westerners to publish a permanent collection of their work for the general public.

Jeff C. Dykes
Chairman, Publications Committee

Index

Note: Indian tribal names appear so frequently throughout this book that there has been no attempt made to index each reference. Following each entry here you will find the pages in which each tribe played an important role.

Ackland, Sgt. Kit, wounded, 43
Adobe Walls, first battle of, 104–6; second battle of 203–13
Ahdilohee. *See* Carson, Kit
American Fur Company, posts, 28; Rendezvous, 28 *et. seq.*; monopoly, 31
Angel, Eugene, killed, 77
Apaches, 163–74, 201–13, 255–66
Apache Scouts, 20 *et seq.*, 104; praised, 263; imprisoned, 264
Applegate, Jesse, 195
Applegate, Lindsay, agent, 190
Arapahoes, 22, 84, 117, 163–82, 201–20
Arikara Scouts, 244

Bandera Pass, 39–45
Bankhead, Lt. Col. Henry C., 172–74
Bannacks, 268–80
Bannack Indian War, 270–80
Beaumont, Capt. Eugene B., 216
Beckwourth, James P., 134–35
Beecher, Lt. Frederick H., 164–70; killed, 171
Beecher Island, fight at, 165–74
Bell, Lt. James M., 179
Bendire, Capt. John, 273
Bennett, Capt., killed, 279
Bent, William, 104–5, 293
Benteen, Capt. Frederick W., 178, 241, 243–44; counterattacks, 251; rescued, 252–53, 293

Bernard, Capt. R. F., 193, 271–73; engages Indians, 275–76, 277
Betzinez, Jason, 259
Big Bow, Chief, 204
Big Foot, Chief, 309–11; killed, 313
Bighorn Road. *See* Bozeman Trail
Bishop, Lt., 279
Blackfoot Indians, 21, 27
Black Hawk, Chief, 20
Black Hills, gold found (1874), 222
Black Kettle, Chief, killed, 179
Blanket Indians, 88
Bloody Knife, scout, killed, 245
Bonneville, Capt. Benjamin E., 37
Bourke, Capt. John G., 226, 230–32; praises Apache scouts, 263
Boutelle, Lt. F. A., 189, 192–93
Bozeman, John M., 109; killed, 135
Bozeman Trail, 109 *et seq.*, 183
Bradley, Lt. James H., 253
Bridger, Jim, 23, 113, 119
Brisbin, Maj. James, 238
Brooke, Gen. John R., 310
Brown, Capt. Frederick H., 121–22; killed, 126
Brule Sioux, 156, 183–88
Bruneau, John, 272
Buffalo hunters, 201–13
Buffalo Horn, Chief, 270–73
Bull Hump, 299–300
Burgess, William, 186
Burnett, Finn, 139 *et seq.*
Bradley, Lt. Col. L. B., 137, 144

Calhoun, Lt. James, 242
California Joe, scout, 177, 180
Camas Prairie, 268, 270
Campbell, with Sublette, 32, 35
Campbell, Walter S. (Stanley Vestal), 232

Canadian River, 103
Canby, Gen. E. R. S., 96, 194–96;
    shot, 197
Canyon de Chelly, 94
Captain Jack, 189 *et seq.*; shoots
    Canby, 197; surrenders, 199
Captain Jack (Ute), 285
Carey, Capt. Asa B., 97
Carleton, Gen. James H., 95; letter
    to Kit Carson, 99, 103
Carpenter, Capt. Louis H., 173
Carrington, Col. Henry B., 111;
    departs Fort Kearny, 112, 115,
    119; suspects attack, 127; finds
    dead, 128; relieved, 130
Carson City Rangers, 75
Carson, Col. Christopher (Kit),
    92; orders, 96–7, 103; Adobe
    Walls, 104–5, 106
Carter, Capt. Robert G., 219–20
Case, Samuel, 195
Cator brothers, 212
Chapman, Amos, 206–7
Charging Cloud, grave of, 317
Charlton, Sgt. John B., 202
Chatto, Sgt., scout, 258
Cheyennes, 117, 156, 293–94, 163–
    82, 201–20, 225–54, 293–317
Chihuahua, 258, 264
Chiquito (Little Winnemucca), 74,
    77; out of action, 78
Chiricahua Apache scouts, 255–66
Chivington, Col. John, 84, 163
Cochise, Chief, 255
Coeur d'Alenes, 47–72
Colby, Gen., 307, 315
Collins, Dennis, 295
Collins, Maj. Patrick, 272–73
Colter, John, 28
Colvin, D. A. (Al), 141–47
Colvin, Zeke, 139–40
Comanche (Keogh's horse), 253
Comanches, 39–46, 102–7, 210–20,
    163–74
Comancheros, 204
Condon, Thomas F., Jr., 75
Connor, Col. Patrick E., 84, 111
Cooke, Lt. William W., 180, 241–
    43, 248
Corbin, Jack, scout, 177, 180

Crawford, Capt. Emmett, killed,
    260
Crazy Horse, Chief, at Rosebud,
    232; 234, 249; joins Gall, 250
Creeks, 21
Crook, Gen. George, 222, 225–27;
    recalls Mills, 232, 233; resumes
    campaign, 234, 236–37, 238;
    pacifies Apaches, 255, 259–60;
    resigns, 262; on Bannack War,
    280, 285
Crow, 297
Crows, 132–47, 221–54, 267–80,
    303–17
Crow King, Chief, 241
Crow's Nest, 240–41
Curly Headed Doctor, 196
Custer, Lt. Col. George A., 175;
    plans campaign, 176–77; attacks,
    178, 179; tactics, 179–80, 222,
    237, 239, 240, 243; in action,
    248–49; at the last, 250; body
    found, 253
Custer, Lt. Thomas W., wounded,
    179; killed, 242

Davidson, Lt. Henry B., 64–65
Davidson, Col. J. W., 202
Davis, Lt. Britton, 255–56
Davis, Col. Jeff C., 198
Deming, Dexter E., 48
Dent, Capt. Frederick T., meets
    Steptoe, 59–60; at Four Lakes,
    63–64
DeWolf, Dr. J. M., killed, 246
Dixon, Billy, 208, 209, 210, 213
Dodge, Capt. Francis S., 289–90
Dog Soldier Society, 167
Donovan, John, 172–73
Dove, Capt., 278
Doyle, Pvt. Thomas, 155, 158
Dull Knife, Chief, captured, 296;
    escapes, 297; parleys, 298; sur-
    renders, 299; starves, 300, 301
Dyar, L. S., 195

Eastman, Dr. Charles, 315
Egan, Capt. John, 273, 278
Egan, Chief, 272; killed, 277
Egbert, Capt. Harry, 273, 278

Elliott, "Abe," 76
Elliot, Maj. Joel H., 177, 179
Estes, Stephen T., 188

Fairchild, John A., 195
Farmer Indians, 88
Far West, steamer, 238, 253
Father Kraft, killed, 313
Fetterman, Capt. William J., 121;
  overzealousness of, 122; killed,
  126
Fetterman Massacre, 115, 124;
  described, 124–27; Carrington
  on, 129–30
Finnerty, John J., 226, 230, 232
Fisher, Isaac, 121; killed, 125
Fitzpatrick, Tom (Broken Hand),
  32–33
Fleming, Lt. Hugh B., 65
Fontenelle, Lucien, 32, 37
Forsyth, Maj. George A. (Sandy),
  recruits, 164, 165; regroups,
  169; wounded, 170, 172;
  rescued, 173
Forsyth, Col. James W., 308, 310,
  315; court-martial, 316
Fort Apache, 256
Fort Canby, 99
Fort C. F. Smith, 115, 133
Fort Fetterman, 226
Fort Phil Kearney, 113–14, 120
Fort Ridgely, 89, 93
Fort Taylor, 62
Fort Wallace, 166, 172
Fort Walla Walla, 47
Fort Wingate, 98
Four Lakes, battle of, 63–65
Fourth Cavalry, 204, 214, *et seq.;*
  destroys Dull Knife band, 223
Free, Mickey, 258
French, Capt. Thomas, 242

Galbraith, Major, 88
Gall, Chief, 241, 249
Garry, Chief, 67, 68, 69
"Garry Owen," song, 178, 180
Gaston, Lt. William, 55, 57
Gatewood, Lt. Charles B., 259;
  meets Geronimo, 263
Genoa Rangers, 75
Gerard, Fred, scout, 243, 248

Geronimo, Chief, 255, 258; sur-
  renders, 260; escapes, 262; meets
  Gatewood; surrenders, 263
Ghost Dance, 22, 304, 308; mas-
  sacre at, 313–14; burial at, 316
Gibbon, Col. John, 237–38; ad-
  monishes Custer, 239; at Reno
  Hill, 253
Gibson, Lt. Francis, 243
Gibson, Lt. Horatio G., 63, 66–67
Gibson, Sgt. Samuel, 150, 155–56
Gillem, Col. Alvin C., 194–95, 197;
  replaced, 198
Godfrey, Lt. Edward S., 242, 250,
  314
Godin, Antoine, scout, 34
Goodale, Lt. G. A., 191
Goodnight, Charles C., 220
Good Thunder, arrested, 305
Gordon, John, supplies burn, 288
Greeley, Horace, 282
Green, Maj. John, 192, 278
Gregg, Lt. David McM., 54, 55
Grier, Capt. William N., 63–66, 70
Grinnell, George Bird, 119, 173,
  209, 293
Gros Ventres (Big Bellies), 27–38
Grouard, Frank, 226, 228, 230
Grover, Abner T. (Sharp), 164,
  166
Grover, Col. C., 273
Grummond, Lt. George W., 121,
  126
Gunther, Capt., 216, 218

Hagerty, Pvt. Henry, killed, 158
Hamilton, Capt. Louis Mc., 179
Hanrahan, 205–9; moves out, 213
Hard Rope, Chief, 177
Hardie, Capt. James A., 63, 66
Harper, Capt., 273
Hartz, Capt. Edward S., 144–45
Hasbrouck, Capt. H. C., 198
Hayden, Dr. F. V., 278
Hayfield Fight, 137; account of,
  139–43, 145; compared, 147
Hays, Capt. John C., 41–43, 81
Headly, killed, 78
Hen eggs, incident of, 87–88
He-who-looks-at-the-calf, 21

Highsmith, Ben, 43–44
Hines, Dr. C. M., 123
Hodgson, Lt. B. H., killed, 245
Horton, Dr. Samuel M., 160
Howard, Gen., 270–76
Hudson's Bay Co., 28
Hump, Chief, 241
Hungate family, 84
Hunkpapa Sioux, 84
Hunter, J. Marvin, 41
Huntington, Supt. J. W. P., 190

Ihrie, Lt. George P., 64
Inkpaduta, Chief, 241
Isatai (Little Wolf), 203–6, 209;
    strategy, 210; disgrace of, 212,
    296

Jackson, Capt. James A., 192
Jacobs, John M., 109
Janis, Antoine, 188
Jenness, Lt. John C., 150, 155,
    156; killed, 157
Johnson, Capt., parleys, 298
Johnston, Capt., 75
Joseph, Chief, 268
Joset, Father John J. A., intercedes
    with Steptoe, 54–55, 68, 69

Kamiakin, Chief, 67, 69, 70
Kanipe, Sgt. David, 243, 248
Kanseah, Jasper, scout, 263
Karnes, Capt. Henry W., 42
Kauffman, Anton, reports, 78
Kayitah, scout, 262; imprisoned,
    264
Keogh, Capt. Myles W., 242, 243,
    248, 250
Keyes, Capt. Erasmus D., sent to
    build fort, 62–63
Kicking Bear, reports Sun Dance,
    305, 310
Kicking Bird, Chief, 204
King of Spain, appealed to, 40
Kinney, Capt. N. C., 114, 132;
    leaves Fort C. F. Smith, 137
Kiowas, 22, 164–74, 201–20
Klamaths, 189–200
Knapp, O. C., agent, 191

Lame Deer, Chief, 241
Lame White Man, 249
Lava Beds, 193 et seq.
Lawton, Lt. H. W., 202
Lawyer, Chief, offers aid, 59
Lease, Henry, 212
Lee and Reynolds, traders, 206–7
Leighton, A. C., 135, 137
Lewis, Meriwether, 21
Lincoln, Pres. Abraham, 81, 82;
    message to Congress, 83–84;
    commutes Sioux sentences, 93;
    urges revised policy, 163
Little Beaver, Chief, 177
Little Bighorn, battle of, 235–52;
    tribes at, 241; Custer's action at,
    248–50
Little Crow, 87–90; retreats, 92
Little Hawk, 228
Little Shield, 301
Little Wolf. See Isatai
Little Wound, Chief, 305
Littmann, Sgt. Max, 153, 155, 156;
    in a duel, 159
Lone Wolf, Chief, 204
"Long Walk," the, 100
Lost River, 196 et seq.
Lower Agency (Sioux), 88–89 et
    seq.
Lyon, Lt. Lylan B., 63

Mackenzie, Col. Ranald, 202, 215;
    destroys village, 216; destroys
    herd, 217; strategy, 218, 219;
    destroys Dull Knife band, 223
Malheur Paiutes, 267–80
Marsh, Capt. Grant, 238
Martine, scout, 262, imprisoned,
    264
Martini, Giovanni, 244, 246; takes
    message from Custer, 249
Mason, Maj. E. C., 193, 197
Massacre Canyon, battle of, 185–
    88
Masterson, William B. (Bat), 210
Mathey, Lt. Edward G., 242
Maus, Lt. Marion P., 260
McDonald, Capt. Archie, 75
McDougall, Capt. Thomas, 242,
    243

McGregor, Capt. Thomas, 190, 273, 276

McIntosh, Lt. Donald, 242, 244; killed, 245

McLaughlin, James, agent, 308

Meacham, A. B., 190; shot, 197

"Medicine Fight" (Indian name for Wagon Box Fight), 162

Meeker, Josephine, 269; violated, 281, 290

Meeker, N. C., agent, 269, 281, trouble with Utes, 283; found dead, 290

Meredith, killed, 77

Merritt, Gen. Wesley, rescues troops, 290

Mexican War, veterans of, 22

Miles, Gen. Nelson A., 201; negotiates surrender after Little Bighorn, 223; relieves Crook, 262; meets Geronimo, 263, 277–79; on Wounded Knee incident, 316

Milk Creek, battle of, 281 *et seq.*

Milkapsi, Chief, 69

Mills, Capt. Anson, 230–32; is recalled, 233

Minneconjou Sioux, 156; 235–54

Modocs, 189–200; war, 193–99

Mooar brothers, 204, 206, 207; leave Adobe Walls, 208

Mooers, Dr. John H., 164, 170; dies, 171–72

Morningstar. *See* Dull Knife

Moses, Chief, 277

Moylan, Capt. Myles, 242

Mullan, Lt. John, 62, 63

Myers, A. C. (Charlie), 205–7; leaves Adobe Walls, 208

Myrick, Andrew, 88; killed, 89

Naiche, son of Cochise, 255, 258; escapes with Geronimo, 262

Navajos, 94–101

New Mexico Volunteers, 94

Nez Perces, as scouts, 62; 267–80

Nixon, Tom, 212–13

Nokoni Comanches, 202

North, Frank, 186

North, L. H., 186

Northern Paiutes, 267–80

Numaga (Little Winnemucca), 74, 77

Nye, Gov. James W., breaks up last Paiute assembly, 81

Odeneal, T. B., 192

Ogg, Billy, 209, 210

Oglala Sioux, 112, 156, 183–88, 235–54

O'Keefe, Tom, 205, 207

Old Schonchin, Chief, 189

Olds, William (Mr. & Mrs.), 210, 213

Ord, Capt. Edward O. C., 64, 66, 67

Ormsby, Maj. William M., 75–76, 78; retreats, 79; killed, 80

Osages, 177

Owhi, Chief, 70

Paiutes, territory of, 48; 73–82

Palo Duro Canyon, site, 214–15; village destroyed, 216; horses killed, 217; after battle, 220

Palouses, 47–72; map of military campaigns against, 52

Pawnees, 20, 183–88

Payne, Capt. John S., 287, 288; rescued, 290

Peno Creek, 116

Perry, Capt. David, 193

Pfeiffer, Capt. Albert, 98, 100

Phillips, John (Portugee), 127

Piegans (Blackfeet), 21

Pierce, Capt. F. E., 257–58

Pierre's Hole, 21; site of, 28–31; occupants of, 32; Rendezvous of 1832 at, 32 *et seq.*; fighting at, 34–5

Pike, Zebulon M., 183

Pine Ridge, 307, 310, 315

Piney Island, 116 *et seq.*

Pitkin, Governor, 283–84

Platte, L. B., 186–87

Pliley, Allison P., 172–73

Poito (Old Winnemucca), 74

Polotkin, Chief, parleys with Wright, 68; taken hostage, 69

Pontiac, Chief, 20

Porter, Dr. H. R., 250, 252

Porter, J. R., 149
Pourier, Baptiste, guide, 226, 228, 230
Powder River Expedition, 111
Powell, Capt. James W., 116; replaced by Fetterman, 121; assigned to Piney Island, 149; tries to save wood party, 154, 155–60; returns to fort, 160
Presidential Peace Commission, 194–95
Price, Major, 202
Price, Mrs. Shadrick, 281
Pyramid Lake, battle of, 73–82

Qualchan, son of Owhi, 70
Quanah Parker, Chief, 204, 212

Randolph, Dr., 58
Rankin, Joe, scout, 285, 286; goes for help, 290
Ransome, Lt. Dunbar R., 64
Rath, Charles, 205–7; leaves Adobe Walls, 208
Red Cloud, Chief, 112; describes Indian losses in Fetterman fight, 130, 139; at Wagon Box Fight, 157, 183, 305
Rendezvous, the, 28–31; breaks up, 34
Reno Creek, 242
Reno, Maj. Marcus A., 237–38; on review, 239, 243; prepares to fight, 244; at Little Bighorn, 245–46; is trapped, 251; counterattacks, 252; rescued, 253
Renville's Rangers, 89, 91, 92
Republican River, 184–88
Reynolds, Charlie, scout, 240; killed, 245
Reynolds, Col. James, 226, 237
Richards, Louis, guide, 226
Riddle, Frank, 196–97
Rocky Mountain Fur Co., 29–31; race of the supply caravan of 1832, 32; under William Sublette, 32–33; arrives at Rendezvous, 33–34
Roman Nose, 167; superstition of, 177, 173–74

Roop, Isaac, 48
Roosevelt, Theodore, 19
Rosborough, Judge, A. M., 195
Rosebud, battle of, 221–34
Rosebud River and Canyon, 225, 227
Rowland, James, interpreter for Dull Knife's band, 300, 302

Sand Creek Massacre, 85, 163
Sanford, Major, 278
Sans Arc Sioux, 156
Santa Fe Trail, 102
Santee Sioux, 235–54
Sawyer, Col. James A., 111
Scott, Lt. Gen. Winfield, censures Maj. Steptoe, 51
Seminoles, 21
Seventh Cavalry, 176 et seq.
Shadler brothers, killed, 210
Sharrow, Sgt. Maj. W. W., 242, 248
Sheridan, Gen. Philip H. (Phil), 164, 176, 180; strategy of, 221; plans Sioux campaign, 237; censures Crook, appoints Miles to succeed, 262
Sherman, Gen. William T., 23, 101, 162
Short Bull, Chief, 310
Shoshones, 20, 84, 221–34, 267–80
Sibley, Col. H. H., 86; organizes forces, 89; pursues Sioux, 90
Silver City Guards, 75
Sinclair, Alexander, joins Sublette, 33; death of, 35
Sioux, 83–93, 109–74, 183–88, 221–54, 303–17
Sitting Bull, Chief, 222–24; at Sun Dance, 227; at Rosebud, 232–34; settles down, 303; arrested, killed, 308
Sky Chief, 186; killed, 187
Slowiarchy, Chief, 71
Smith, Lt. Algernon E., 242
Smith, Capt. Allen, 259
Smith, Maj. Benjamin F., leads rescue party, 160
Smith, Capt. Deaf, 42

Smith, Col. John E., 149
Smith, Lewis H., 111
Smyth, R. J., 153, 155
Spears, William, killed, 79
Spokanes, 47–72
Spokane Plains, battle of, 65–67; results of battle at, 71
Spotted Tail, Chief, 112, 184
Steele, Elisha, 195
Stephens, of Gant & Blackwell, killed, 37
Stephens, Gov. Isaac J., signs treaty of 1855, 47
Steptoe, Maj. William J., 48, 50; leaves Fort Walla Walla, 51; at To - hoto - nim - me parley, 53; forms troops, 56; retreats, 58–59; declines Nez Perce aid, met by Dent, 59; returns to fort, 60
Sternberg, Lt. Sigmund, 140; killed, 145
Stewart, Maj. Joseph, 273
Stillwell, Simpson E. (Jack), 167, 169, 170; goes for help, 172
Strong Left Hand, 299
Sublette, William, 32–33; joins battle at Pierre's Hole, 35; wounded, 35, 37; detours train, 38
Sullivant's Hills, map, 118, 120
Sumner, Col. E. V., forces Sioux to agency, 309
Sun Dance, 201, 227

Tangle Hair, 299
Taylor, E. B., 111
Taylor, Lt. Oliver H. P., 56; wounded, 57; dies, 58; fort named for, 62
Taza, son of Cochise, 255
Tecumseh, Chief, 20
Tendoy, Chief, 271
Ten Eyck, Capt. Tenedor, 113; sent to join Fetterman, 123; finds the battlefield, 126–27
"Tennessee," 74
Tenth U. S. Cavalry, 173
Terry, Brig. Gen. Alfred H., 222, 239; divides Seventh Cavalry, 238; arrives at Reno Hill, 253

Texas Rangers, 21, organization, 39; survivors of Bandera Pass fight, 44–45
Third Colorado Volunteer Cavlary, 84
Thomas, Capt. Evan, killed, 198
Thomas, Rev. Eleaser, 195; shot, 197
Thompson, Lt., 202
Thompson, Pvt. James W., 134–35
Thornburg, Maj. T. T., 281; marches to White River agency, 285; under fire, 286; killed, 287
Three Tetons, 28, 30; location of Pierre's Hole, 31
Throckmorton, Capt. C. B., 276
Tilcoax, Chief, 68, 69
Timothy, Chief, 51; aids troops, 59
Tobey. See Winema
To-hoto-nim-me, parley at, 53; battle at, 55–59; losses at, 60
Tonkaway Scouts, 217
Traveling Hail, Chief, 88
Treaties, 22; Apache-Spanish, 40; of 1855, 47; mutual aid with Nez Perce, 62; Coeur d'Alene peace treaty, 69–70; with Sioux, 87; with Navajos, 95–96; with Kiowas, Comanches, and Apaches, 107; with Pawnees, 183; of 1868, 184; with Klamaths and Modocs (1864), 189; with Sioux and Cheyenne (Laramie treaty), 221, 236
Trudeau, Pierre, goes for help, 172
Two Moons, Chief, 119, 241
Tyler, Lt. Ogden, 65, 66

Umatillas, 267–280
Utes, 281–92

Varnum, Lt. Charles A., 240–41, 244, 246
Victor, Chief, killed, 56
Vincent, Chief, meets Steptoe, 55
Virginia City Hearties, 75
Virginia City Road. See Bozeman trail

Wagon Box Fight, 148–62

Wallace, Lt. George D., 244; 252–53; killed, 313

Warrior Creek, 135

Washita, battle of, 175–82

Washita River, 176 *et seq.*

Watkins, Capt. Richard G., 75

Weir, Capt. Thomas B., 242, 246, 248, 250

Weiser tribe, 272

Wessells, Lt. Col. Henry W., replaces Carrington, 130; cuts Indian rations, 300, 301

West Point, former students of, 22

West, Thompson J., Co., 74–75

Wheatley; James S., with Fetterman, 121; killed, 125

Wheaton, Lt. Col. Frank, 193, 276, 277

Wheeler, Lt. James C. Jr., replaces Taylor, 57

White, Barclay, 187–88

White, Lt. James L., 63

White River Agency, 282–91

Wild Hog, 299

Williams Station, trading post, episode of, 73–74

Williamson, John W., 186–87

Wilson, Jack. *See* Wovoka

Winema. *See* Tobey

Winder, Capt. Charles S., joins Gregg, 56; at Four Lakes, 64

Winnemucca. *See* Chiquito, Poito, Numaga

Winters, Capt. W. H., 276, 279

Woman's Heart, Chief, 204; killed, 217

Wood Lake, battle of, 83–92

Wooden Leg, 228, 232

Wounded Knee Creek, 301; map, 312

Wounded Knee, battle of, 22, 303–17

Wovoka, teachings, 304, 305

Wright, Col. George, background of, 61; at Four Lakes, 62–66; makes treaty with Coeur d'Alenes, 69–70; denounces renegades, 71

Wright, Robert M., 206

Wright's Hill, 64

Wyeth, Nathaniel J., joins Sublette, 32; leaves Rendezvous, 34

Wyeth, John, 35

Wyse, Capt. Francis O., 62

Yakimas, sign treaty of 1855, 47; parley at To-hoto-nim-me, 53, 61–72

Yanktonnai Sioux, 235–54

Yates, Capt. George W., 242, 250

Yellow Bird, medicine man, 311; killed, 313

Young Man Afraid, Chief, 305